THE Cure
FOR Alcoholism

THE SINCLAIR METHOD

A MEDICALLY PROVEN CURE FOR ALCOHOLISM

THE Cure
FOR Alcoholism

The Medically Proven Way to Eliminate Alcohol Addiction

Roy Eskapa, PhD

FOREWORD BY
David Sinclair, PhD

INTRODUCTION BY
Claudia Christian

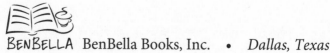
BenBella BenBella Books, Inc.   •   *Dallas, Texas*

BenBella Books, Inc.
10440 N. Central Expressway, Suite 800
Dallas, TX 75231
www.benbellabooks.com
Send feedback to feedback@benbellabooks.com

Printed in the United States of America
10 9 8 7 6 5 4

Library of Congress Cataloging-in-Publication Data is available for this title.
ISBN 978-1-937856-13-7

Proofreading by Stacia Seaman, Jennifer Canzoneri, Michael Fedison,
    and Cape Cod Compositors, Inc.
Cover design by Kit Sweeney
Text design and composition by John Reinhardt Book Design
Index by Shoshana Hurwitz and Clive Pyne
Printed by Lake Book Manufacturing

Distributed to the trade by Two Rivers Distribution, an Ingram brand
www.tworiversdistribution.com

Special discounts for bulk sales (minimum of 25 copies) are available.
Please contact Aida Herrera at aida@benbellabooks.com.

Contents

SECTION ONE
Alcoholism: Who Says It's Incurable?

SECTION TWO
Five Steps to Curing Alcoholism

SECTION THREE
Real Stories of Real Cures

SECTION FOUR
A Sober, Happier Future

*In loving memory of Rosemary Eskapa,
Clive Beck, and Rodney Barnett.*

Dedication

THIS BOOK IS DEDICATED to all those who have suffered, directly or indirectly, from the effects of alcohol. It's also dedicated to David Sinclair, without whom we would not have the first truly effective treatment for this terrible affliction—a treatment based on highly original discoveries made over forty years of meticulous research. Lives are already being saved as a result of Sinclair's breakthrough, a treatment that solves the riddle underlying addiction right where it begins—deep in the physiology and biochemistry of the brain. With the Sinclair Method (or pharmacological extinction, as it is also known), the craving and suffering can now end.

Acknowledgments

MANY PEOPLE have contributed to the science on which this book is based. One of the most outstanding was Ivan Pavlov, the Russian physiologist and Nobel Prize winner who described how learning and extinction occur. Jack Fishman and Harold Blumberg isolated the first opioid antagonist medications.

David Sinclair was the first to demonstrate how these compounds reverse alcohol addiction in the brain. Sinclair's discovery of the Alcohol Deprivation Effect and pharmacological extinction led to a proven, cost-effective, and dignified cure for alcoholism—without abstinence and unpleasant, dangerous withdrawal symptoms.

I would like to acknowledge the Finnish National Public Health Institute (KTL, formerly Alko Labs) for its vision in providing massive funding over forty years for research into alcoholism.

All those dedicated researchers who worked on the use of opioid antagonists (naltrexone, nalmefene, naloxone) in addiction research also deserve acknowledgement. In particular, Project COMBINE in the United States stands out as the largest clinical trial ever conducted in addiction research. Although Project COMBINE is just one of more than seventy clinical trials affirming the power of naltrexone treatment in alcoholism, its team—led by Raymond Anton and Stephanie O'Malley—deserves special mention. The pioneering work performed by the group at the University of Pennsylvania, headed by Charles O'Brien and Joseph Volpicelli, and by Pekka Heinälä and the team in Finland, must also be acknowledged.

Much appreciation is due to Dr. Kshama Metre and Pankaj Dogra of the Chinmaya Organization for Rural Development, who had the foresight and the courage to put the Sinclair Method into practice by using naltrexone in the correct way—in combination with ongoing drinking—in poor areas of rural Himachal Pradesh, India. Thanks to their efforts, we now know that the treatment can work just as well in developing regions as it can in Helsinki, New York, or London.

I would like to express very special appreciation to my mother, Shirley Eskapa, and to Claire Cazier, for their valuable comments. Tara Foss proved to be a talented professional editor.

I am greatly appreciative of the staunch goodwill of my father, Raymond Eskapa, and my uncle, Graham Beck, for their whole-hearted conviction that this was a book that had to be written. The tremendous enthusiasm of my late uncle, Rodney Barnett, inspired me onward, and I am deeply indebted to him. My gentle and inspiring aunt, Rhona Beck, believed from the outset that the Sinclair Method is the long-overdue breakthrough in the search for a cure for alcoholism for which we have all been waiting. She also helped me keep faith when I was faced with several daunting hurdles, and I am enormously grateful to her.

I would like to express my gratitude to Kevin Mitnick for his introduction to David Fugate of Launch Books, who proved to be an exacting, professional, and tenacious agent. I would also like to thank Glenn Yeffeth, Jennifer Canzoneri, Yara Abuata, and Laura Watkins of BenBella Books for their professionalism and for their unflagging commitment to this work.

Akiko Takahashi, Linda and Richard Grosse, and Anil Metre offered unique support and helped me more than they can ever know. I would also like to express my gratitude to several of my most distinguished teachers: my mentor, Professor Arnold Lazarus; Professors Allen Neuringer, Les Squier, Dr. Raymond E. Anderson, and the great physician, Professor Mosie Suzman.

I would like to acknowledge the support I received over the years from my brother, Robert Eskapa; my young buddy, Max Cazier; his grandparents, Edward and Yvonne Cazier. Thanks also to Isaac Kaye for his introduction to David Sinclair, and also to the following for their friendship over the years: Julian and Jo Spector, Lisa Kaye, Tony and Michal Leon, Lisa Chiat, Mark and Sandy Cohen, Jean Fleming, Jill, Sandra, and Geoffry Wolf, Amikam and Miriam Levanon, Shlomo, Doron and Miriam Angel, John and Lucy Richards, Abe Mahlangu, Betty Brown, Sheleen O'Meara, Olga Faure, Pinky, Georgina Jaffee, Harold Nakin, Dr. Steve Herman, Dr. Kenneth Jacobson, Dr. Marios Panos, Dr. Rama Murthy, Drs. Roy and Kathy Aaronson, Nawang Dorje, Olivia Gibbs, Prasado Munch, Stephanie and Paul Cohen, Helen Burton, Hassan Granmayeh, Vivek Narang, Munu Kasliwal, Kirsti Sinclair, Lorette Scheiner, Jill Samuels, Professor John Lazarus, Reena, Kartik, and Tanwi Metre, Ren Yaar Takahashi-Or, Bupa Patel, Dr. Ming Pang, Pat Barnett, Dr. Frank Ferrise, Philip Gillamond, the late Harvey Martin and late Philippa Pullar, Dr. Josh Berkowitz, W. L. Tollman, Athar and Cornelia Sultan-Khan, and of course my lovely niece and nephew Antonia and Nicholas Grosse, and cousins Anthony Beck, Oliver, and Leah Barnett, and Terri Kramer.

Finally, I would like to acknowledge my grandparents, Masha and Pepo Eskapa and Lea and Harry Barnett, who taught me so much.

Foreword

David Sinclair, PhD

ON THE DAY that the first draft of this book was due to the publisher in Texas, Dr. Roy Eskapa was in the foothills of the Himalayas, introducing the method for treating alcoholism to CORD, a non-governmental organization working in rural northern India.

I was in Finland and had been checking scientific points in the manuscript. Naturally it had taken me twice as long as anticipated, and Roy got my comments only shortly before the deadline. The delay created a problem. He could, with some difficulty, get my simple e-mail messages through his mobile phone even in the small village near Dharamsala. A broadband Internet connection would be needed, however, to transmit the entire manuscript to the publisher, and there was none.

The only nearby access to the Internet was further up the mountain, in McLeod Ganj, the village where the Dalai Lama lives with his followers. I could not even find the road up to McLeod Ganj on Google Earth, but apparently it does exist. It's just small—winding, full of potholes, Tibetan monks, goats, and cows. And motorbikes. So Roy found a fellow in Dharamsala who would rent him an old Royal Enfield motorbike.

With the book stored on a USB memory stick in his pocket, Roy got on the Enfield and started up the mountain. Past the goats and cows. But as he neared McLeod Ganj, the motor sputtered and died.

The bike could go no further up the road, but it could go downhill. So Roy turned around and coasted back down the slope, past where he had started in Dharamsala, until he finally found a mechanic.

In five seconds the spark plug was fixed, and Roy was on his way up the road again.

Halfway to McLeod Ganj, the Enfield stopped again. This time the chain had come off. Roy coasted back down the hill one more time. The repair this time took an hour, but in due course Roy was back on the road and up the mountain, past Dharamsala and the fellow who had rented him the bike to begin with. And this time—since this was his third try—Roy succeeded in reaching his destination, the Green Cyber Café in McLeod Ganj.

Transmitting the whole manuscript was still difficult: the computers at the Internet café were all occupied, but the owner allowed Roy to use his own terminal. The connection was slow and spotty and just as the manuscript was almost completely sent, there was a power failure. Roy tried again and there was a second power failure. On the third try (of course!), the entire book flew from the Internet café at the roof of the world, went halfway around the world in a heartbeat, and arrived safely at BenBella Books in Dallas.

Dr. Eskapa has faced many obstacles in writing this book, though few of them involving broken motorbikes, and his tenacity, energy, and dedication (not only with the book, but also in promoting its new and effective treatment for alcoholism) are the reason you're holding *The Cure for Alcoholism: The Medically Proven Way to Eliminate Alcohol Addiction* in your hands today.

I have been most fortunate in that I've been involved in the development of this new treatment method since the beginning. It is very rare that a scientist gets to see his work go all the way from theory to laboratory experimentation to clinical trial, and then on to a safe and approved application. But there is one more step I hope to see, and it is this step that I hope this book will help accomplish. If this method for treating alcoholism is going to fulfill its potential, doctors and patients must know about it and understand it.

The Cure for Alcoholism should also reduce the problem that currently only a small fraction of those people who need help ever seek treatment. This is understandable with the traditional treatment method, which I call the "D Method." Consider the steps involved in most current treatments and imagine if you would want to sign up:

Detect. Before you are allowed to start treatment, you have to admit that you are an alcoholic, with all the stigma that unfortunately (and incorrectly) is associated with that label.

Delay. Once you have finally agreed to say, "I am an alcoholic," and developed enough courage and motivation to go into treatment, you may be told that the earliest opening in the program is three months or more away. This is more of a problem in some countries than in others, but where it does exist, it takes the heart out of seeking help.

Detox. You start with the horrible experience of alcohol withdrawal. If no medications are used, detoxification is painful and disturbing; it may even be fatal. It also destroys brain cells. If medications are used, they're usually addictive drugs: benzodiazepines such as diazepam (Valium) or chlordiazepoxide (Librium) or barbiturates such as phenobarbital (Luminal) and pentobarbital (Nembutal); these drugs will help you through the alcohol withdrawal, but you may end up—as many do—with two addictions rather than one.

Detain. Next you are put away for weeks in a place—rehab— where it is supposed to be impossible to drink. You have to put your life on hold to do so, forcing you to choose whether to lie to friends and coworkers or else tell them you're an alcoholic and risk their reactions. If you're lucky, your job will be waiting for you when you return. But only if you're lucky.

Don't Drink. All this time, the main thing you want to do is to drink. Nothing has weakened the craving and now, after weeks of alcohol deprivation, it is even greater. Yet, the main thing everyone tells you is, "Don't Drink!"

Denigrate. Some treatment facilities will attempt to break your spirit and resistance, for example, by insulting you, waking you up at odd hours, making you perform demeaning jobs, and forcing you to confess all your past sins in public.

Disulfiram. You are in treatment because you cannot resist drinking. Now, without doing anything to improve your ability to resist drinking or to reduce your craving, the facility's doctors may put you on a prescription of disulfiram (Antabuse®), where if you do what every fiber of your body insists you must do—drink alcohol—you will suffer agonizing torture and may even die. You must face this ordeal every day for the rest of your life. The disulfiram will do nothing to abate your craving, and if you ever stop taking the disulfiram, your craving will probably be greater than it was before you started taking it.[*]

Dollars. The treatment, especially because of the inpatient detoxification and detention steps, is very expensive. You have to be able to afford this even though, during your detention, you won't be collecting your regular paycheck and may even lose your job.

And finally: Do it all over again. The odds are very high that within a year or two you will be back where you started, deciding whether to go through the treatment again, and then again....

The new method detailed by *The Cure for Alcoholism* changes all of the **D** steps. There's no **D**etection. Our method is for anyone who wants to control their drinking. No **D**elay. The treatment is

---

[*] Soon after I first wrote this, an old friend, Pat, asked me about Antabuse capsules because the alcoholic husband of a friend of hers had been given one. I told her that I thought its use was similar to the treatment of the Abu Ghraib prisoner told he must keep his arms raised or else suffer agonizing torture and even die. I met Pat again recently and she said, "You remember the alcoholic who was given the Antabuse capsule and told that if he drank, he would die? Well, I just heard that he drank, and he died." She went on to explain that he had abstained for about a month, but eventually could take it no longer and started sipping alcohol. Personal problems arose. Finally, he bought and drank a large amount of alcohol. And died. I suspect his action was similar to that of a prisoner who finally chooses death over further torture.

completely outpatient and can start immediately. No Detox. You drink as you normally do, but because of this method, your craving slowly decreases, so your drinking also decreases gradually and safely. No **D**etention. No **D**isulfiram. No addictive or dangerous drugs. No **D**enigration. Your dignity is emphasized. Costs are reduced. And there is no revolving **D**oor: the method works the first time around and instead of relapsing, patients get progressively better the longer they have been undergoing treatment.

We should not blame doctors and clinicians for this **D** Method. Until now, it was the best they had to offer.

Let me give an example. I had just given a lecture to the staff of a hospital in Massachusetts explaining pharmacological extinction, the key concept in this new method, and how to use it to help their patients. The head physician, Dr. Michael Pearlman, liked our results and was excited about using the extinction method. On the way out, he introduced me to one of the patients, Kathy, and told her I had developed a new medicine for treating alcoholism.

Kathy looked at me suspiciously. "Is that one of those medicines where you can't drink anything?"

I replied that ours was almost the opposite. You had to drink for our medicine to work. She thought that was an interesting idea.

I described how drinking was learned. She agreed: she'd been there and done that.

Then I explained how learned behaviors could be removed by extinction. She had heard about Pavlov and how he used extinction with his dogs to eliminate their conditioned responses.

The new treatment made sense to her. "I think I might like to try that...but I don't want my usual doctor here giving it to me. He steps on me for my being a mother and all."

I assured her that degrading patients was not part of the procedure. "Indeed, one of the rules I insist upon is that patients must be treated with dignity."

She looked up at me with a surprised glow. The idea of being treated with dignity had not occurred to her in a long time.

More important, however, was what Dr. Pearlman told her: "You see, Kathy, before we did not have naltrexone and extinction.

So we used any hammer we had to try to make you stop drinking, including telling you that you are a bad mother if you drink. But now we have a better way."

The goal of this book, at least initially, was to inform folks in America about this new method. Developed countries, like the United States and Finland, would certainly benefit from it. For most patients, it does—as the book's title says—provide the cure for alcoholism. It is safer, cheaper, more humane, and more effective than other treatments.

Where the method has the greatest potential benefit, however, is in developing countries.

The situation is similar to that with mobile phones. They provide benefits in countries like America and Finland where there is already an existing infrastructure of landlines, although to some extent landlines are in competition with mobile phones and can hinder their development. Mobile phones really shine, however, in places where there is no infrastructure, as in much of Africa. Mobile phones in these places provide the capacity for "leapfrog technology," connecting people to one another and to the world without first having to spend a fortune stringing cables across the land. They allow developing countries to skip that intermediary step entirely.

The same is true for our treatment. It does not require prior detoxification or detention. The first clinical trial in the world treating alcoholics without prior detoxification was the one we conducted here in Finland: patients who were drinking yesterday are simply told to take naltrexone or nalmefene before drinking today.

I once gave a presentation at an alcoholism treatment hospital in Virginia. The staff understood how pharmacological extinction worked and accepted the results I showed them, but mentioned one problem: "What are we supposed to do for a living?" The hospital received a certain amount of money for each alcoholic it detoxified. Where would the money come from with a treatment that skipped inpatient detoxification?

This may have been an obstacle to the spread of the treatment in America and other developed countries, but it is a major advantage in developing countries. They have not invested millions building facilities for detoxifying and detaining alcoholics. They do not have large numbers of people already trained to work in such facilities. Our method, therefore, could provide developing countries with another form of "leapfrog technology," allowing them to help their people with alcohol problems without first having to spend a fortune building a treatment infrastructure.

Using the new method where traditional treatments have not been established sounds good on paper, but would it work in practice? Dr. Eskapa has shown it probably will. He introduced the treatment to the clinicians working with CORD in northern India. CORD's national director, Dr. Kshama Metre, recently sent me the results from their first twenty-eight patients. They had a 75 percent success rate. This is virtually the same as the success rate we found in our clinics in Finland and close to the rate reported by clinics using the method in Florida. Of course, the sample from India is still small, but there is no reason to suspect the method will work differently in different countries. Unlike many alcoholism treatments, extinction with naltrexone or nalmefene should be relatively independent of cultural factors.

Recently, I was describing the science behind the new method to a young visiting scientist in our lab in Helsinki. It was gratifying to find that he accepted without hesitation each of the major discoveries and conclusions leading to pharmacological extinction, but I was not really surprised. Today, these points are generally accepted by most of the leaders in the field. After my talks, I am often told that the top clinicians in alcoholism treatment knew all of this all along. The consensus for decades has been that alcoholism is a learned behavioral disorder and that the endorphin or opioid system at least played a role in the reinforcement of drinking. Extinction has been known for over a century to be the mechanism for removing learned behaviors. The obvious conclusion to anyone putting these points together is that naltrexone and nalmefene could be used to extinguish alcohol drinking. I am not sure why others, with the notable exception of Abram Wikler in the field of heroin addiction, did not previously speak out more about the use of extinction in de-addiction treatment, but it is more important that most of the alcoholism experts agree with the conclusions today. Such approval within the field may mean that the time has come for this method's general acceptance among doctors and patients. *The Cure for Alcoholism* may well play a critical role in establishing this acceptance. And hopefully, with this acceptance will come a more enlightened era—of truly *curing* addictions.

David Sinclair, PhD
National Public Health Institute
Helsinki, Finland

Introduction

by Claudia Christian,
author of *Babylon Confidential*

From 2003 to 2009 I tried every available treatment for alcoholism on the planet.

I tried rehab, detox, hypnosis, psychotherapy, vitamin treatments, yoga retreats, spiritual intervention, A.A., prayer, church, acupuncture, past-life regression, diets, cutting out sugar, nutritionists, electrical-current therapy...well, you get the point.

Nothing worked for me. I continued to remain sober for anywhere from a month to 11-and-a-half months (never quite got to the year mark), then fell off the wagon after convincing myself that I was not actually an alcoholic at all—I was just an emotional drinker. That's the insidious thing about the disease: it makes you think that if you can remain sober for a period of time, then you're not an alcoholic. So you have a drink, and you're fine with one, so you have two the next time, then three. Then, lo and behold, you're nipping in the morning to get rid of the hangover, and, the next thing you know, you're lying in bed detoxing with hallucinations, puking your guts up, and crying like a two-year-old. Well, at least that's what I did.

I am not ashamed to admit that I was an alcoholic. In fact, I am thrilled to be able to say just that: "I *was* an alcoholic." I *was* an alcoholic and no longer am. Alcohol does not rule my life anymore.

Wouldn't it be wonderful to stand up at an A.A. meeting and shout: "Hi, I'm Bob, and I used to be an alcoholic!"

You can say that now. The Sinclair Method (TSM) does cure alcoholism, and I am living proof. I have been on it since that fateful day in March of 2009 when I stumbled across Dr. Roy Eskapa's book *The Cure for Alcoholism* while researching the ingredients in the long-acting injectible shot Vivitrol that I was considering trying. The shot cost $1,000 a month, and it was supposed to inhibit cravings for alcohol. I really wanted that shot, but the detox center I kept calling thankfully—and fatefully—never returned my calls.

I bought the book and read it. Then, I copied a few chapters and brought it in to a doctor. The doctor had to look naltrexone up in his little black drug book, and he was very wary, to say the least. He had never heard of TSM, nor had he had any experience with opiate blockers. But he reluctantly gave me a prescription for 15 pills, and the rest is history.

Now I can drink safely, and I still enjoy a glass of wine and socializing with friends. I am not 100% abstinent, although there are times when I quite literally "forget" to drink; other times, though, I have more than one glass of wine—just like a normal drinker. TSM has made me the person I was *before the disease came creeping in.* I no longer think about alcohol, and, because I am not on a strictly enforced abstinence program, I no longer resent being sober. TSM has achieved the impossible. I can drink, or I can choose not to drink. The key word here is "choose." I have a choice now. I am free from the chains of addiction and from the chains of enforced abstinence.

I have many friends who, like me, found that as they got older, they began to abuse alcohol. It's not surprising that both of my grandfathers abused alcohol in their 40s; my addiction began in my late 30s but, before that, I was a normal person. I didn't drink during the day or every night; nor did I pass out or throw up or poison myself. I was just a moderate social drinker. Many of my friends who notice that they are on their way to becoming addicts or who are seriously abusing alcohol have gone on TSM. All of them who have taken the medication correctly have cut back greatly on their drinking: it works.

The one thing is that you *must* follow the simple yet massively critical directions; take naltrexone or nalmefene 1 hour prior to having your first drink in a 24-hour period. This is the Golden Rule. You might take 50 mg, like me, or you might, like some people (a small percentage), need 75 mg. That should be decided by you and your physician.

It is an excellent idea to keep a drinking diary, In fact, I think it is imperative to your recovery process because it really shows you the facts in black and white. For me, the graph was radically down in the beginning. Then I was abstinent. Then, a few months later, I began drinking like I did in my 20s: some wine a few times a week and no binges. I am what Dr. Eskapa calls a "fast responder," and I am blessed that TSM worked, literally overnight, for me. But, for some of you, it might take several months.

One of my friends only saw a difference after 9 months (the average time from beginning to cure is 3–4 months); another had to up the dosage to 75 mg and then saw huge results after 6 months of frustration. So you must keep the diary to see how it's working for you personally and then adjust things as needed. Please do not make the (surprisingly common) mistake of thinking, "Oh, I'll take the medication *with* my first drink," or, "Oh, I'll skip it this time."

You must take it one hour prior to your first drink for the rest of your life if you continue to drink. I cannot stress this enough. Follow the directions—please!

It's not that hard if you prepare a little. Diabetics manage their disease, so you can manage alcoholism. Simply put your medication everywhere: in your car, in your wallet, in one of those pill-keeper key rings, in your desk at work, at home, and at your best friend's house. Seriously…you need access to your medication if you know you will be in a situation where you will have a drink. I know one fellow who has a necklace with a little silver bullet on the end that holds two capsules of naltrexone, and he doesn't even drink anymore.

So, there you have it: go to a physician, get the prescription, and take a pill an hour before your first drink. In a few months you will be cured. It's that simple.

If I had known about TSM back in 2002, when the first signs of alcoholism were showing, I would have saved myself from years of agony, ruined relationships, loss of trust, physical pain, family discord, financial drain from treatments, weight gain, debilitating guilt and misery—to name but a few of the horrors I endured.

We cannot get those years back, but we can move forward. I did, and so can you or your loved one who is suffering from alcoholism.

In the spring of 2009, after being cured of alcoholism, I contacted Dr. Eskapa through his publisher, BenBella, and was thoroughly surprised that he responded not only quickly but with an open heart and mind and a tremendous amount of kindness, integrity, and passion. We spoke about why TSM is not better known and what I could do to help. I told him that I planned on writing a book about my journey through addiction and asked if he would mind if I used some of his research in my book. He generously offered an entire appendix, access to Dr. David Sinclair (another saint who deserves the Nobel Prize for his tireless efforts and years of hard work), and we began a friendship and working relationship that has seen me through some of the most inspiring times of my life. These two men are utterly devoted to saving lives with this miraculous treatment, and I intend to do everything in my power to help spread the word.

My dream is that, someday soon, you will overhear someone in a bar or restaurant ask, "Did you take your pill?" Or you'll see a young kid turn to a new friend at a club and say, "Oh, you're a TSM-er? Me, too!"

That is my dream: a world where people no longer suffer from this dreadful disease. A world where families reunite with their loved ones; where children no longer suffer abuse at the hands of an alcoholic; and where youth and beauty and talent and intelligence are not wasted on abuse and addiction. A world where car accidents are halved, medical bills chopped in pieces, and the collective cost of alcoholism on society reduced to a mere blip.

That is my dream, and I hope you, reader, will help achieve that dream.

I wish you health and happiness and freedom from addiction. I did it, and so can you.

Claudia Christian
January 5, 2012
Hollywood, California

Alcoholism: Who Says It's Incurable?

1

Introducing Yourself to the Cure

THE CURE FOR ALCOHOLISM is intended as a guide to understanding the complexities and subtleties of the Sinclair Method and how it works. It is a scientifically proven treatment that, for the first time in history, actually *cures* alcohol addiction. Dozens of clinical trials prove that the Sinclair Method cures alcohol addiction. Success rates in clinics are 78 percent or higher.[*] By contrast, current rehabilitation methods yield success rates of around 10–15 percent, according to the National Institute on Alcohol Abuse and Alcoholism (NIAAA) and the World Health Organization (WHO).

The book's title, *The Cure for Alcoholism: The Medically Proven Way to Eliminate Alcohol Addiction* means what it says. Addiction to alcohol can now be cured—not through abstinence, but by always taking a medication called naltrexone an hour before drinking alcohol. Naltrexone is not addictive and seldom produces side effects.

---

[*] This figure is based on success rates at clinics in both Finland and Florida.

The reduction in craving and drinking is progressive. Benefits can be seen as soon as ten days after first use, but the effects are more than three times stronger after three to four months. By that time, your cravings for alcohol will have diminished so much that you are no longer obsessed with alcohol. Some people will choose to stop drinking completely; others continue to drink at safe, controllable levels. The benefits continue increasing indefinitely so long as you take naltrexone if and when you drink.

Since the early 1990s, the Sinclair Method has cured thousands of patients, many of them so-called hopeless cases. The treatment is supported by more than seventy published clinical trials, which are discussed later in the book. The first clinical trials using naltrexone for alcoholism, conducted at the University of Pennsylvania and at Yale, included extensive counseling; consequently, when the FDA approved the use of naltrexone in 1994, it stipulated that the medicine was to be used as part of a comprehensive program of alcoholism treatment. In May 2006, the *Journal of the American Medical Association* published the results from Project COMBINE with 1,383 patients, making it the largest trial in the history of alcohol addiction.[1] The results once again showed that naltrexone was safe and effective, but they also showed that extensive counseling was not needed. As a result of this study, naltrexone is no longer just for large clinics specializing in alcohol problems; now, any licensed doctor can ethically and safely prescribe naltrexone for problem drinking.

One of the objectives for this book is to provide these doctors and their patients with the information they need in order to use naltrexone properly. The clinical trials have shown clearly that naltrexone only works when it is used in a particular way, and it is not the way most doctors would use it intuitively. If you want patients to stop drinking, you tell them "don't drink," you give them as much support for maintaining abstinence as possible, and then you tell them to take the medicine. That is the intuitive solution. Moreover, it is the way doctors have given Antabuse®, the only medicine previously approved for treating alcoholism. Clinical trials in Finland and America have shown naltrexone is not effective when used this way. The trials proved that naltrexone only worked when it was taken at the same time that alcohol was being drunk.

Until now, most doctors and addiction experts were *unaware* that to cure alcoholism, one has to drink alcohol while naltrexone is in the bloodstream. How, they ask, can it be ethical to allow alcoholics to continue drinking? Even if drinking is monitored and combined with a special medication, how can it produce a cure? In America, a nation with a temperance tradition so powerful that it once produced Prohibition, the idea may seem outrageous. In particular, it runs counter to cultural notions that the only answer to alcoholism is cold turkey withdrawal followed by rehabilitation and abstinence for life.

The Cure requires a basic understanding of three key concepts discovered by David Sinclair:

1. **The Alcohol Deprivation Effect**—explains how abstinence leads to a progressive increase in craving and eventually to a relapse to excessive drinking and why addiction has never before been curable
2. **Pharmacological Extinction**—Sinclair's proven method for removing the addiction
3. **Pharmacologically Enhanced Learning**—for strengthening healthy alternative behaviors

The Cure for Alcoholism may enrage the $6.2 billion alcohol rehabilitation industry and all those people who are, in principle, opposed to medication because they are ideologically wedded to a philosophy of abstinence. Despite the fact that Finland has routinely used the method to treat an estimated seventy thousand patients successfully, the treatment remains largely unknown in the United States, much of Europe, and Japan. *The Cure for Alcoholism* is intended to change this and, above all, to save lives.

Alcoholics Anonymous and the Sinclair Method

The term "cure" is not used lightly or without deep consideration. Sinclair's method is equivalent to a cure because it actually restores the brain to a condition in which the craving and interest in alcohol are similar to the way they were before alcoholism was learned.

Bill Wilson founded Alcoholics Anonymous (A.A.) in 1934, sixty years before naltrexone was approved by the FDA in 1994. A.A. is not a cure and has never pretended to be one; it says instead that the people in its program remain alcoholics. From an A.A. perspective, though, anything that can save people from the ravages of alcohol addiction must be worthwhile—even if it means patients continue to drink at medically safe levels.

Alan Franks, a reporter for the *Sunday Times Magazine* (London) after coming to Finland to interview Dr. Sinclair, wrote that A.A. and the Sinclair Method "could be even more complementary than Sinclair was suggesting."

Many of the first doctors and clinicians using the Sinclair Method were themselves A.A. members. They had been frustrated because A.A.'s Twelve Steps did not work for many of their patients but now, with pharmacological extinction, they were able to help practically all of their patients.

Antabuse and the Sinclair Method

Disulfiram or Antabuse was initially thought to be an excellent and logical way to deal with alcohol addiction. Antabuse is a prescription drug given to recovering alcoholics to help them abstain from drinking alcohol. If someone drinks alcohol while taking this medicine, it quickly causes a severe, unpleasant, and potentially dangerous reaction. It was thought that knowledge of this fact could help to stop people from drinking, but this treatment is wildly unsuccessful. It's the equivalent of locking up a patient in a prison or mental facility where no alcohol is available. Enforced abstinence produces an Alcohol Deprivation Effect (discussed in chapter 2), which increases the craving. Indeed, animal studies have shown that disulfiram and similar medicines increase the craving even more than the level of craving produced by the abstinence alone. Therefore, although most patients cannot drink while on disulfiram, they become very anxious to get rid of the medication and start drinking again. The craving induces people to quit taking Antabuse so they can start drinking again. There are stories of alcoholics cutting open their arms or abdomens to remove slow-release capsules in order to be free to start drinking. Antabuse, therefore, is *not* a cure because it fails to remove the basis for alcoholism, as proven by the fact that it fails to reduce the craving. Instead, Antabuse actually leads to an increase in craving. It attempts to establish a logical barrier against drinking: patients are told they will become very nauseated and may even die if they drink while taking it, so logically the patients should abstain. Unfortunately, alcohol abuse is not a logical behavior.

The Sinclair Method removes the neural changes that have caused alcoholism—the over-strengthened pathways of neurons that have developed in the brain, causing alcohol craving and excessive drinking.

How I "Discovered" the Sinclair Method

In the early 1990s, I began searching for an effective treatment on behalf of a beloved childhood friend who had been battling a severe alcohol addiction since his early twenties. My training as a clinical psychologist in California had merely touched on addiction. The conventional wisdom was that addiction was virtually impossible to treat and, unless you were an expert, the best course was to refer patients with addictive disorders to Alcoholics Anonymous (A.A.) and specialist care.

As a graduate student in clinical psychology, I had been required to attend Alcoholics, Narcotics, or Gamblers Anonymous meetings as an observer. I was stunned by the extraordinary lengths to which addicts would go to get a fix, whether it was of alcohol, heroin, or gambling. After numerous sessions as an observer at a leading addiction treatment facility, I decided to avoid working professionally with addicts. Yet, several years after I had graduated with my PhD in psychology, my friend's addiction to alcohol intervened. I began to search for help.

After several false starts and long searches, I found Dr. Sinclair and his research team in Finland. Sinclair claimed he could *cure* alcohol addiction. Addiction is a learned behavior that has been reinforced so often and so powerfully that the addicted person is no longer able to control it. Alcohol drinking produces reinforcement and is learned through that reinforcement.[2] At first, I thought the claims were extraordinary when Sinclair told me that alcohol produces reinforcement through the same system in the brain as morphine (an opiate), but he showed me his research findings— starting all the way back with his doctoral dissertation and then published in the distinguished scientific journal *Nature*[3]—that morphine acts as a substitution drug for alcohol. This is because alcohol releases endorphins that bind to the same opioid receptors in the brain as morphine and other opiates.

While visiting Sinclair's laboratory in Helsinki, I saw images and graphs that depict how alcoholism is learned by strengthening pathways in the brain, and how, once learned, these pathways that cause craving and drinking remain powerful and able to dominate other behaviors for a lifetime. This is the basis for the A.A. precept that once people become alcoholics, they remain alcoholics forever. Abstaining from alcohol did not get rid of the alcoholism; indeed, Sinclair showed me how it made the pathways more sensitive, making a person crave alcohol more than ever. "Addiction does not happen overnight," Sinclair explained. "It takes time and practice to learn it. By the time it has taken root, all conventional methods can only attempt to overcome the ever-strengthening addiction—like trying to stop a knee-jerk reflex with willpower— but they cannot remove the cause of the drinking and they prove almost futile in combating alcohol addiction."

There was only one way known, Sinclair said, to reverse the changes caused by learning. The nervous system has a mechanism called extinction for weakening previously learned behaviors. "Extinction is the brain's eraser for removing those behaviors that no longer produce the reinforcement you expect." Extinction begins when a person does something that used to give reinforcement but now, for some reason, the reinforcement is blocked. In the case of drinking, the reinforcement can be prevented by medicines, such as naltrexone, that block the receptors for endorphins. "The person drinks, and endorphins are released, but the endorphins just bounce off of the receptors that are blocked with naltrexone." The nervous system then reacts by weakening the neural connections that cause craving and drinking.

Sinclair showed me graphs demonstrating how craving and drinking gradually decreased over months in patients always taking naltrexone before drinking.[4] The graphs also showed how administering naltrexone without drinking had no effect on addiction.[5] Patients had to drink to get any benefit from the medication!

Sinclair gave me several of his publications and explained how alcohol causes the release of endorphins—the body's naturally produced opiates—in the brain whenever we drink alcohol. Endorphins are opiate- or morphine-like "local hormones" that provide a shortcut for learning. For example, animals can learn to get food from the slow reinforcement given after the food is digested and hunger is eliminated, but endorphins provide a faster, more precise way. For example, as soon as you bite into a ripe apple, the sweet taste causes a release of endorphins, thus providing rapid reinforcement. Our brains use this shortcut for reinforcing many behaviors; endorphins are released when we exercise vigorously, have sex, taste sweet and spicy foods, cuddle babies and cute little animals, place bets, go shopping, or try risky activities. Endorphins also serve as "natural painkillers"; for instance, women's endorphin levels rise when they give birth.

My Personal Encounter with Alcoholism

Most of us know at least one person very well who is addicted to alcohol. In my case, it was a childhood friend, James. He was a much loved, highly successful, and charismatic man who displayed outstanding willpower—and humor—against his craving for alcohol. Over the years, he admitted himself for inpatient treatment at several highly reputable clinics. When he relapsed, he would bravely—and cheerfully—get back on his horse to try again. His goal was always abstinence. He carried the A.A. book *Twelve Steps and Twelve Traditions* with him wherever he went throughout the world.[6] The inscription in his book reads: "James, Expect a Miracle. Love, Jane." He diligently attended

A.A. meetings no matter where in the world his life and business took him.

I remember his uncle tearfully telling me how he had driven James to a clinic where he was given an Antabuse implant. They both believed that the implant would help by putting him into a "chemical prison"—it would physically prevent him from drinking. He drank through the implant. Then he tried a famous therapist in London who was said to have "that special touch with addicts." When that did not work, he became an inpatient at the renowned Father Martin's Ashley rehabilitation clinic in Maryland. My friend resorted to alternative practitioners, priests, and even mystics. He implored the Divine to intervene on his behalf, and he continued to make a brave and gallant effort in his fight against alcohol.

His family and friends tried equally hard in many different ways to continue to help. People, including virtual strangers, prayed for him. They begged him to stop drinking. He begged himself to stop, even going as far as hiring a personal assistant to physically prevent him from getting alcohol. Although he certainly did not "choose" to carry on drinking—as some addiction experts would claim—the craving won in the end. In the prime of his life and after a magnificent struggle, he lost this agonizing battle against the bottle. He died at the age of thirty-five. No one imagined this would happen.

My Contribution to James's Struggle

In June 1995, six months before his death, I visited James to discuss "my discovery" of Sinclair's little-known cure for alcohol addiction. At the time, he was recovering from a severe leg injury sustained in an alcohol-related auto accident; I could see the shiny titanium pins jutting out of his leg. "It's a new treatment," I told him. "You have to take naltrexone, which has only recently been approved by the FDA. The medication will block the jolts of reinforcement your brain gets from the endorphins released each time you have a drink. In fact, you may be amazed to hear this—and maybe even pleased—but you actually have to carry on drinking when you take this medication. Slowly but surely, each drink you have while you take this medication will be 'good medicine for you.' Sinclair has put his theories into practice—and they are now getting incredible results in de-addiction. The treatment actually seems to be reversing or erasing the addiction from the brain."

I can still see the hope and warmth in his eyes. He looked off into the distance and considered what I had said. Many people had come to him before. All sorts of solutions, potions, and prayers were proffered. Well-meaning doctors had offered their advice. Everyone was an *expert*. He looked at me directly and simply said, "It makes sense. I would like to try it." But James died of sudden cardiac arrest after a heavy drinking session—not uncommon in advanced alcoholism—before he could even begin treatment. How I wish I had known how effective naltrexone with pharmacological extinction—the Cure—really was. Sometimes I feel that somehow, if only I had been more insistent, not only with James but with his family and the doctors, he might still be alive. But I was up against the conventional wisdom of our age: aim for abstinence. The formula of Naltrexone + Drinking = Cure seemed totally crazy and, at the time, impossible for many people— including his family—to accept.

It is now just over twelve years since James died. It feels both ironic and personally tragic that I am writing this in what is still known as "James's room." Located at the top of a house once almost demolished by German bombs during World War II, it has a beautiful view over a green London square with magnificent trees on all sides. Roses in the garden now bear James's name. I now know with a certainty I did not possess at the time that had he been able to take advantage of Sinclair's discovery—that Naltrexone + Drinking = Cure—he could still be using this room. Before he became gripped by the tightening vise of alcoholism, he was so full of fun that once, after a heavy snow, he ran out into the square with his tennis racket and used it to write "I love you, Mum" in the snow. That image remains fresh in his mother's mind's eye.

I wrote this book for James and for all of the other friends, brothers, mothers, and fathers who can benefit from the Cure. The proof is in the scientific trials and in personal accounts: Naltrexone + Drinking = Cure. The next chapter discusses the background and ideas behind The Cure.

(Please refer to www.cthreefoundation.org for updates and on-line support.)

The Genesis of the Cure for Alcoholism

No great discovery was ever made without a bold guess.
—ISAAC NEWTON (1642–1727)

I *CAN QUIT any time I want. I'm not addicted; I just like to drink.* How often have you said these words, either to yourself or to those around you? Well, you may not be addicted, but you can't quit either. You're somewhere in between. You know that drinking too much alcohol is dangerous for your health, you know that sometimes you drink too much and say things you wish you hadn't, and you know the hangovers are getting worse. But you also know that quitting "cold turkey" and never drinking again would be too hard for you; you think it would be a nightmare. You think there's no other way. Read on.

Sinclair Discovers What Drives Alcoholism

Who would have thought that a little boy taunted on a school bus in West Virginia for having a speech impediment would one day crack the code behind a bewildering addiction that, according to the World Health Organization, kills 1.8 million people every year?

At the same time when most people could not understand what he said, Sinclair's "right brain" activities were advanced. His drawings were comparable to those created by students twice his age. At the age of eleven, he was accepted into art classes at the local college. His grade-school principal named him the "Official Artist of the School," mainly to encourage him to stick around and at least learn how to read and write. With his special aptitude for visual and spatial concepts, he started to catch up academically and eventually graduated at the top of his class. He also overcame his speech problem and today is noted for his ability to speak eloquently about abstract ideas.

Sinclair subsequently won scholarships to study physics at the Carnegie Institute of Technology in Pennsylvania in 1961. At that time, Carnegie had one of the first computers, the Bendix G-20, equipped with 32,000 vacuum tubes. That is about half the capacity of my cell phone, but it was a marvel for its day; Sinclair's experience with it had a profound influence on his later work in neuroscience. When you program a computer, you cannot just draw in a black box labeled *reward* or *punishment*; you have to describe exactly how the process works. On the other hand, observing the complex "behavior" that the G-20 could produce with mere wires and vacuum tubes led Sinclair to suspect that it might be possible to understand the physical basis for our own human behavior.

Sinclair's interest in behavior led him into alcohol research, first at the University of Cincinnati and then at the University of Oregon. An important, although essentially accidental, factor was his discovery of the Alcohol Deprivation Effect (ADE).[7] The ADE turned out to be the first step in cracking the alcohol addiction code.

Dr. R. J. Senter at the University of Cincinnati had a grant for doing alcohol research and hired Sinclair as an eager undergraduate student in 1964 to help look after the laboratory rats. The pervasive belief at the time was that rats and other animals did not like alcohol and, therefore, were not relevant to the study of human alcoholism. And that was indeed what they were finding in Cincinnati. The rats had a choice of two bottles from which they could drink, one filled with water and the other with an alcohol solution. The rats took about 70 percent of their fluid from the water bottle and only about 30 percent from the alcohol bottle. Rats *seemed* to prefer water to alcohol.

Sinclair had an idea for an experiment of his own and asked Senter if he could have some rats. Senter agreed but said he would have to use animals that had been used as controls in an earlier study because there were no funds for additional animals. In the previous experiment, the rats had been given a choice between water and alcohol for several weeks. At the end of that experiment, these rats were left in their cages for a few weeks with free access to food and water but no alcohol.

It was then that Sinclair first made a chance observation that would have major ramifications on research into the causes of and eventual solution for alcoholism in humans. In evoking an entirely new way of understanding the mechanisms driving addiction, it must have come as bold a revelation as that of Isaac Newton when he noticed an apple falling from a tree—an observation that is said to have triggered the creation of the theory of universal gravitation in Newtonian physics.

Sinclair recounts what happened:

So, in the middle of the afternoon, when rats normally are sleeping, I went down to the rat room and started putting alcohol bottles back on the cages. Much to my surprise, the rats immediately woke up, came to the front of the cage, and began drinking the alcohol solution vigorously. They paid no attention to the water bottle next to it. Their preference for alcohol gradually returned to normal levels over the next week, but having seen that high level of drinking when the alcohol was first returned, I could have no doubt that these rats had shown a high motivation for alcohol. (Sinclair, 1997)[8]

The Alcohol Deprivation Effect (ADE) turned out to be one of the most robust, powerful factors controlling alcohol drinking. Today, forty years later, it is still one of the most studied effects in alcohol research. The data from these experiments conclusively demonstrated that abstinence from alcohol in rats already used to drinking increases their motivation for alcohol. This happens not only in rats and other animals but also in people. The implication was that the more an alcoholic is deprived of alcohol, the more he is liable to crave it.

Since the 1968 publication of the paper describing the Alcohol Deprivation Effect, it has become recognized as central to understanding why alcoholism and many other addictions become lifelong conditions. To establish an alcohol craving in the first place, it's necessary to drink alcohol repeatedly for a long time—in rats for several weeks. After that, as T-k Li, the director of the National Institute on Alcohol Abuse and Alcoholism (NIAAA), has said, the motivation for alcohol is purely a matter of scheduling. It is similar to the motivation for food and water. If you want to study hunger, you do not look for it immediately after the Thanksgiving meal. You look at people who have gone many hours or days without eating. Similarly, if you want to see high motivation for alcohol, you study rats or people who have been deprived of it for weeks.

The motivation for alcohol is seen most clearly when the alcohol is first returned. The rats cannot tell you that they are dying for a drink, but as soon as you reopen the bar by placing their alcohol bottles back on their cages, they immediately start vigorously drinking again. The rate of alcohol drinking during the first few minutes after the end of deprivation is more than fifteen times the rate seen daily without deprivation.[9]

Once the initial binge drinking in deprived alcoholic rats has run its course, they return to their previous drinking levels. The Alcohol-Deprivation Effect (Figure 1) is seen not only in animals but also in human alcoholics. The curves show how craving increases over time if the alcoholics—rats or humans—are deprived of alcohol and how they binge when they regain access.

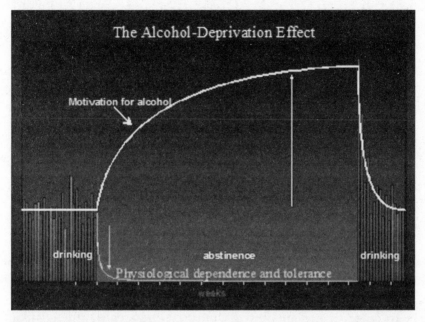

Figure 1. (Sinclair, JD. PowerPoint presentations, Finnish National Public Health Institute, 1997–2008). Original data are from published studies by Sinclair and Senter.[10, 11]

The ADE has profound implications for treatment. The typical treatment for alcoholism has been detoxification followed by weeks of forced abstinence. The ADE suggests why forced abstinence is not an effective treatment. It does not cure alcoholism but actually causes an increase in craving that helps produce relapses. An effect with cocaine that is similar to the ADE has recently been found at the National Institute on Drug Abuse (NIDA); the director, Nora D. Volkow, has pointed out that it suggests incarceration alone is also not a suitable treatment for cocaine abuse. The ADE explains how already addicted alcoholics increasingly crave alcohol when they abstain from alcohol for a period of time. The deprivation or abstinence may be the result of imprisonment or hospitalization. Many times, the deprivation is self-imposed through abstinence-based or faith-based methods like Alcoholics Anonymous, which encourage participants to employ a Higher Power to help them stay dry "one day at a time." Other therapies also rely on abstinence and the use of willpower to go cold turkey.

Sinclair's experiments and all the ADE research that has followed it prove abstinence does not remove the craving for alcohol and, therefore, why abstinence is not a successful treatment for the vast majority of individuals.

The ADE also has important theoretical implications for the causes of addiction. At the time when the ADE was discovered, the prevailing view was that alcoholism was caused by physiological dependence on alcohol. It was already clear to the experts of the day that alcohol abuse could not be explained by the pleasure produced by alcohol. Most alcoholics report that they feel very little if any pleasure. Maybe alcohol drinking had been pleasant at one time, but not when it reached the stage of alcoholism—clearly, whatever remnant of pleasure still remained was insufficient to counteract all of the pain and suffering they knew their alcohol drinking was causing. Nevertheless, once addicted, they continued drinking.

In order to explain this discrepancy, the idea developed that the reason alcoholics drank was to prevent, or stop, the very unpleasant effects of withdrawal from alcohol. This hypothesis produced the semantic confusion we still have today: alcoholism is called "alcohol dependence," but that doesn't mean alcoholism is a simple physiological dependence produced by the body when it adapts to the prolonged presence of alcohol. This hypothesis was also one of the justifications for the usual treatment. It was supposed that once the alcoholics had been taken through the painful process of withdrawal—had been subjected to detoxification—the primary reason for drinking would be removed. Indeed, if alcohol dependence (meaning alcoholism) were caused by alcohol dependence (meaning physiological dependence produced by adaptation), detoxification would have been the cure.

The ADE showed that physiological dependence is not important for the motivation to drink. Simple physiological dependence is reversed by only a few days of abstinence. The motivation for alcohol in animals that have learned to drink, however, does not go away when the dependence is removed, but instead increases. Moreover, the time frame for it increasing differs from the time frame for withdrawal.

Another factor often associated with alcoholism (and indeed included as one criterion for alcoholism) is an increased tolerance for alcohol. Sometimes the idea was advanced that alcoholics drank so much simply because they could; they had such a high tolerance that they could drink massive amounts before showing much intoxication. The ADE is contrary to this idea as well. Tolerance—the ability to consume increasing amounts of alcohol—like dependence, decreases during abstinence. But craving does not diminish over months or years, as one might surmise based on reductions in physical dependence and tolerance after a few weeks of abstinence.

Common sense would also seem to indicate that if you want to stop someone from drinking, you put him or her away in a place where there is no alcohol. Based on the earlier hypotheses about dependence and tolerance and on common sense, this has been the usual treatment for alcoholism. Common sense, however, does not apply here. In fact, depriving alcoholics of alcohol actually *increases* their craving or urge to drink. Detoxification and putting them away in an alcohol-free facility may stop their intake of alcohol while they are there, but when they get out—and especially when they encounter sudden triggers, such as sudden stressful situations or passing a favorite bar—they invariably relapse.

Pharmacological Extinction—How the Cure for Alcoholism Was Discovered

By the late 1960s, Sinclair had already established the Alcohol Deprivation Effect as a fundamental driving force in alcohol addiction. To take his research forward, he needed to use specially bred Alko Alcohol (or AA) rats, which were genetically predisposed to learning alcoholism. These rat lines were developed in the Alko Laboratories in Finland, the best facilities in the world for studying the science of alcoholism. Alko Laboratories were part of the national alcohol monopoly, which had set aside vast funds—ironically, derived from taxes on alcohol—for research "to reduce the harm caused by alcohol."

At the time, Alko's premises in Helsinki were located in a large building that overlooked the frozen white Baltic Sea in the winter and crystal blue waters in the summer. Wines and other imports arrived through the basement; on the middle level, vodka was exported, with smartly dressed executives working in minimalist Scandinavian offices. Sinclair's laboratory, along with those of other Alko research teams, was near the top. I found it rather ironic that they were trading alcohol in the basement while searching for a cure for its abuse on the top floors.

Sinclair's brief at Alko was simple: discover a cure for alcoholism—a condition that affects one in ten people who drink. One of the main research advantages was that the Finns had already spent years breeding the special rats, the AA line, that clearly preferred alcohol. This in itself was a major scientific advance because, like the Alcohol Deprivation Effect, it challenged the assumption that rats could not be used to study alcoholism because they simply did not like to drink alcohol.

Dr. Kalervo Eriksson started the AA rat line in Finland in the early 1960s. The high level of alcohol drinking by the AA rats brought Eriksson to the same conclusion that Sinclair had reached in America: rats can develop a primitive drive for alcohol that is very similar to human alcoholism. Eriksson and Sinclair exchanged reprints of their publications in the late 1960s. Then, in 1972, when Sinclair completed his doctoral dissertation on the alcohol research, he leaped at the opportunity to study these special rats in Finland. We owe a great deal to these animals because they enabled the research to proceed successfully, finally leading, as you will see, to a *cure* for this dreaded addiction.

Eriksson developed two lines of rats. The AA line was bred to drink large amounts of alcohol when they had a free choice. Over several generations, they eventually came to get nearly all their fluid from the alcohol bottle. The other line, the ANA rats, was developed by selecting rats for breeding that drank very little alcohol; eventually, they were avoiding nearly all alcohol. Eriksson's work led to the conclusion that genetic factors play an important factor in alcohol drinking. A large body of research, first in rats and then in humans, has now shown that heredity and experience are about equally powerful in determining how much alcohol is consumed and who becomes an alcoholic.

Now, Sinclair had the AA rats for his research, and Alko had given him virtually unlimited funding and free rein to proceed independently—more than any research scientist could wish for. He knew from his research on the Alcohol Deprivation Effect that alcoholism was not caused by physiological dependence or tolerance. He had never considered the old idea that alcoholism was a moral weakness, jokingly saying that he did not have any "bad rats." He had evidence from his research in his dissertation that there was a connection to opiate addiction and also some interaction with zinc. He did not, however, know the underlying cause of alcohol drinking. In retrospect, the answer was simple and rather obvious—as hindsight makes most discoveries—but at the time, no one saw it.

The answer came as the result of a bit of luck, followed by a lot of hard work. Kalervo Eriksson had gotten the impression from his reading that American psychologists all worked with operant conditioning chambers, also known as Skinner boxes. Consequently, Eriksson had a present waiting for Sinclair—a beautiful new Skinner box imported all the way from Lafayette, Indiana. Contrary to Eriksson's preconception, Sinclair had never done any Skinner box research of his own. Fortunately, however, one of Senter's grants while Sinclair was working for him had involved operant chambers. The big advantage Sinclair had was his belief that rats do like alcohol, so he didn't do anything to force the animals to drink; he simply left the rats in the Skinner box where they could press a lever for alcohol or water and where they also had a bottle of water and food available so they were not hungry or thirsty.

Within a day, each of the AA rats had learned to lever press for alcohol.[12] They soon were pressing the lever several hundred times every day to get alcohol, and almost completely ignoring the free water and the lever that gave water. Later, he tried putting weights on the back of the levers. The usual way to make a response more difficult is to use punishment; for example, a researcher might study how much electric shock a rat would withstand in order to get the alcohol. Sinclair never tried that, partly because he liked the rats, but also because the stress would have confounded the results. The weighted levers showed the AA rats had a high amount of motivation for alcohol; they continued pressing when up to a third of their body weight was on the back of the lever and the only way the animal could get it to go down was to put its nose and front paws on the lever and then jump.

These studies and later ones by his student Petri Hyytiä showed that alcohol produces reinforcement. The rats had learned a new response in order to get the alcohol, so by definition, alcohol drinking was producing reinforcement. A simple extension of this conclusion was that alcoholism is a learned behavioral disorder. Some people who had enough experience with alcohol drinking and who, like the AA rats, had genetic characteristics that led to them obtaining large amounts of reinforcement from alcohol learned the behavior of alcohol drinking so well that it could not be controlled.

It is only one step from this notion that alcohol drinking is learned to Sinclair's discovery of pharmacological extinction and eventually to the cure for the addiction. It has been known since the time of Pavlov that if a response is learned, the way to weaken and remove the response is with extinction. The Sinclair Method uses a medication, naltrexone or nalmefene, to trigger pharmacologically the body's own mechanism of extinction. The result was that, for the first time in history, it was possible to remove the responses causing alcoholism.

Learning and Reinforcement

Sinclair drew on the early experiments of Ivan Pavlov, the Russian physiologist who was awarded the Nobel Prize in 1904 for his work on how behaviors are learned and extinguished. Pavlov's famous experiments showed how dogs *learned* to salivate when a bell was rung because previously the bell had been rung before the dogs were given food (reinforcement). The learning is contingent on the dog being rewarded with food whenever the bell is sounded. Once the behavior had been *conditioned* and the dog would salivate at the sound of the bell, Pavlov rang the bell but gave no food. Soon, the dog was salivating progressively less each time it heard the bell. By not giving food to the dog when the bell was sounded, Pavlov prevented its brain from receiving positive reinforcement. Each time this happened, the dog's nervous system reacted by weakening the previously learned behavior. Less and less saliva was produced and eventually none was released at the sound of the bell. This mechanism was called *extinction*—a deceptively simple, yet particularly powerful biological mechanism for reversing learned behavior.

Extinction is not simply learning that the bell no longer means food. Extinction is a separate mechanism from learning and obeys different rules.[13] For example, learning works best when there is a lot of time between each trial, but extinction requires "massed trials." If Pavlov had only rung the bell once a week without giving food, there would have been little or no reduction in the amount of salivation. Instead, he had to ring it over and over again in a short period of time.

Experiments with AA rats genetically predisposed to becoming alcoholic led Sinclair to the conclusion that the addiction to alcohol was learned and could be removed by extinction. He knew that extinction occurs when a response is made but the expected reinforcement is blocked. The question then is, how can one block the reinforcement? How can you have a rat or person drink alcohol, taste it, feel the intoxication, but still not get the reinforcement? If Sinclair could figure out a way to do this, he could *extinguish* the addictive drinking and cure the problem.

To answer this question, however, it was necessary to know how alcohol causes reinforcement. The answer was suggested by the research Sinclair had already started back in Oregon on the effect of morphine on alcohol drinking.[14] If morphine satisfies the desire for alcohol (and alcohol satisfies the desire for opiates), then it is likely that both drugs produce reinforcement in the same way. The scientific evidence showed that morphine and other opiate substances (such as heroin) produced their rewarding or reinforcing effects by binding to special receptors—known as opioid receptors—in the brain. Of course, the brain did not develop opioid receptors for the purpose of binding extracts of opium poppies. As was soon discovered, the body has its endogenous opioids, called endorphins, which are the natural substance binding to opioid receptors.* The reason opium, heroin, morphine, and other opiates are able to affect the brain is that these chemicals all have molecular shapes similar to endorphins and consequently, like endorphins, can bind and activate the opioid receptors.[†]

It seemed likely, therefore, that alcohol was producing reinforcement by releasing endorphins.[‡] *The solution to the addiction was simply a case of blocking reinforcement from the endorphins each time alcohol is consumed.* Sinclair figured that the way to do this would be to *block* the opioid receptors in the brain from binding with the endorphins released each time alcohol was consumed. The next step was to find a way to do this.

Fortunately for Sinclair, the tools for getting inside the brain to block the endorphins already existed, in the form of compounds called *opioid antagonists*. These are medications that literally block opiates, such as morphine or heroin, and opioids, like endorphins, from binding to the opioid receptors in the brain. These medications had been around since the early 1960s.[§] By taking advantage of the ability of these drugs to block the effects of endorphins, Sinclair was to begin the most successful endeavor in

---

* For a fascinating history of the discovery of opioid receptors, see Candice Pert's *Molecules of Emotion: The Science Behind Mind-Body Medicine,* New York: Touchstone, 1997.

† Neurons fire; receptors are activated. If enough glutamate receptors are activated, they cause the neuron containing them to fire. Opioid receptors, however, never make a neuron fire. They are inhibitory, preventing the neuron from firing; thus, they can block pain transmission. When activated, the opioid receptors cause reinforcement–strengthening–not of themselves but of recently used synapses with glutamate receptors.

‡ Before the discovery of endorphins, it was suggested that alcohol might produce reinforcement by causing the production of a morphine-like alkaloid. This idea has stimulated a great deal of research and even now cannot be positively eliminated. Finding that the brain produces its own morphine-like substance (endorphins), however, provides a simpler explanation for alcohol reinforcement and has come to dominate most thinking today about the question. Naltrexone and nalmefene produce extinction in the same way in either case.

§ Please refer to *Essays of an Information Scientist,* Vol. 6, pp. 121–130, 1983. Current Contents, 16, pp. 5–14, April 18, 1983 at http://www.garfield.library.upenn.edu/essays/v6p121y1983.pdf for the history of Fishman and the origin of opioid antagonists. Harold Blumberg of Medical College, Valhalla, New York, was also a major figure in the opioid antagonist research. Thousands of patients who took heroin overdoses or were given too much morphine during anesthesia were saved by opioid antagonist medication. Endorphins were simultaneously discovered in 1975 by John Hughes and Hans Kosterlitz in Scotland and by Rabi Simantov and Solomon Snyder in the United States.

alcohol research—the extinction of alcohol addiction. The opioid-blocking or antagonist medications Sinclair used to accomplish the de-addiction process were short-acting naloxone and its longer-acting cousins, naltrexone and nalmefene.

Opioid antagonists had long been used in routine anesthesia to reverse the effects of opiates like morphine. Opioid antagonists have the ability to block opioid receptors in the brain from accepting opioids. Sinclair uses the analogy of putting the wrong key in a lock. So long as naltrexone is in the lock designed for endorphin, endorphin itself and other opiates bounce off and have no effect; at the same time, the naltrexone itself is the wrong key and is not able to open the lock. In other words, once opioid antagonist medications like naltrexone have been absorbed by the body, the brain's opioid system is locked down. Thus, the endorphins cannot activate or stimulate the brain's opioid receptors.

Opioid antagonists do not cause any other effects and do not make you feel either high or low. Yet they are so powerful that they can reverse the effects of opiates in the brain, even if you have already taken an opiate overdose. In fact, the short-acting opioid antagonist naloxone is used in hospitals throughout the world as a life-saving antidote to reverse the effects of narcotic intoxication from heroin overdoses.*

Pharmacological Extinction: De-Addiction and Cure

Prior to running the clinical trials on people, Sinclair first conducted dozens of experiments testing naltrexone, nalmefene, and naloxone on the high-drinking line of AA rats and other rats already addicted to alcohol. Sinclair's experiments showed that when addicted rats were given the antagonist to block the opioid (endorphin) receptors

---

* I once had the sobering experience of observing the powerful effects of naloxone on an overdosing heroin addict who had been brought into a central London hospital emergency department in the early hours of a cold January morning. The patient appeared gray and comatose and may have been on the brink of death. As soon as paramedics injected him with naloxone, he came around; the naloxone had dislodged all of the heroin from his opioid receptors, making him go into instant acute withdrawal. There was no question; he was displeased and very angry with the doctors and nurses for disturbing his narcotic sleep. The attending physician said that the naloxone had saved this man's life and that there would be more cases like this.

in their brains, the animals reduced their drinking of the alcohol solution. That was an important finding because it suggested that the
medicines would also help alcoholics. Just as important, however,
was the pattern for how drinking decreased because that showed
the mechanism through which the antagonists work, and consequently the way the medicines should be used by humans.

Figure 2 illustrates the results of a typical experiment. The rats
had been drinking alcohol solution for many weeks and now got it
only one hour a day—sort of a "happy hour." They had water and
food available all the time, but every day when the alcohol bottles
were put on the cages, the rats would rush up and start drinking
vigorously, thanks to the Alcohol Deprivation Effect. The first bar
shows the average amount of alcohol they drank in each happy
hour during the week before treatment.

The rats then had an antagonist medication (nalmefene in this
case) administered shortly before each of the next five daily sessions. Notice that alcohol drinking was not reduced on the first
session; indeed, in this experiment, the drinking on the first treatment day was slightly higher.

This is important. *The medicine itself did not reduce the rats' craving.* When the alcohol bottles were put on the cages, the rats all
came running up to the front of the cage and began drinking rapidly.

The medicine did not have an effect until *after the rats had drunk
the alcohol*, the alcohol had been absorbed and gone to the brain,
and endorphins had been released. At that point, the medicine
blocked the effect of the endorphins—it blocked the expected
positive reinforcement the endorphins normally produce.

As a result of this effect, the behavior of alcohol drinking and
the craving for it were weakened a little by the mechanism of
extinction. This shows up for the first time only on the second
treatment day. This time, when alcohol was given, the rats were
slower at coming to the bottles, and they drank significantly less
of it. Then, after that alcohol had been absorbed and caused endorphins to be released, the medicine once again blocked the reinforcement. Consequently, the behavior was weakened still further,
so that on the third day the rats were showing still less interest
in alcohol. Each day when alcohol was consumed and was not

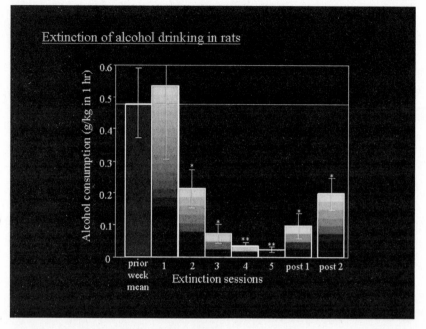

Figure 2. Extinction of alcohol drinking in rats

   Prior Week Mean → Rats are given alcohol one hour a day but no opioid antagonist medication = High drinking

   Extinction Sessions → Rats are given alcohol after opioid antagonist medication = Drinking eventually decreased but not on the first daily session

   Post Sessions → Rats are given alcohol but no opioid antagonist medication = Drinking is still significantly decreased but begins to increase

   * Less than 5% probability that the decrease from the prior week is caused by chance.
   ** Probability <1%.

(Sinclair, JD. PowerPoint Presentations, Finnish National Public Health Institute, Department of Alcohol Research, 1997–2008). An earlier version was published in 1998.[15]

followed by reinforcement was one more extinction trial weakening the drinking and craving still further. By the fifth day, only one of the rats bothered coming up to the alcohol bottle during the not-so-happy hour.

On the next day, labeled "Post 1" in the figure, the rats were not given any antagonist before access to alcohol. Almost all of the medicine from the previous day should have been eliminated, but the rats still drank very little alcohol. The next trial, "Post 2," was a week later, when all of the antagonist definitely would have been gone from their systems, but the drinking was still significantly reduced.

This also is important. *It shows, once again, that it was not the medicine itself that was reducing alcohol drinking; the medicine was gone, but the drinking still was decreased.* Instead, the combination of drinking while on the medicine—Naltrexone + Drinking—had weakened the wiring in the rats' brains that causes drinking and craving.

Notice, however, that the drinking on the post days is going back up. On these days when no antagonist was given and alcohol was consumed, it produced reinforcement again and the drinking behavior was being relearned. This came as no surprise because it is known that extinguished behaviors can be easily relearned.

The addicted animals stopped drinking because the antagonist prevented *reinforcement* from endorphins after they drank. Sinclair called this de-addiction process pharmacological extinction, which has now come to be known as the Sinclair Method.*

Sinclair clearly demonstrated that extinction was responsible for the reduction in addictive drinking. He went on to repeat these experiments in every conceivable way. The same pattern of reduced consumption was always observed for alcohol and saccharin, which both release endorphins in the brain. In addition, when used correctly, opioid antagonist medications eliminate the consumption of other substances, like the opiate methadone, which is similar to morphine.† Learning and extinction curves are identical in rats and humans—except that extinction happens more quickly in rats that have learned drinking in only one laboratory setting (Figure 2) than in humans (Figures 3 and 4), who have been learning to drink for years in a wide variety of situations.

Drinking Drops in Alcoholic Rats—Extinction

The curve in Figure 3 shows the downward pattern in 115 patients with alcoholism. Drinking is reduced from an average of thirty-seven units to nine units per week (see chapter 9 for descriptions

---

* See Appendix C for Sinclair's formal scientific description in the U.S. Patent, substantiating the scientific claims behind pharmacological extinction of alcohol.

† Morphine and other opiates, like synthetic oxycodone, can also be thought of as "external" or exogeneous endorphin-like substances.

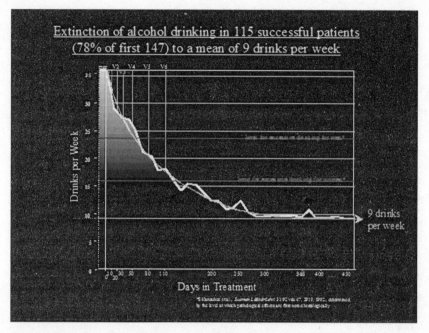

Figure 3. Extinction of alcohol drinking in alcoholics

(Sinclair, JD. PowerPoint Presentations, Finnish National Public Health Institute, Department of Alcohol Research, 1997–2008). Not previously published. Similar data from the first forty patients were published in 1997. [16]

of measures of alcohol). The same downward pattern, which is called an *extinction curve*, was observed in rats given naloxone, nalmefene, or naltrexone before drinking (Figure 2).

Drinking Reduction in Real Patients

Notice that alcohol drinking was not reduced much when the patients first started taking naltrexone before drinking. When they returned for their first visit after about ten days, their drinking diaries showed they were still drinking about thirty-two units. As in the rats, naltrexone does not immediately reduce craving and drinking. Instead, the combination of drinking while the reinforcement is being blocked by naltrexone gradually weakens the behavior. The data are from an analysis of the first 147 patients treated in Finland; the treatment was successful in 115 of them,

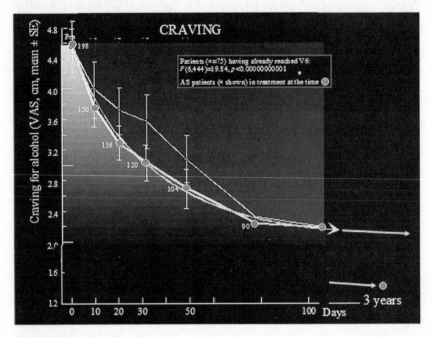

Figure 4. Extinction of craving

(Redrawn from Sinclair, JD. [2001] Evidence about the use of naltrexone and for different ways of using it in the treatment of alcoholism. Alcohol and Alcoholism, 36: 2–10, 2001.[62])

that is, the 78 percent shown in the graph. Many of the failures, but not all, were in patients who did not take the medication.

Sinclair also asked patients to rate their subjective craving as they progressed through treatment. Patients reported that their craving diminished as they continued drinking while on the naltrexone. Here, we can see how craving levels reported on the Visual Analog Scale (described in chapter 9—Step Four: Charting Reduced Craving and Drinking) diminish (Figure 4). At the time when the data were collected, seventy-five patients had completed their first six visits (about 100 days). The white line indicates their results. Meanwhile, other patients had been entering treatment and were at earlier stages; the results from all patients, including those still at early stages, are shown as the red circles and yellow line. In both cases, the decrease in craving followed an extinction curve (blue line). Approximately three years later, craving was measured again and was still lower, as would be expected because every time when the patients had drunk alcohol in the intervening period while on naltrexone was one more extinction session that was further suppressing drinking and craving.

Reduction in Craving with Real Patients

As outlined in Figure 5 on the next page, external triggers (like seeing a bottle of wine or passing a bar) and internal triggers (such as thoughts and images of oneself drinking, or certain mood states, such as feeling in a party mood or feeling depressed) can trigger the urge to drink. In physiological terms, they cause certain pathways of neurons to fire, and when these neurons fire, the person experiences a craving for alcohol. If these neurons fire enough, the person starts drinking.

When alcohol is absorbed into the bloodstream and then carried to the nervous system, it causes endorphins to be released. The endorphin molecules diffuse around the brain, like a local hormone, and bind to opioid receptors. This activates the receptors, causing them to reinforce pathways of neurons that had just been used. In this case, the pathway that had just been used is the one causing drinking and the feelings of craving for alcohol. The more this happens, the stronger the pathways causing drinking and craving become.

Being reinforced makes these neurons easier to fire in the future. Initially, the sight of a wine bottle or the sense of being in a party mood are unlikely to make people think about alcohol and seldom make them drink. However, after the pathway of neurons has been reinforced over many drinking sessions, when people are in the same situation again, they want to drink and actually do so.

After many months and years of drinking and getting reinforcement from endorphins, the pathways producing all of the behaviors related to drinking become permanently hard-wired into the brain. Once this stage has been reached, people have little or no control over drinking; they have become addicted to alcohol.

Drinking alcohol leads to addiction much more easily if there is a genetic predisposition to alcoholism. Without the "right" genetic

13 STEPS FOR BEGINNING TO LEARN ADDICTION TO ALCOHOL

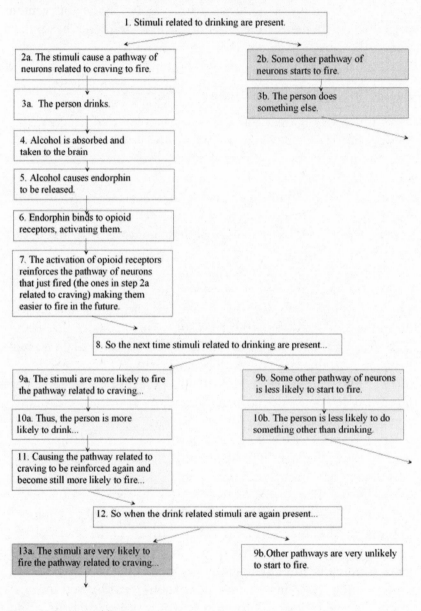

Figure 5. Steps to addiction

predisposition, it is possible but unlikely someone will ever develop a drinking problem. Even people who have the "right" genetic constitution for alcoholism will not become addicted if they never drink in the first place.

In those who have inherited the potential to become addicted *and* who drink, the pathways in the brain producing drinking will eventually broaden into "super-highways." Once learned over years of drinking, these super-highways remain open for life, never going dormant or disappearing. They are with someone forever, which is why it is so hard for alcoholics to remain abstinent. No matter which secular or spiritual therapy they embrace, the majority of alcoholics relapse within months of beginning their treatment. Alcoholics Anonymous states: "Once an alcoholic, always an alcoholic." Alcoholism is a permanent condition—unless and until the addictive neural pathways controlling it can be removed.

Fortunately, it is now possible to delete these addictive nerve pathways hard-wired throughout the brain. If these superhighways are gradually closed down, the addiction is reversed. Sinclair managed to show that this de-addiction process could be achieved through the process of pharmacological extinction, which is made possible by using naltrexone to block the reinforcement from endorphins released in the brain each time someone drinks.

Pharmacological extinction treatment requires the combination of Naltrexone + Drinking to reverse the over-strengthened alcohol-drinking system, gradually restoring it to its earlier, pre-addicted state. The process of pharmacological extinction happens gradually and incrementally each time alcohol is drunk while naltrexone is in one's system blocking the action of the endorphins on opioid receptors in the brain. The super-highways are cut back, becoming one-lane country roads once again.

In the outline in Figure 5, naltrexone acts at Step 6, preventing endorphins from binding to the opioid receptors. Consequently, the receptors are not activated and there is no reinforcement; therefore, Step 7 does not occur. Instead, the mechanism of extinction is triggered, weakening the pathway that failed to provide reinforcement. In this case, it weakens the neurons producing craving and drinking.

Naltrexone has essentially no "anti-craving" effects if taken on its own without drinking. If one does not drink alcohol, endorphins are not released into the brain. If naltrexone is taken without drinking, it simply sits on the opioid receptors without having anything to block.

Actually, that is a bit of an oversimplification because other things also release endorphins. Taking naltrexone without drinking may reduce one's interest in sweets or sex a little, but it will not reduce the craving for alcohol. *Extinction only affects those endorphin-mediated behaviors that occur while on the medication.*

Even if naltrexone is taken with alcohol, the anti-craving effects occur gradually and progressively. In human alcoholics, the results are not seen immediately.

Figure 6 shows the similarity of the results obtained with laboratory rats to those obtained with human alcoholics. In both cases, the medication produced significantly greater benefits than placebos when combined with drinking—making extinction possible—but not when given along with abstinence—thus preventing extinction.

The lower part of Figure 6 illustrates the efficacy of the Sinclair Method (Naltrexone + Drinking = Cure) in comparison to the lack of benefits when naltrexone is given along with abstinence.[17] The team in Finland conducted two placebo-controlled clinical trials simultaneously. In one, the patients were allowed to drink, with a goal of controlled drinking. In the other, the patients were told they had to abstain while on the medication. The results show that naltrexone, taken along with controlled drinking, produces significantly better results than either naltrexone with instructions to abstain or taking a placebo (such as an inactive sugar pill) along with controlled drinking. Those who aim for controlled drinking and are on the placebo have the highest chance of relapsing to heavy drinking. Thus, just as A.A. says, social drinking is not an attainable or realistic goal for alcoholics—if they are not getting naltrexone. But taking naltrexone together with drinking changes the rules. Controlled drinking then is an appropriate goal; Naltrexone + Drinking is the formula for obtaining benefits from the medication. In the case of pharmacological extinction or the Naltrexone + Drinking formula, patients remain in control of their drinking indefinitely as long as they follow Step Five (in Section Two)—the "Golden Step"—and never drink without the medication. In fact, many patients report that after a month or two of treatment, they are able to abstain altogether, and those who do drink on the medication do so moderately. In the Finnish follow-up study, about three years after the start of treatment, those patients still taking naltrexone before drinking averaged a maximum of only about 1.5 drinking occasions per week, and on those occasions averaged a maximum of four drinks.

Naltrexone Works If You Drink On It but Not If You Abstain

Notice that with abstinence, the results for naltrexone tended to be worse than those for placebo in the Finnish clinical trial[19] and in earlier laboratory studies. Almost identical graphs were produced by the results of the alcoholism clinical trial at Yale[20] and a University of Texas clinical trial of naltrexone for the treatment of cocaine addiction.[21]

The specific benefit in the clinical trial data shown here is the reduction in the rate of relapse to heavy drinking. This has been the clearest measure for the success of naltrexone in the clinical trials. The main reason for this is that there is no extinction until the patients are actively drinking on naltrexone. Most other trials have started by first detoxifying the patient before commencing treatment. After that and before the first drink, the naltrexone patients were no better off than the placebo patients. Consequently, in almost all of these trials, naltrexone did not help delay the relapse to the first sampling of alcohol again, but after alcohol had once again been consumed, naltrexone did significantly delay the relapse to heavy drinking.

Professor Schumsky's Students Extinguish His Behavior

Many laboratory research studies contributed to the development of the alcohol de-addiction treatment. Surprisingly however, Sinclair points to another influential study. It was not one

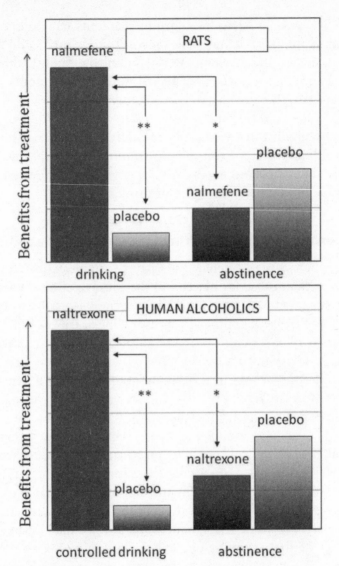

Figure 6. Consistent results from preclinical study and the Finnish dual double-blind placebo-controlled clinical trial.[18] In both cases, the medicine (naltrexone in the human trial, nalmefene in the rat study) produced significantly greater benefits than placebo when extinction was possible, that is, when given along with alcohol drinking, but the medicine tended to be worse than placebo when given during abstinence.

* Means the result is significant and would not have happened by chance one time in twenty.

** Means the result is highly significant and would not have happened by chance one time in a hundred.

done with rats. Instead, according to Dr. Don Schumsky, one of Sinclair's psychology professors at the University of Cincinnati, it was an experiment his students once performed, with Schumsky as the subject.

Schumsky had been lecturing the students on reinforcement, learning, and extinction. One morning, the students collaborated to test what their professor had been teaching. They decided to alter Schumsky's own behavior with reinforced learning and then extinction. For the first half hour of the class, the students all reinforced Schumsky by looking up whenever he moved to the left. They smiled at him and at least pretended to be interested when he moved left but not if he moved to the right or stood still.

It worked beautifully. By the end of the half hour, Schumsky had been reinforced to move to the left side of the room, finally squeezing his large body into the window alcove, trying to go further to the left. Over the next twenty minutes, the students changed tack and stopped reinforcing Schumsky for being on the left side of the lecture hall. He eventually moved away from the left wall, back to the middle of the room.

The students then informed Schumsky what they had done to him. He remembered being on the left side and trying to sit on the windowsill. He had not, however, realized what was happening: "I did notice that you all seemed to be paying more attention this morning, but I just thought I had done a good job on the lecture."

So, what did the experiment show?

- Reinforcement has a powerful effect on a person's behavior at a non-conscious level; Schumsky did not consciously decide to go to the left. He was not consciously trying to get more pleasure. Nevertheless, he learned the behavior very well.
- Extinction, produced by preventing the previous reinforcement, has an even more powerful effect—it removes the learned behavior. Extinction also works at a subconscious level; Schumsky was not *consciously* aware that he was undergoing extinction, and he made no *conscious decision* to stop going to the left. Nevertheless, the learned behavior was extinguished.

Just as alcoholism is learned through reinforcement via release of endorphins in the brain when we drink, so can it be extinguished through blocking of reinforcement by taking naltrexone when drinking. This is the process of extinction. It is not a conscious choice, and many people may not even be aware of it happening.

Finally, many years after Sinclair started his experiments, his Naltrexone + Drinking formula is helping thousands of people to break their addiction to alcohol. It is rare for any laboratory researcher to see the fruits of his labor in action. Sinclair has seen numerous lives saved and has had personal contact with many grateful patients and their families. Naltrexone's usefulness in the treatment of drinking problems was endorsed in 2006 when the *Journal of the American medical Association* published the results of the largest ever clinical trial in the history of addiction research. The Sinclair Method has been adopted by several clinics outside Finland, including some in the United States. But sadly, for many patients and their families, the treatment is not yet as widespread as it should be. Although relatively new, the treatment is grounded in orthodox scientific methods and should be available as a safe option for the treatment of alcohol addiction.

Other Researchers Continue Testing the "Naltrexone + No Drinking Allowed" Hypothesis

Sinclair published numerous scientific articles showing how the method works—by giving the medication together with drinking—and presenting laboratory data confirming that this was the first truly effective treatment for alcoholism. The first two clinical trials, at the University of Pennsylvania[22] and at Yale University[23] showed that naltrexone worked. Furthermore, the results of both trials supported the conclusion that naltrexone works if the patients drank while on the medicine, but not if they took it while abstinent. (This is discussed further in chapter 3.) Based on the theory, results from laboratory animals, the findings in the clinical trials, and with alcoholics in the real world agreeing on how to use naltrexone correctly, one might think the question of pre-scribing Naltrexone + No Drinking Allowed (i.e. not allowing for extinction to occur) would have been settled back in 1992 when the results of the clinical trials were published, or at least in 1999 when the Finns published their clinical trial specifically testing and confirming the conclusion.[24]

It was not. Researchers continued to conduct clinical trials of naltrexone in conjunction with abstinence. For example, it was tested on sixty-three alcoholics who were inpatients at a treatment center and was found to be of no benefit.[25] Other trials detoxi-fied the patients first and gave naltrexone while the patients were abstinent, finding again and again that there was no benefit until after the patients started drinking again. Naltrexone did not help to delay the time until the detoxified patients again took a drink, just as Sinclair predicted. The treatment absolutely requires that patients drink while on the medication.

Nevertheless, despite eighteen publications or reports by 2000 that naltrexone is not effective clinically along with abstinence and two more using nalmefene, another group of distinguished re-searchers at Yale University proceeded to run a huge trial in which 627 veterans were tested using the Naltrexone + Abstinence ap-proach.[26] Essentially, the researchers retested this already-refuted proposition: Take naltrexone but do not drink when you do. The results were, of course, abysmal.*

Patients initially took their medication and abstained, as in-structed, but since they were getting no benefits, eventually they gave up on the treatment: they relapsed to drinking and at the same time did not bother to take the medication when they start-ed drinking again. After all, why would they after correctly con-cluding that naltrexone had no effect on their drinking or craving levels?

It is a pity that patients told (1) to abstain and (2) to take na-ltrexone usually stop taking the medication at the same time as

---

* In view of the current evidence supporting pharmacological extinction for alcoholism (see Appendix 1), in my view, it is unethical to prescribe oral naltrexone with instructions to abstain—because doing so is a formula for failure and there is no scientific evidence to prove this approach is effective.

they start to drink again because this results in the worst possible combination of effects. They start off the trial with high motivation, obeying both instructions: avoiding all alcohol and taking their naltrexone every day. The craving does not go down and eventually they give up, stopping the naltrexone and starting to drink at the same time. This may also be caused by some of them confusing naltrexone with Antabuse. With Antabuse, it is true that you have to stop the medication when you start drinking; otherwise, the combination of drinking and Antabuse produces extremely unpleasant and sometimes even fatal effects. In the case of naltrexone, however, stopping the medication when starting to drink prevents the patients from benefiting from extinction.

Furthermore, their first return to drinking produces extraordinarily high amounts of reinforcement, making the drinking behavior and craving worse than ever. This is the result of the Pharmacologically Enhanced Learning mentioned previously as one of the three discoveries Sinclair had made that contribute to the success of his method. Used correctly, Pharmacologically Enhanced Learning can be very beneficial in helping alcoholics learn alternative behaviors. Along with Naltrexone + No Drinking Allowed, however, it could be detrimental. For example, it is why, in the results of the Finnish clinical trial illustrated in Figure 6, the Naltrexone + Abstinence group tended to do worse than the Placebo + Abstinence group.

Misdirected research such as this simply serves to delay getting real help to patients. It costs lives and does not diminish the trauma associated with alcohol addiction. Indeed, it would be very much like conducting a clinical trial in which the polio vaccine were given *after* the patients contracted polio. Vaccines do not work this way; if administered in this way, one would mistakenly conclude that the polio vaccine was useless, it would never have been approved by the FDA, and thousands would still get the disease, even though the vaccine works if administered correctly. The same reasoning applies to the use of Naltrexone + Drinking = Cure. The trials that required abstinence while on the medication are doomed to fail, and the researchers concluded that naltrexone didn't work in curing addiction. Even worse, doctors and clinicians who are out in the field treating alcoholics read the negative results and conclude naltrexone doesn't work. This is probably one of the reasons so few alcoholics in America are being treated with the medication.

One important feaure distinguishes the Sinclair patient from those treated with traditional methods. A group of patients treated with any other method will be at their best at the beginning of treatment, but after that they will get worse and worse. The typical graph of the results of traditional treatments is called a "survival curve." It shows the ever-diminishing number of patients who, over time, are still in the program—who have not dropped out and returned to abusing alcohol.

Such graphs are of no use with the Sinclair patients because they are headed in the opposite direction; they are progressively improving with time. During the first week, all of them are drinking. After that, the levels of craving and drinking decrease.

The scientific data prove that it's possible to recover from alcohol addiction fully through pharmacological extinction. Its simple formula, Naltrexone + Drinking = Cure, requires continued drinking while simultaneously taking naltrexone to block reinforcement in the brain from the endorphin released by alcohol.

The reasons the Sinclair Method is an effective and viable treatment for alcoholism should be clearer now.

The Hard Evidence
Behind the Cure

Intellectuals solve problems; geniuses prevent them.
—ALBERT EINSTEIN (1879–1955)

THE EVIDENCE FROM CLINICAL TRIALS around the world confirms the findings from research with alcoholic animals completed more than two decades ago. The conclusion is that combining active drinking with naltrexone is the most vital ingredient for success. There are several other essential features:

- No prior detoxification or withdrawal is required before naltrexone is prescribed.
- Naltrexone is taken only when drinking.
- Other behaviors reinforced by the opioid system are avoided while on naltrexone but occur on days when no naltrexone or alcohol is taken.

- Naltrexone is taken before drinking for the rest of the patient's life. A patient does not take naltrexone if he or she is not going to drink.

This approach to treatment has now been shown in clinical trials to be safe and effective. These procedures work without any need to punish or demoralize the patient.

Prior to conducting clinical trials with people, laboratory experiments proved that when alcoholic rats drank alcohol after they had been given opioid antagonists such as naltrexone, nalmefene, or naloxone, their drinking steadily decreased. These medications blocked the effects of endorphins and opiates such as morphine in the brain. By doing this, they prevented the endorphins released each time alcohol is consumed from reinforcing the system in the brain that leads to drinking.

As long as the alcoholic animals always had the medication before drinking, their drinking levels decreased and then remained down indefinitely. But if the medication was stopped and they were given access to alcohol, they gradually relearned the behavior and eventually began drinking heavily again. All of this was exactly as predicted by Sinclair's learning model of addiction and his pharmacological extinction method for treating it. Also as expected, naltrexone, naloxone, or nalmefene were of no benefit if they were given during abstinence—if the addicted rats were given the medication but not allowed to drink alcohol. In fact, giving these opioid antagonist medications *without drinking* tended to increase drinking levels slightly in already addicted laboratory animals because of pharmacologically enhanced learning.

Pharmacologically enhanced learning is produced from increased reinforcement because of a phenomenon called *receptor upregulation*. The body responds to having any particular variety of receptor blocked by producing more of that type of receptor. Consequently, naltrexone administration causes an increase in the number of opioid receptors ("upregulation") and the brain becomes super-sensitive to endorphins or opiates. *The clinical implications are that opioid antagonists such as naltrexone should therefore generally not be prescribed together with abstinence.*

The failure of naltrexone with abstinence was seen in the first clinical trial of its use for treating heroin addiction, as reported by Renault in 1980.[27] Naltrexone was prescribed to heroin addicts with instructions to abstain from taking heroin while on the medication. The overall results showed that naltrexone produced no significant benefits over placebo. It worked very well, however, for those patients who disobeyed the doctor's orders and took heroin (or methadone) while on the medication!

The first clinical trial of naltrexone for alcoholism, reported in 1992 by Volpicelli and associates at the University of Pennsylvania, gave naltrexone to alcoholics who had first been withdrawn from alcohol.[28] As might have been predicted from Sinclair's laboratory experiments, naltrexone was of no benefit so long as the patients took the medication while abstinent. In other words, naltrexone was no better than placebo in keeping them abstinent. However, naltrexone worked well after the patients began drinking together with the medication. The treatment was particularly effective in preventing patients who had sampled alcohol from progressing to a heavy drinking binge. The paper concluded: "the primary effect of naltrexone was seen in patients who drank alcohol while attending outpatient treatment." The study also found that "naltrexone was not associated with mood changes or other psychiatric symptoms."

The second clinical trial, reported in 1992 by O'Malley and associates was, by accident, a direct test of Sinclair's extinction treatment.[29] Two groups of patients were prescribed naltrexone or placebo and received strong instructions to abstain from drinking. Two additional groups were prescribed naltrexone or placebo but given instructions that inadvertently encouraged them to drink while on the medication. (These patients were told that falling off the wagon was not serious—it should almost be expected—but the important thing was to learn to cope with a slip so it did not turn into a binge.)

The results were the same as those Sinclair's team had found with alcoholic rats (shown in Figure 6). Naltrexone had significant benefits over placebo only in the group accidentally encouraged to drink while on the medication, but it was worthless with instructions to abstain. The most powerful results in the paper were the ones comparing the two naltrexone treatments and showing that it worked better with drinking than with support of abstinence. In addition, on some measures, like craving and number of drinks per occasion, naltrexone with abstinence tended to be even worse than placebo—just as it was in the results of the Finnish clinical trial shown earlier in Figure 6, and as Sinclair had found in rats, because naltrexone plus abstinence produces enhanced learning of alcohol drinking.

An open-label test on people who were not alcoholics but nevertheless were heavy drinkers gave naltrexone without prior detoxification and produced results that look almost identical to those Sinclair had found in rats (see Figure 2): alcohol drinking was reduced progressively along what appears to be an extinction curve, and it remained suppressed a month after the end of naltrexone treatment.[30]

A subsequent Swedish trial also compared naltrexone prescribed with abstinence groups with naltrexone prescribed with drinking groups.[31] Again, the results were the same: naltrexone worked when patients were inadvertently *encouraged to drink while on the medication, but it was worthless with instructions to abstain.*

The Finnish clinical trial by Heinälä (2001) was the first based on an understanding of extinction and thus to use controlled drinking deliberately as the goal for half of the subjects. The result, previously shown in Figure 6, shows that naltrexone was beneficial when combined with drinking but not when given with instructions to abstain.

Similarly, a trial in Chicago by Maxwell and Shinderman found no benefits when naltrexone was given to alcoholics with instructions to abstain, but there were positive results when alcoholics, also suffering from mental illness and usually hard to treat, were given naltrexone but not made to abstain.[32]

In another confirmation of the Sinclair Method, Henry Kranzler of the University of Connecticut's Department of Psychiatry and his colleagues confirmed that the treatment was highly effective when naltrexone was taken on an "as-needed" basis in high-risk drinking situations—always *before* the urge to drink became overwhelming. The study conforms to Sinclair's Naltrexone + Drinking model of de-addiction and was published in the journal *Addictive Behaviors* in 1997.[33] Beneficial effects were still evident three months after treatment—patients were either not drinking or drinking far less than before treatment combining naltrexone with drinking.

Another team of researchers led by José Guardia in Spain published similar findings in 2002.[34] The multicenter, double-blind, placebo-controlled trial—the gold standard in clinical trials, where neither doctors nor patients know if they are taking an active ingredient—showed lasting benefits from naltrexone in 202 alcoholics. However, *the only patients who showed a significant benefit were those who drank while taking the medication.* The study concluded that naltrexone was well tolerated and reduced relapse to heavy drinking. "The most significant finding of our study," said Guardia, "was that naltrexone-treated alcohol-dependent subjects showed a reduced relapse rate to heavy drinking in comparison with those patients treated with a placebo. We know that alcoholism is a recoverable disease."

A study published in the *American Journal of Psychiatry* in 1997 by Lifrak found that naltrexone was safe and effective in adolescent alcoholics.[35] Oslin reported that naltrexone was effective in older alcoholics who were allowed to drink on the medication, but as with younger subjects, it was of no use during abstinence in delaying the first drink.[36]

All together, successful results have been reported in seventy-two of the seventy-four clinical trials with naltrexone or nalmefene to date that had conditions allowing extinction.* In contrast, thirty-five of the thirty-six trials that had conditions preventing extinction (such as treating hospital inpatients, strong instructions

---

* Nalmefene is the "sister" drug. It is not yet fully approved by the FDA, but it is currently approved for human trials in the United States and is expected to be released soon in Europe. Nalmefene, unlike naltrexone, is not metabolized in the liver and so does not stress the liver. Also, nalmefene has a stronger binding affinity for opioid receptors than naltrexone. Naltrexone is now generic (the patents have expired), so it has not been pursued by large pharmaceutical companies because the right to manufacture it is not exclusive. In other words, any legitimate pharmaceutical company could make naltrexone, which has brought the price of the medicine down by virtue of open competition.

to abstain, or during a period, such as before the first drink, when extinction could not occur) failed to find any benefits from naltrexone or nalmefene. Most of the successful trials—fifty-eight of them—were in the treatment of alcoholism; the others were for addiction to heroin, cocaine, or amphetamine or for pathological gambling (see Appendix A). This is an amazingly consistent set of findings. The theory, the animal results, the clinical trials with addiction to heroin and other drugs, and the clinical trials with alcoholism show that naltrexone is successful when used according to the Sinclair Method. And they show naltrexone is not useful when used with abstinence.

Unfortunately, many doctors have prescribed naltrexone along with instructions to abstain. This is partly because the manufacturer did not instruct doctors to use naltrexone in combination with active drinking, and also because of the presumption that naltrexone should work with abstinence. Even many doctors in America who worked on the clinical trials showing naltrexone does not produce significant effects with abstinence still say that they prefer having naltrexone being given with instructions to abstain. Acknowledging the role of extinction as the reason naltrexone works, one alcohol researcher was categorical: "it might be true that naltrexone only works with drinking," he said, "but this is only of 'academic interest' because you can't tell an alcoholic to start drinking again and you can't predict when the patient would relapse." Fortunately, most researchers today understand that naltrexone works through pharmacological extinction.

Often, treatment protocols have been based on the assumption that medications can only be given after patients have already been through withdrawal and detoxification and are currently abstaining alcoholics. This is the way disulfiram or Antabuse (the largely ineffective drug that causes nausea or even death if the patient drinks while taking it) is administered. Naltrexone is often prescribed as a *substitute* for Antabuse, which it is not. It is also the way naltrexone must be given to opiate addicts.

Naltrexone can be given in another, more effective and ethical way to alcoholics. This way offers a practical solution for having the patient drink while taking naltrexone, and also benefit from both taking naltrexone and instructions to abstain.

Naltrexone can be given to alcoholics who are still actively drinking. These patients were drinking yesterday and they almost certainly will be drinking tomorrow. They do not need to be told to drink. Indeed, they may be told to try to control their intake. But most important, they are told always to take naltrexone before drinking: "If you feel the urge to drink, take your naltrexone before you do."

This is how naltrexone has been used since 1995 in Finland. It is also how naltrexone was given in the Finnish clinical trial by Heinälä et al. All of the earlier controlled trials with alcoholics had first put the patients through detoxification, which meant that patients had to stop drinking for a period (three weeks) before being allowed into the clinical trial. These alcoholic patients had only inadvertently been encouraged to drink, because one cannot ethically tell an abstinent alcoholic to drink. The Finnish trial, however, moved the onset of naltrexone treatment back in time, before detoxification, when the alcoholics were still drinking.

The safety of starting naltrexone without first getting rid of physiological dependence had, of course, first been checked in rats. The clinical trials not only confirmed that this was a safe procedure, but produced the initially surprising result that naltrexone caused fewer side effects in drinking patients than in patients told to abstain.[24]

Patients treated with the Sinclair Method are, in fact, slowly detoxified over the course of treatment. They start the treatment with a physiological dependence on alcohol, but after several months of gradually reducing their drinking, they are consuming so little that they no longer show withdrawal symptoms. Thus, giving naltrexone to drinking alcoholics can be viewed as a new, improved form of gradual detoxification.

Alcohol withdrawal is a severe condition, sometimes causing hallucinations, tremors, anxiety, depression, and seizures. It can even be fatal. The usual way to deal with severe withdrawal symptoms is to prescribe benzodiazepines like Librium® or Valium®. Although these drugs help with the withdrawal symptoms, there is the very real risk that the patient will become seriously addicted to these drugs. Inpatient detoxification is also very expensive. A study published in 1997 found the cost then ranged from $6,336 with no medication to $9,630 when both lorazepam and phenobarbital were used.[37]

It has always been known that the safest way to withdraw from alcohol would be to reduce gradually the amount of alcohol taken each day. Then the body would have time to adapt. There would be no severe withdrawal reactions, and it would not be necessary to expose the alcoholics to other addictive medicines. The trouble was that alcoholics would not be able to taper off their drinking on their own. After all, the core of the problem is that they cannot control their alcohol intake.

Extinction with naltrexone, however, automatically produces this safer form of detoxification. Thus, the actual amount of alcohol drunk each day while taking naltrexone is reduced automatically, gradually, and rather effortlessly. Naltrexone, unlike benzodiazepines and barbiturates, is not at all addictive. No one ever gets high or develops a craving for naltrexone.[*]

The Sinclair Method—taking naltrexone before drinking—safely and effectively detoxifies the patient. It gradually removes the physiological dependence on alcohol with less risk than the traditional inpatient or outpatient detoxification programs.

The Sinclair Method is a safe and effective detoxification procedure with one additional benefit: the patient is also cured of alcoholism. The craving for alcohol and the obsessive drinking—the basis for the alcoholism—are also removed.

Seventy-two clinical trials consistently show that naltrexone and nalmefene, when used according to the Sinclair Method, are effective in treating addictions.[†] This is generally understood to be the most powerful way of treating alcoholism. Again, the trials consistently show naltrexone must be used along with drinking,

---

[*] The litmus test for an "addictive substance" is whether rats or humans will "work" to get it. Will they work to receive reinforcement from alcohol, cocaine, nicotine, or heroin? Yes. But they will not work for naltrexone or nalmefene.

[†] See Appendix A.

and the Finnish clinical trial shows the best way of using it in conjunction with drinking.

Finally, the results of Project COMBINE, the largest clinical trial in the history of alcoholism research, consisting of 1,383 diagnosed alcoholics and conducted by an assembly of the top American researchers in the field, were published in the *Journal of the American medical Association* (May 3, 2006).[38] This trial confirmed that naltrexone was effective but did not find significant benefits for another medicine called acamprosate. Most important, Project COMBINE found that naltrexone is effective for compulsive drinking with only basic medical management—no intensive psychotherapy is required. Naltrexone had originally been tested only within comprehensive programs of alcoholism treatment, including intensive counseling and therapy; consequently, the FDA approved it for use as an adjunct within such programs.

Project COMBINE clearly shows that this restriction is not correct. Naltrexone works without counseling. This has also been found in a smaller Australian study[39] with naltrexone and in a Finnish trial[40] with nalmefene. Therefore, the original restriction of prescribing the medication only within the context of highly specialized treatment or rehab has been removed. Now, your family doctor can safely prescribe naltrexone.

The Finnish clinics using the Sinclair Method have found that it is effective in 78 percent of the patients. Clinics using it in Florida report 85 percent efficacy. The first results from CORD,* a nongovernmental organization (NGO) using the Sinclair Method in India, indicate a 75 percent success rate.

About half of the cases in which naltrexone was not effective involve a failure to take the medication or a patient dropping out of treatment. This is a very low rate of noncompliance for alcoholism treatment. There is, however, a small minority of patients—perhaps 10 percent—who, according to their "drinking diaries," are using naltrexone properly but do not benefit from it. One of the hot research areas today is trying to find "markers" to identify these individuals who do not respond to naltrexone. There

---

* Chinmaya Organization for Rural Development, Sidbari, Himachal Pradesh, India.

is evidence that they tend to be people who do not have close relatives who are alcoholics, who do not like very strong sweet solutions, and—according to Project COMBINE—who have a particular form of opioid receptor.

The positive clinical trials, the results of Project COMBINE, and the reputation of the *Journal of the American Medical Association* mean that the use of naltrexone—and eventually, its sister medication, nalmefene—should increase greatly in the months and years to come. In other words, once the word that Naltrexone + Drinking = Cure gets out, alcoholism's days are numbered.

The American Medical Association usually restricts access to published studies on its Web site, but at the time of publication, it considered the results of Project COMBINE to be so important that it made the study freely available for download.

The Project COMBINE study began in 2001. When its results were published in May 2006, it was immediately recognized—even picked up by the media—as a landmark in alcohol research. Raymond Anton of the Medical University of South Carolina and Stephanie O'Malley of Yale University led the trial in collaboration with twenty other leading alcohol researchers.

Although Project COMBINE did not specifically set out to test the Sinclair Method formally, it concluded that naltrexone is invaluable in the treatment of alcoholism and recommended that the medication should now be prescribed for alcoholism in general medical practice, even without the requirement for intensive counseling or A.A. meetings. Although less than 2 percent of alcoholics in the United States have ever had the opportunity of being prescribed naltrexone, the indications are that it could become the new gold standard for treatment to reach the millions of alcoholics in America, Europe, and beyond who would otherwise be left untreated and unprotected from the ravages of this progressive illness.

Even in the United Kingdom, where naltrexone can—scandalously—only be prescribed for alcohol abuse on a private basis (that is, not subsidized by the government's National Health Service*), the treatment now offers a brighter future for alcoholics,

* Some parts of the National Health Service in the UK are now authorized to prescribe naltrexone for alcoholism, but still with instructions to abstain—not the The Sinclair Method (TSM) way.

heavy drinkers, and those who simply need more control over their drinking.

David Sinclair reported on the lasting benefits of naltrexone three years after the start of treatment, in which patients continued to take naltrexone an hour before drinking.[41] The patients did not take the medication on days when they were not drinking. The patients' craving, drinking levels, and liver damage markers were all way down. Indeed, these patients were drinking and craving alcohol less after three years than they had been after the first five months of treatment. Traditional abstinence-based alcoholism treatments had always found that the results were best at the beginning of treatment, and then gradually, week after week, the patients would relapse and the drinking would increase to the level it had been before treatment. Pharmacological extinction produces exactly the opposite pattern, as shown by this three-year follow-up study. The drinking and craving is highest in the first weeks of treatment, but becomes progressively lower as the weeks on treatment progress because each intervening episode of drinking while on naltrexone was one more extinction trial. In other words, the more often people drink while on naltrexone, the less they will want to drink.

The clinical trials demonstrating the efficacy of naltrexone continue coming out. For example, Morley et al. published an Australian double-blind, placebo-controlled study of 169 alcoholics in 2006.[42] Like the earlier studies, it showed naltrexone was effective in preventing alcoholics who were drinking while on the medication from relapsing to heavy drinking, but taking naltrexone during the initial period of abstinence did not delay the first sampling of alcohol.

The United States now has 1,630 drug courts; they are beginning to use naltrexone for alcoholic defendants who, rather than serving custodial sentences, can be monitored to ensure they take the medication. California Superior Court Judge Stevens was one of the first to institute mandated naltrexone treatment. He was so impressed with the results that he said, "We have had too much

---

* Naltrexone and the law. See http://youtube.com/watch?v=a88oFbHZS4E.

success not to use it." Describing himself as conservative, Judge Stevens is emphatic that imprisonment and standard therapies leave addiction intact. In his view, they basically do not work because they cannot prevent alcohol and opiates from "lighting up the brain"—which is why he believes most offenders relapse and find themselves back before the courts. An interview with Judge Stevens can be viewed on the Internet.*

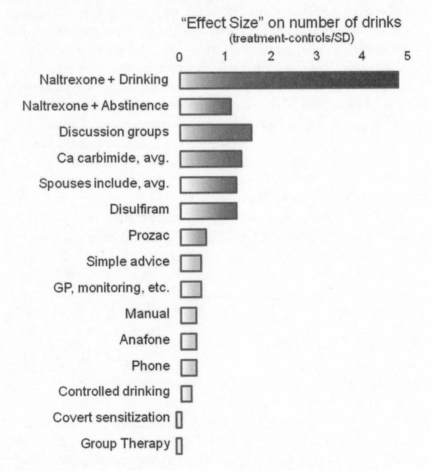

Figure 7. The "Effect Size" on reduction of the number of drinks shows that Naltrexone + Drinking (that is, the Sinclair Method) is more effective than giving Naltrexone + No Drinking Allowed and also that it reduces drinking far more effectively than other medications or other therapies (Agosti, 1995).

The Sinclair Method fulfills the cost-effective requirements as "evidence-based medicine"; more detailed scientific and academic references to published journal articles on the clinical trials can be found in Appendix A, the annotated bibliography of the clinical trials published prior to March 2008.

The graph in Figure 7 plots the results from an article by Agosti (1995) comparing the power of different forms of alcoholism treatment to reduce the number of drinks, as measured in various clinical trials. The naltrexone data are from the O'Malley et al. 1992 study. The article is rather old—1995—so it does not include data for newer treatments such as the use of the medication acamprosate. There have, however, been no similarly broad analyses made since then, and Agosti's conclusion, that naltrexone used appropriately is the most powerful treatment, is still valid today.

4

Why Haven't I Already Heard of the Sinclair Method?

"IF THERE IS A CURE for alcoholism, why has it not been splashed across the front pages of the *New York Times*? Surely, if there was a cure for alcoholism, and amphetamine, cocaine, and gambling addictions, we would know about it. If it sounds too good to be true, then it probably is too good to be true."

This refrain was raised by my agent, David Fugate, by my mentor, Professor Arnold Lazarus, by ordinary people wherever I traveled, and by experts like my friend, the renowned physician Dr. Marios Panos, who knows a great deal about liver cirrhosis. He has managed liver transplants made necessary as the result of excessive drinking and recently said: "It's just simply too good to be true—it's too simple. It's hard to believe. How come I haven't heard about it? I keep up with the scientific journals."

Even though naltrexone was recently featured in a *Newsweek* article[43] that presented drugs as possible cures for addiction, the

Sinclair Method still has not reached the 50 million people in North America and Europe trapped in the vise of alcohol and other addictions for a number of reasons.

History

The problem goes back long before the Sinclair Method and the use of naltrexone in alcoholism treatment. A major clinical trial, sponsored by the National Institute on Drug Abuse (NIDA), on the use of naltrexone in treating opiate addiction was conducted in the 1970s. The results were published by Renault in 1978[44] and again by NIDA itself in 1980.[45]

The doctors who designed the experiment were not thinking about extinction but rather imagining that drug abuse was a rational behavior (more on that later) chosen to produce happiness and avoid pain. Consequently, the patients were given a card telling them not to use heroin or any other opiate while on the medication. The card said that if they were to use a small dose, they would feel no pleasure; if they took a large dose, they would die.

If naltrexone had any ability to reduce craving on its own, the patients on it should have shown better results than those on placebo. In fact, in the entire population studied, there was not one significant benefit of naltrexone over placebo. Naltrexone does not work that way.

There was, however, a small subgroup of seventeen naltrexone patients and eighteen placebo patients who disobeyed these instructions. They took heroin or methadone while on the medication. Renault reported:

- In this sub-sample, the naltrexone patients had significantly fewer urine samples that tested positive for methadone or morphine.
- The pattern in the naltrexone group was to test once or twice with heroin or methadone and then to stop.
- The naltrexone patients reported significantly less craving toward the end of their evaluation than did the placebo-treated patients.

Renault concluded that naltrexone works by extinction, as Wikler[46] had theorized earlier. Extinction requires that the response—the drug-taking behavior—actually take place in the presence of naltrexone. Therefore, it was quite reasonable that only those patients who made the response of taking opiates while on naltrexone benefited from the medicine. Similarly, a recent clinical trial confirmed that naltrexone is effective but only in patients who take opiates while naltrexone is in the bloodstream, thus blocking the opiates (morphine or heroin) from reinforcing the opioid system in the brain.[47]

No one, however, has told the doctors or patients that this is the way to use naltrexone.

Instead, thirty years later, the package insert for naltrexone still reads:

"If you attempt to self-administer heroin or any other opiate drug, in small doses while on naltrexone, you will not perceive any effect. Most important, however, if you attempt to self-administer large doses of heroin or any other opioid (including methadone or LAAM) while on naltrexone, you may die or sustain serious injury, including coma."

The package insert does not mention that the scientific evidence shows only opiate addicts who disobey these instructions benefit from naltrexone!

Meanwhile, because of this missing information, a generation of addicts who could have been helped has been lost.

Information Overload—Large Oil Tankers Turn Around Slowly

Appendix A lists more than seventy studies confirming that opioid antagonists (naltrexone or nalmefene), when administered correctly according to the formula of Naltrexone + Drinking = Cure, are effective and also reviews concluding that naltrexone is the best treatment for alcoholism. Appendix A also lists more than thirty trials confirming that incorrect administration of the medications according to the Naltrexone + No Drinking Allowed paradigm leads to relapse and abysmal failure. If this degree of evidence for cure were presented, for example, for a medication (even a generic one) for a virulent cancer, it would have been shouted out loud from the world media, and we would hear about it.

It does not work like this for alcoholism.

Even though we live in a fast information-based world, society has not *yet* benefited from the research showing that pharmacological extinction is the most cost-effective and proven solution for alcoholism to date. One reason is that there is simply too much literature—thousands of scientific journal articles are published annually—for medical professionals to read and put into action.

Most primary care physicians are not even aware of the largest multicenter study in addiction research ever conducted, Project COMBINE—mentioned throughout this book—which was published in the *Journal of the American Medical Association* in May 2006. The American Medical Association concluded that "naltrexone with medical management could be delivered in health care settings, thus serving alcohol-dependent patients who might otherwise not receive treatment." There is simply too much information for physicians and patients to keep up with it all.

Changing the way in which society deals with alcoholism can be exceedingly cumbersome—much like altering the course of a huge supertanker. It is a dreadfully slow process reminiscent of the way it took a century for the world to accept William Harvey's (1578–1657) observation that blood was circulated around the body by the action of a pumping heart. It took decades for Edward Jenner's (1749–1823) ideas on smallpox vaccination to be fully appreciated. Now, vaccination against life-threatening diseases is routine around the world. Leading surgeons of the day rejected Lister's (1827–1912) notion that we should sterilize instruments before surgery and that we should use carbolic acid to keep hospitals free of germs after surgery to prevent infections like gangrene. Sterile operating theaters are now routine in every reputable hospital. Louis Pasteur (1822–1895) traveled around the French countryside for ten years demonstrating how his vaccine against rabies worked before farmers would believe him. Everyone now accepts his ideas on pasteurization—heating milk and other liquids to prevent diseases such as tuberculosis—but it took decades before pasteurization became routine and a legal health and safety requirement.

Despite our fast-paced world, the Sinclair Method is no different. The world of de-addiction treatment is still firmly entrenched in an ideology based on the religious dogma of "abstinence only" and "no drugs for addiction" and the belief that there is one and *only one solution* for addiction: complete abstinence—through submission to a higher power, isolation in prison, restrictive rehabilitation, stigmatization, humiliation, and other punishments.

Patents and Profits Make the World Go Around

If naltrexone had been a proprietary medication with a long patent life that could still be exploited for decades—as Prozac* once was for depression—there would have been a stronger financial incentive by pharmaceutical companies to exploit the medication. Instead, DuPont obtained only a short period of exclusivity for its ReVia brand and naltrexone now is a generic medication—meaning it is non-exclusive and, therefore, inexpensive for the customer and with low profit margins for the manufacturer. What pharmaceutical company executive in his or her right mind would waste hundreds of millions of dollars promoting a medication that would yield low profits that would soon be undercut on international markets by competitors? Not one. Shareholders are in the business of securing financial returns—not in giving charity.

It is ironic that the reason for patenting the Sinclair Method (see Appendix C, which presents the original patent) was to get the treatment out to more people more rapidly, but patenting it may, in retrospect, have delayed the process—and cost lives in the process. In an e-mail about why people have not heard about his method, Sinclair responded:†

---

* Prozac was a $3-billion-a-year, blockbuster medication when Eli Lilly introduced it in the United States. It is now off-patent, a generic medication, and the pharmaceutical companies have been driven to introduce newer SSRI antidepressants with long patent lives to retain market exclusivity.

† My editorial additions are in parentheses.

One reason could be the fact that the Method is patented. I have often wondered what the effect of patenting was. It was, of course, intended to hasten the spread of the procedure. But it may have delayed the process. I understood that DuPont was discussing the possibility of signing a contract with ContrAl (which owned the patents), but then decided instead to go around the patent. They stopped all communications with ContrAl and me...and their package insert and promotional material were carefully designed not to suggest extinction and the proper way to use their medicine.

When naltrexone went generic, the representative for Mallinckrodt (which manufactures generic naltrexone) told me he agreed with extinction (Naltrexone + Drinking) but said they could not change anything from what DuPont had in its prescribing leaflet (i.e., Naltrexone + No Drinking Allowed). I asked, but he could not even give copies of the Heinälä (2001) clinical trial paper to doctors—although that is now being changed with the new FDA regulations.[*]

There is a nice coincidence here. My initial American patent expires on June 13, 2008. So the book (*The Cure for Alcoholism*) coincides with the end of patent coverage. So at least now everyone is free to use the Method.

Patenting cannot, however, explain the similar suppression of information about the correct way to use naltrexone for treating opiate addictions. That suppression started more than a decade before Sinclair got his patent related to alcoholism, and there was no similar patent related to opiate addiction encouraging any misleading of doctors and patients about the scientific evidence showing how naltrexone had to be used to be effective.

---

* The FDA is altering its regulations to allow pharmaceutical companies to present research on applications for their products other than those specifically approved for a particular condition.

Vested and Commercial Interests—Confronting Marketing Obstacles

Although naltrexone requires a medical prescription, it is an un-scheduled, non-addictive safe medication with few side effects. Yet, when launching it in 1995, DuPont's sales reps had to approach naltrexone with extreme caution. First, the manufacturer's labeling stated that it should be considered as only one of many factors determining the success of treatment of alcoholism and that it was to be used as adjunct to a comprehensive program of alcoholism treatment. This impeded the marketing effort because naltrexone could only be advertised to specialists, and not to family practitioners or primary care physicians. This automatically cut the majority of doctors and patients out of the loop. Second, fears surrounding medical malpractice ensured that doctors would avoid the risk of writing prescriptions for naltrexone just in case they were sued. This restriction was lifted in May 2006 with the publication of the results of Project COMBINE in the *Journal of the American Medical Association*.

Third, the inserts accompanying the medication stated that it could cause liver damage. Increased liver enzymes were noted at doses greater than 300 mg—six times the recommended safe dose of 50 mg! The idea that naltrexone *might* cause liver damage further impeded the medication from reaching patients. Family doctors had more reason to steer clear of prescribing naltrexone, even though the recommended dose was well within safety limits. Despite a review of the literature and "adverse effects" reporting from DuPont that the recommended dose poses no health risk, the warning label is still included along with the medication. Who wants to prescribe or take a medication that might damage the liver even if it cures alcoholism? Furthermore, the warning led to the requirement of blood tests for liver damage before starting naltrexone, which added to the expense and hindered acceptance. In fact, one of the benefits from treating alcoholics with naltrexone is the improvement shown (using those same blood tests) in their livers.

DuPont branded naltrexone as ReVia™, but faced additional marketing obstacles. The company may or may not have known that naltrexone was effective only when combined with active drinking. But even if the company did know this, it did not have FDA permission to say so. Therefore, when patients were given naltrexone, they were told *not* to drink alcohol. If they complied with these instructions, they experienced no benefit—no reduction in their craving or drinking levels—good reason for them to abandon the treatment. It also proved a "catch-22" situation for doctors. Doctors could only prescribe naltrexone in a highly specialized setting, such as an inpatient addiction clinic. Besides, they were not permitted to give directions enabling their patients to benefit from the way the medication worked—"if you drink alcohol, always take this medication an hour before you do." Clearly, DuPont had its hands severely tied while trying to market naltrexone.

Another major hurdle involves health insurance, which often covers expensive inpatient rehab, but not less costly outpatient treatment with naltrexone. Tania Graves, a spokesperson for the Arizona Medical Association, said this: "Insurance companies often don't allow naltrexone to be prescribed by a primary care physician. Their point of view is that drug or addiction problems should be sent to a specialist."[48] Other insurance companies reject it outright. For instance, a chain of California treatment centers based on using naltrexone as a primary treatment for alcoholism had to suspend its operations after only six months because health insurance would not cover the treatment.

Pharmacological extinction is unattractive to the $6.2 billion dollar rehabilitation industry, which is quick to cite ideological reasons against using naltrexone: "abstinence is the only way" and "we don't believe in using drugs to treat addicts." The Sinclair Method does not attract anything like the kind of profit the pharmaceutical industry and the rehabilitation industry have come to expect. The pharmaceutical industry's return of 39.4 percent on equity means that it is five-and-a-half times more profitable than the average Forbes 500 company. Private facilities, such as those based on the Minnesota Model (Hazelden, Betty Ford, Cottonwood de Tucson) rely on income generated by new and repeat patients. An unfortunately high failure rate means there are plenty of repeat patients in need of more of the same treatment.

The rehabilitation industry typically charges $30,000 to $42,000 per twenty-eight-day rehab in the United States (for example, Hazelden, Betty Ford, Cottonwood de Tucson) and $36,000 in the United kingdom (for example, the Priory Group). Business projections were so attractive that the Dutch Bank, ABN Amro, bought the Priory Group in the United Kingdom for the equivalent of $1.5 billion in 2005. A rehab clinic treating 400 patients a year can expect to generate income on the order of at least $10 million a year. The Betty Ford Clinic has the capacity for 800 patients for a gross income of $20 million per year!

Such facilities stand to lose if a simple outpatient, non-intensive, and cost-effective treatment like the Sinclair Method—which requires only one outpatient visit with a physician (and if possible, some visits with a trained counselor)—were to replace the standard twenty-eight-day detox- and abstinence-based models of treatment. This is by no means intended to be an attack on the dedicated professionals who genuinely want the best for their alcoholic patients. It is simply the way the present treatment infrastructure works.

Because patients gradually reduce their drinking, the Sinclair Method eliminates the need for conventional "shock-to-the-system" inpatient detoxification, which causes brain damage in itself. The Sinclair Method is effective for patients but is not a money-spinner for addiction clinics focused on high occupancy rates. If it were universally adopted as the treatment of choice for alcohol addiction, the Sinclair Method and its 80 percent first-time success rate would transform the addiction industry. It would mean that millions of addicts could be effectively cured without abstinence, withdrawal, or the need for willpower. But it would also mean that, in addition to money lost through the closure of private inpatient rehab centers, thousands of addiction professionals and inpatient clinics would be out of business. Could this at least partly explain why the Sinclair Method has not yet been adopted by governments (apart from Finland) on a wider scale? Just because the Sinclair Method is unattractive to big business does not mean it should be prevented from helping all those in need of it.

The loss of detoxification business does not, however, explain why the extinction treatment of opiate addiction has also been suppressed. A major difference between the treatment of alcohol and opiate addictions is that prior detoxification is definitely needed when treating people who are physiologically dependent on opiates. Nevertheless, the use of pharmacological extinction with naltrexone has not been widely accepted for opiate addiction either. When naltrexone was first approved by the FDA, too little was known about its mechanism of action and effectiveness to merit extensive publicity. The manufacturer, DuPont, provided minimal promotion in the form of press releases.

Igniting the "Tipping Point"—Revealing the Sinclair Method and Naltrexone

Malcolm Gladwell, a bestselling author, borrowed the term "tipping point" from epidemiology to describe the point at which "social epidemics"—like the sudden reduction in New York City crime rates in the mid-1990s or an unexplained new trend in fashion—attain critical mass. Gladwell explains it this way: "I'm convinced behaviors, ideas, and products move through a population like a disease does, and even the smallest change…can get them started." It takes only one famous person to start a chain reaction and give birth to a new trend—such as laceless running shoes, Botox® injections, or a new gadget. During the 1990s, it suddenly became fashionable to be "in recovery." Once sinning celebrities were seen at A.A. meetings, joining the recovery movement was seen as legitimate. Even though being "an addict" carried a stigma—a sign of personal weakness—it was also perceived as "cool." The number of private rehab centers—like Hazelden and the Betty Ford Clinic—and A.A. groups swelled. According to Gladwell, anyone can start a "positive epidemic"—which is what happened when Lister unleashed carbolic acid and the rules of hygiene to end the gangrene epidemic that had been spreading in hospitals around the world.

Imagine for a moment the positive social consequences if Nancy Reagan had promoted the effective Sinclair Method rather than the ineffective "Just Say No" national campaign against alcohol and drugs. Some influential leaders in New England had plans for possible promotion schemes, for example, in the military, but for one reason or another, their discussions with the Finns promoting the method never worked out and the plans never materialized.

The United States Is Ahead of the United Kingdom but Still Lacks Knowledge about Naltrexone

America may be slow in adopting naltrexone and slower still in accepting its correct usage, but it still is far ahead of Great Britain. Given that the United Kingdom has one of the highest rates of alcohol bingeing and addiction in the world—and with perhaps some of the youngest drinkers—it is scandalous just how much naltrexone and nalmefene have been ignored by government and industry.[*]

Although naltrexone is specifically approved for alcohol treatment in the United States and almost all European countries, including Russia and the countries formerly part of the Soviet bloc, in India, Australia, and beyond, it has not been approved for alcoholism in the United Kingdom. It boils down to this: because naltrexone is a generic medication, it was simply not worth a pharmaceutical company's investment in the clinical trials specifically needed for approval—in a market already open to competition. It is a mystery why, in 2005, the government spent $400 million treating sixty-three thousand alcoholic patients in specialist care—at more than $6,000 per patient—yet ignores all the positive data on naltrexone.

Just as baffling is the fact the British National Health Service (NHS) does not permit its general practitioners to prescribe naltrexone for alcoholism in a country said to be "losing the battle

---

* Children as young as eleven are reported to be in A.A. groups for children. See "11-year-olds treated for alcoholism," March 9, 2008, by Sarah Manners, Wales On Sunday: http://icwales.icnetwork.co.uk/news/wales-news/2008/03/09/11-year-olds-treated-for-alcoholism-91466-20585094/ Retrieved: March 9, 2008.

with the bottle." After all, with the United Kingdom's advanced technology, it would be particularly easy to implement such a program. Even if you knew how to use it for a drinking problem, naltrexone is only available in the United Kingdom if you can afford it. Naltrexone is approved in the United Kingdom for narcotic addiction (heroin, morphine), but it can only be prescribed for other purposes, such as alcoholism, by private prescription. This means that any registered medical doctor in the United Kingdom can write a prescription for naltrexone, but the patient would have to pay for the medication. According to Alcohol Concern, a UK charity, one in three government NHS hospital beds is occupied as a result of excessive drinking. It is ironic, to say the least, that the NHS will not yet pay for naltrexone in alcohol treatment.

I recently met with an American alcohol researcher who has worked with the British National Health Service for more than twenty years. Although she knew a great deal about the literature on alcoholism, she had hardly heard of naltrexone, and had never heard about the Sinclair Method or pharmacological extinction. "I called two of my colleagues in the United States before our meeting—real hot-shots in the field. They told me that there was just no evidence for what you and Sinclair are saying," she challenged. When asked, she had no idea why her colleagues did not know about the seventy clinical trials or even about Project COMBINE (1,383 alcoholics—a major study by any standard). She held her colleagues in such high esteem that she believed they could not possibly be wrong, saying, "Where are the data? I need to see the references. If what you and Sinclair are saying is true, this is a total revolution in addiction. It will change the world."

As we saw in chapter 3, many of the top researchers in America are now studying and prescribing naltrexone in a manner that allows extinction to occur. Naltrexone is being seen as the treatment of choice for patients who are actively drinking, especially for those who do not aim for total abstinence. The technique of starting naltrexone without prior detoxification was first studied among alcoholics in the Finnish clinical trial (Heinälä et al., 2001), and first made available to the public by clinics using the Sinclair Method in Finland. Now it is being adopted by more clinics and by physicians in general medical settings. The ingrained assumption that alcoholics must stop drinking instantly and that abstinence is the only way has been a major handicap in implementing the Sinclair Method. This misinformation is only just beginning to dissipate.

Nevertheless, it is scandalous that fewer than 2 percent of problem drinkers in America and even fewer in the United Kingdom have ever been given the opportunity to use naltrexone for their addiction. Is withholding effective treatment for alcohol addiction, even through ignorance, unethical? Illegal? Perhaps. But the major thrust must be in correcting the situation. *The Cure for Alcoholism* could make inroads into addiction by informing the world that a highly effective cure for alcohol addiction is already here.

Alcohol Abuse Is Not Rational

The extinction of alcohol drinking and opiate addiction may have been ignored because it was contrary to a common attitude epitomized by the "Just Say No" campaign. This attitude assumes that all behavior is rationally chosen to maximize pleasure and minimize pain. People always have a choice about drinking or taking drugs, and all they have to do is just choose not to do so: to just say no. Furthermore, the reasoning goes, if the consequences of drinking and drug taking were made sufficiently horrible, everyone—including alcoholics and addicts—would abstain. So the secret to treating alcoholics is simply to be tough enough to be ready to administer enough punishment in the form of Antabuse (producing a very nasty, painful reaction if you drink while taking it), prison (bad enough in most countries), "Tough Love" boot camp, or a Spartan abstinence-based rehab regime.

The Sinclair Method is diametrically opposed to the punishment of alcoholism (and alcoholics) and a moralistic absolutist attitude. The Method does not force alcoholics to do anything. It subjects them to no pain. Instead, it eliminates the agony of forced, often dangerous, withdrawal. It allows them to continue drinking; it permits them to have a goal of moderate drinking—of not being different from most members of our society. It does not punish alcoholics for the sins of their intemperate behavior. Such an approach is not popular in many circles.

The fact is that not all behaviors are chosen rationally. There is a behavior continuum ranging from those over which we do have conscious control—like going to get a cup of coffee—down to autonomic reflexes—like having your heart beat or your stomach contract. These reflexes are wired into the nervous system and are not under rational control. If you were offered ten dollars to make your heart stop beating, you could not do so. You could not even make your stomach stop contracting. It does not matter what the consequences are. You still could not control these responses consciously for a million dollars or if you were threatened with severe pain.

In between the extremes are behaviors that are partially under rational control. In many cases, the response initially is almost completely voluntary, but control is lost with the duration of deprivation. For example, you can easily start to hold your breath, but the response (to breathe) then becomes progressively more automatic and after a minute or so is no longer subject to conscious control. Of course, individuals differ as to their degree of domination over their reflexes, but for most people, a "Just Say No to Breathing" campaign could not work.

Behaviors often start out being consciously controlled but become progressively more automatic as they are learned. Driving is a well-known example. Drinking alcohol is another such behavior. The young boy taking alcohol for the first time has conscious control over the behavior. He may be influenced by what he has heard or by peer pressure to imbibe, but that too is part of rational control.

After much experience with drinking and having the behavior reinforced so often, it may come to be progressively more automatic. One of the first signs is having thoughts about drinking or having some particular beverage suddenly spring to mind, as in: "Gee, a cold beer would taste good right now." You do not choose to have these thoughts. They are an automatic product of your nervous system and its prior learning with alcohol. You become more observant of things related to alcohol and may find your-self with a glass in your hand without really planning to do any drinking.

(Interestingly, one of the effects reported by patients being treat-ed with the Sinclair Method is the reversal of these processes. For example, after a while in treatment, they no longer are continually being pestered by thoughts about drinking.)

Some people are so good at this learning process that alcohol drinking moves into the class of behaviors where occasionally the response is no longer under conscious control. Most of the time, they can abstain if the circumstance demands it, but sometimes, in the right setting and after a long time without alcohol, the drink-ing is beyond the point of conscious control.

This threshold probably provides the best definition there is of alcoholism. An alcoholic is a person whose drinking is no longer under rational control.

Beyond this point, alcohol drinking is wired in. No amount of reward and no threat of punishment can stop the drinking.

The drinking no longer makes logical sense. It continues even though the amount of pleasure is far less than the pain and suffer-ing produced by the drinking. In fact, most alcoholics report that they get little or no pleasure from drinking—and report a great amount of pain—but nevertheless they continue drinking.

Naturally, when the person is an alcoholic and the drinking is no longer rational, it can no longer be controlled by treatments using rational means. Increasing the amount of contingent pain—harsh rehab regimes, boot camp, prison—will be no more suc-cessful in stopping drinking than in stopping breathing. Once drinking is wired in, the only solution is to cut the wires, and that is what extinction with naltrexone does—it literally cuts back and weakens the circuitry driving the addiction in the brain.

Skeptics may question whether patients on naltrexone will take the medication when they know that it may block some of plea-sure from alcohol. This may have served as a deterrent to accep-tance of the Sinclair Method. Taking naltrexone does not make sense, they say.

Indeed, it makes no more sense than alcoholics continuing to drink even when they get much less pleasure than pain (hangovers, accidents, relationship failure, job loss, cirrhosis, legal problems). But in fact they do continue drinking. Alcohol abuse by alcoholics does not make sense. It is not rational. That is why they are alcoholics. They drink because of a learned—wired-in—physiological reflex. They may not want that reflex, but on their own they cannot stop it. Once addiction sets into the brain it is not a choice.

The Sinclair Method provides alcoholics with a rational way to get rid of this objectionable, painful, and unwanted reflex. All they have to do is take naltrexone before drinking. A simple choice. And a rational choice. It does not reduce their pleasure much because they were getting little if any pleasure from drinking. But in the long run, the choice does get rid of a great deal of pain. Excessive drinking by an alcoholic is not rational, but taking naltrexone is rational. Thus, it is not surprising that in practice about 90 percent of alcoholic patients on the Sinclair Method do comply with taking naltrexone before drinking.

The first step in curing alcoholism is recognizing that some responses, like breathing and an alcoholic's drinking, occasionally are beyond rational control. The alcoholic cannot stop imbibing no matter what the promised reward or punishment is. Failure to accept this fact—that craving for alcohol and abusive drinking are learned, unconscious physiological reflexes—has caused most alcoholics to receive painful and ineffective treatments based on the false premise that they really can control their drinking. The treatment of alcoholics has been based on the belief that they really are not alcoholics, but people who consciously choose to drink. Meanwhile, the humane alternative of using the Sinclair Method has been largely ignored in America.

Mind-Set: Passively Taking Medication Is All You Need

Most of us are accustomed to the practice of taking this particular tablet for that specific ailment: daily antidepressants for depression, antihypertensives for high blood pressure, daily insulin for type 1 diabetes, painkillers for pain, antihistamines for allergies. There is nothing extra we need to *do* to make the medications work. They invariably work if we take them. That is how we have become accustomed to thinking about medications, whether they are life saving or simply symptom relieving.

Again, as we have seen throughout *The Cure for Alcoholism,* this is not the way in which naltrexone (or nalmefene) works. These medications require action to be effective: we have to drink while the medication is in our system to get the benefit. In other words, first we need to swallow the tablet (naltrexone or nalmefene), wait at least an hour for the medication to be absorbed into the bloodstream and brain, and then we need to *do* something—in this case, carry on drinking while the medication blocks the opioid system in the brain. By contrast, with antibiotics for infection, we don't *do* anything in particular to activate the medication; taking the medication is enough in itself to conquer bacterial infection.

The medical fraternity and patients have fallen prey to the prevailing mind-set around pill-taking. People assume the power lies exclusively in the drug being absorbed into the body. While it may seem both rational and logical to approach naltrexone as though it were in itself a cure for alcoholism, nothing could be further from the truth. Yet this is the way those who were initially prescribed the medication were instructed to take it—together with abstinence.

Naltrexone also had a bad reputation for its use in the questionable practice of "rapid detoxification." This treatment is based on the disproven idea that addiction is caused by physiological dependence. It is sold at great cost to opiate (heroin) addicts and their families. And it is the frequent subject of medical malpractice suits.*

The Cure for Alcoholism aims to correct these mistakes.

---

* "State's Malpractice Case Against Addiction Specialist Opens," January 4, 2001, Iver Peterson, *New York Times.*

See http://query.nytimes.com/gst/fullpage.html?res=9C01EEDC1E3BF937A35752C0A9679C 8B63&scp=22&sq=naltrexone&st=nyt. "Prosecutors began their malpractice case here in the suburbs of Trenton today against Dr. Lance L. Gooberman, the South Jersey addiction treatment specialist whose unorthodox cold-turkey method of treating opiate addiction cost the lives of at least seven patients, according to the state's complaint." Retrieved April 27, 2008.

Five Steps to Curing Alcoholism

5

An Introduction to the Five Steps— How to Drink Your Way Sober

"Luck is what happens when preparation meets opportunity."
—Seneca (mid-first-century a.d. Roman philosopher)

"We can't solve problems by using the same kind of thinking we used when we created them."
—Albert Einstein

THE FIVE STEPS presented in this chapter equip you with a blueprint to break free of compulsive drinking. Curing your addiction and regaining control over alcohol is not complicated. It does not require *abstinence*. But it does require *meticulous preparation* before, during, and after treatment. The Five Steps do not demand complex psychosocial therapy or an examination of your past to find out why you lost control over alcohol. Unlike standard rehab treatments, there is no insistence on intensive psychotherapy, the trauma of inpatient detoxification programs, withdrawal, or white-knuckling it through arduous abstinence for the rest of your life. The Five Steps guide you through the de-addiction process:

- **Step One**—Understand and think about addiction in an entirely new way.
- **Step Two**—Check the severity of the problem and find out if you need help.
- **Step Three**—Work with your doctor to obtain a prescription for naltrexone.
- **Step Four**—Learn about alcoholic beverage measures and keep a record of your drinking and craving as you begin your journey through de-addiction. Now you are taking naltrexone before drinking alcohol. You become de-addicted—your craving and drinking levels decline gradually.
- **Step Five**—After three to four months—in some cases up to six months—you will be cured. Now your goal is to stay cured once you have completed the program.

(Please note—throughout this section there will be numerous references to the medically proven fact that without the continued consumption of alcohol together with naltrexone, there can be no de-addiction. This is because the use of alcohol to combat alcoholism is so revolutionary. Please refer to www.cthreefoundation.org for updates and information support online.)

6

Step One:
Understanding the Cure

Revolutionary Thinking

The first step toward successful treatment involves profound shifts in thinking about excessive drinking and alcoholism. The Sinclair Method is based on a completely new understanding of how alcohol addiction develops and how it can be permanently cured by removing the addiction from your brain and nervous system.

Understanding how the treatment works will ensure that you solve your drinking problem smoothly and efficiently. It will also show those of you who are only beginning to develop a problem how to prevent or inoculate yourself against one in the first place.

Many people will think it's crazy that if you have a drinking problem, alcohol can actually be necessary for recovery. The research, however, proves drinking is necessary—but only if you take naltrexone whenever you drink.[*]

---

[*] Or nalmefene when it becomes available.

Most of us think of addiction as a deep-seated problem, virtually impossible to conquer. But now, clinical trials based on the Sinclair Method have proven otherwise. While heavy drinking and full-blown addiction to alcohol must be treated as a very serious condition, the latest research proves that it is not nearly as difficult to prevent or cure as it used to be. Now, millions of lives can be freed of compulsive and addictive drinking without resorting to torturous and antiquated treatments.

No Abstinence Allowed

Unlike other alcohol treatments, the Sinclair Method does not demand that you stop drinking. Perhaps you have avoided going into treatment, not only because of the stigma associated with being labeled alcoholic, but because you assume that treatment automatically means that you will have to stop drinking completely. It is perfectly understandable that many people cannot picture their life without alcohol, dread a future of deprivation, craving, and total abstinence. The Sinclair Method is good news for those who wish to carry on drinking moderately—it allows you either to stop completely or to carry on drinking safely.

Many of you may have already tried to control your drinking using some form of higher power, willpower,* with religion, on your own, with professional counseling, or through a traditional support group like A.A. Some of you may have been through expensive private treatment programs, only to find yourselves relapsing back to heavy drinking.

Studies prove that many alcoholics manage to abstain for a few weeks—even months—at a time. This is especially true if you have just started traditional rehab and are feeling optimistic about going straight. But as time passes without having a drink, feelings of deprivation close in and the craving for alcohol intensifies. You might be able to resist the impulse to drink the first time, the second, and the third. But all too soon, you find it impossible to

---

* Willpower refers to any method where your will—your attitudes, values, beliefs—is actively changed. Examples include a "Higher Power," psychotherapy, cognitive therapy, or various group therapies.

resist the craving, and you relapse back to drinking. You may have promised yourself you would drink moderately, but after a drink or two, you end up bingeing, depressed, and hung over.

As chapter 2 showed, when rats already addicted to alcohol are deprived of alcohol for a few days, weeks, or even months, they immediately start binge-drinking much higher amounts than their original daily intake when they are again permitted free access to alcohol. Monkeys also show this Alcohol Deprivation Effect.[49] The same pattern applies to human alcoholics.

The Sinclair Method is about as far away from traditional rehab as you can get; to beat your addiction, you must continue drinking. There is, however, a major proviso: you must only drink while on the endorphin-blocking opioid antagonist medication, naltrexone.[*] As shown in chapter 3 on the hard evidence for the cure, if you abstain from drinking alcohol while taking naltrexone, you will not meet with success because you will not trigger the physiological mechanism causing de-addiction. As you proceed through the treatment, you will notice a gradual reduction in craving and drinking levels within the first few weeks. While this will encourage you to continue, the clinical trials prove that you have to continue drinking while taking naltrexone for at least three to four months until you meet with real success.

Straight Thinking—Undoing the Myths

Like many problem drinkers and alcoholics, you may have come to believe the following about your addiction:

- You are hopelessly incurable.
- Once an alcoholic, always an alcoholic.
- You have a weak "addictive personality."
- Trying to control or reduce your drinking is a delusional pipe dream.
- In general, while about 10 percent of alcoholics are able to stop on their own, the only way to beat your drinking

---

[*] Or nalmefene when it is approved for the treatment of alcoholism.

problem is through a total abstinence regime for the rest of your life. This means you must continually battle the demons that cause craving through the use of some form of willpower to achieve abstinence—your only realistic goal.

- Advanced alcoholism is usually a terminal illness.
- You are born an alcoholic.
- The *only way* to conquer alcoholism is to tough it out, through the Twelve Steps, Tough Love, or similar total abstinence program.
- Alcoholics must go through a rigorous, difficult detoxification and drying-out process.
- You have to come out of denial by hitting rock bottom before you will seek help.

Until the discovery of the Sinclair Method, these statements made sense. Prior to the Sinclair Method, alcohol addiction *was* incurable. Once acquired, the addiction tormented you for the rest of your life. No doubt about it, you had to struggle for lifelong abstinence. Research proved that nearly all attempts at controlled drinking for alcoholics were disastrous. Old-fashioned willpower, an external higher power, or various rehabilitation programs based on total abstinence were the *only* way to go. Sadly, whatever the treatment and despite the best intentions, the majority of alcoholics invariably ended up relapsing.

Before the discovery of the Sinclair Method, difficult and often dangerous inpatient detoxification (drying-out) procedures were compulsory—they simply had to be endured. But now, with the Sinclair Method, there is a safer, cheaper, and easier way to remove the physiological dependence. With the Sinclair Method, you need no longer fear the dreaded customary warnings—"incurable" and "85 percent relapse rates"—so endemic to traditional rehab environments.

The Sinclair Method puts an end to these dangerous myths. You now can expect to beat your addiction:

- Clinical trials show you have reason to anticipate a full reversal of your addiction, in other words, a cure. If you are a heavy drinker or addicted to alcohol, it does not mean you are condemned to remain so for the rest of your life. Your addiction can be conquered through Sinclair's discovery of pharmacological extinction—the formula of Naltrexone + Drinking = Cure.

- Heavy drinking and alcoholism has nothing to do with "personal weakness" or immorality. Rather, you may have inherited an "addictive brain biochemistry."

- Research proves that controlled drinking is a realistic goal with the Sinclair Method. The formula of Naltrexone + Drinking = Cure means that your craving and drinking levels will either end completely or be reduced to safe levels. Even the most severe cases no longer mean a slow death sentence.

- You are not born alcoholic. Excessive drinking is caused by a combination of an inherited genetic predisposition and learning the addiction—installing it into your brain—over many drinking sessions.

- Abolishing the craving and the heavy or addictive drinking no longer demands "hitting rock bottom," "Tough Love," or "Toughing It Out" one day at a time through the Twelve Steps of A.A. or other total abstinence programs. No doubt such programs have helped some alcoholics, but the Sinclair Method offers you a more effective and far less drastic alternative.

- Alcoholics who have managed total sobriety for years without relapsing are in the minority and deserve praise. *But they all remain at risk for relapsing to dangerous drinking—85 to 90 percent will relapse within the first year following treatment.* A single drink for an alcoholic can lead to a major relapse, even after years of abstinence.

- People who attend A.A. regularly report that they encounter fellow alcoholics who have relapsed even after decades of total abstinence. As we saw in chapter 2, the Alcohol Deprivation Effect in the brain means that the addiction remains in the "always on" position. Until Sinclair's extinction treatment, nothing could be done to remove the factor causing alcoholism, to delete the fundamental neural circuitry driving your addiction. No amount of willpower or conventional rehab can remove the over-strengthened addictive wiring in your brain. Without access to the Sinclair Method, the addictive wiring remains intact throughout the brain for life. Thus, even if you have not had a drink for thirty years, you are still addicted and always at risk of relapsing. "One drink and it's over" is your First Commandment for life. The Sinclair Method changes this by *removing the addictive neural pathways* from your brain. After completing de-addiction treatment, your craving will be gone, and you will be cured.

• Detoxification through the Sinclair Method is a gradual, relatively painless process. You will continue to drink while on your medication and your craving and actual drinking levels will subside automatically. Indeed, the ideal way to detox is to do so slowly, bit by bit, so the body gradually adapts to life without alcohol. Pharmacological extinction provides an easier, more dignified way of accomplishing this.

How You Lost Control and How the Cure Helps You Find It

The scientific research from animal and human studies proves that loss of control over drinking, craving, and addiction happen for two major reasons:

1. You probably *inherited* a powerful genetic predisposition that enabled you to be particularly good at *learning* to drink alcohol. In other words, you have inherited a particularly powerful endorphin (opioid) system in your brain. Drinking alcohol causes the morphine-like substances known as endorphins to be released in your brain. Dr. Candace Pert, the acclaimed Johns Hopkins and National Institutes of Health neuroscientist who, in 1973, discovered opioid receptors in the brain, describes endorphins as "Molecules of Emotion."

2. You had considerable experience drinking alcohol. The genetic predisposition for alcoholism combines with drinking experience to produce addiction to alcohol. After you drink, the endorphins *progressively* strengthen the pathways wired throughout your brain that had recently been active,

the pathways that are the neural circuitry producing craving and drinking. Each time you drink, the resulting endorphins make this circuitry stronger, especially if you have the genetic predisposition for alcoholism and receive large amounts of reinforcement from the endorphins. These neural pathways become etched into your brain, just as paths become permanently established as people tramp through the mountains. The more drinking you do—the more you trample down the path—the wider and stronger the pathways become. Eventually, the super-strengthened system becomes so established that craving and excessive drinking are no longer under your conscious control. Now you are addicted to alcohol.

The Cure Also Prevents Alcoholism

The Sinclair Method can prevent or inoculate against alcohol addiction before it has taken root.

Genetically predisposed rats soon go on to become addicted if allowed free access to alcohol. If, however, the rats are given naltrexone before gaining free access to alcohol, they *never* develop the wiring that drives alcoholism.

So what should you do if you think you are at risk of becoming addicted? Let's say that you feel you simply drink too much at parties, on airplanes, on your own, at restaurants, or while driving. Or maybe you say things you later regret or wish you had not had so much to drink, and that this has happened once too often. Moreover, you know that some of your relatives have become alcoholics and you suspect you may have inherited the same heightened risk of becoming addicted. If you want to make sure your drinking does not increase, or indeed if you would like to reduce your drinking to safer levels or stop altogether, say goodbye to hangovers, improve your self-esteem, health, and overall life—the answer is to always take naltrexone before you drink. If you do this, you will soon stop the development of excessive drinking in its tracks. (The "Prevention of Alcoholism" is illustrated in Appendix B.)

You Don't Have to Be an "Alcoholic" to Benefit from the Cure

One of the main advantages of the Sinclair Method is that you do not need to have a serious drinking problem or be an alcoholic to take advantage of extinction treatment. If you tend to drink too much on certain occasions and simply want to reduce your intake, begin taking naltrexone before drinking.*

The research proves that you will find yourself more in control, and you will begin to drink less. You can still drink, moderately and safely—if you choose to do so. The Sinclair Method is easier than dieting because you do not have to avoid the temptation to drink. Naltrexone + Drinking works automatically—it is your formula for successful de-addiction.

Handling the Controversy

It is also important that you be aware that you may encounter a certain amount of controversy surrounding the Sinclair Method. The treatment might not make common sense to everyone—especially if they are unfamiliar with the science behind it. After all, how can instructing compulsive drinkers to continue drinking possibly be helpful, even if they have been given naltrexone? You will probably find people especially skeptical if they know you already have a problem and see you drinking, even if you tell them about the medication and the way it works. You must, above all, have faith in the research data.†

You might also encounter professional health workers and lay counselors who proclaim aggressively that "you can't cure a drug addiction with another drug. Rehab, cold turkey, A.A.'s Twelve Steps, and total abstinence are the *only* way." You may get negative feedback from some health professionals when you tell them about the treatment because knowledge of pharmacological extinction has not yet been widely disseminated around the world.

---

* Of course with a prescription from a physician.

† Please refer to chapter 3—The Hard Evidence Behind the Cure, and the annotated bibliography in Appendix A.

If you are told that you should not be a "guinea pig" for such a treatment, you can safely reply that the guinea pig stage of research has long since passed; tens of thousands have already been successfully de-addicted through Sinclair's Naltrexone + Drinking formula. The scientific data overwhelmingly support the position that pharmacological extinction is the most effective de-addiction treatment ever put into practice.

Other treatment methods have helped some people to cope with craving. They have employed the most powerful tools known to psychology for an individual to overcome drives and desires. However, once the addiction is fully installed in the brain, none of the earlier methods has been able to remove the hard-wired neural circuitry that produces the drive and desire for alcohol. Apart from the Sinclair Method, all current treatments leave your brain in a state of permanent addiction. Prior to extinction treatment, your addiction meant a lifelong battle for abstinence, which was the basis for the truism "once an alcoholic, always an alcoholic." That's why, for an abstinent alcoholic, even a small amount of alcohol is exceedingly dangerous.

Unlike pharmacological extinction, traditional treatments have never been able to cut the addictive mechanism out of the nervous system.* Indeed, the NIAAA, WHO, and other governmental bodies confirm that standard treatments for alcohol prevent relapse for only 10 to 15 percent of alcoholics. Because alcoholism has not been curable, the majority of alcoholics relapse—85 to 90 percent relapse within the first year of treatment. They relapse at the point when the Alcohol Deprivation Effect and environmental stimuli have increased craving to particularly high levels, causing dangerous bingeing. This is when alcoholics are most at risk of harming themselves and others.

Be prepared to face initial puzzlement when explaining how the Sinclair Method actually works. Interestingly, many people who are in the midst of the battle with alcohol seem to grasp the logic

---

* Pharmacological extinction literally "cuts the wires" in the circuitry driving the addiction; therefore, it may be viewed as a sort of "nano brain surgery" to correct over-strengthened neural super-highways by turning them back to more normal pathways, the state they were before addictive drinking was learned.

behind extinction treatment more readily than those without first-hand experience of what it is like to cave in to craving, bingeing, and addiction.

Who Should Not Begin the Cure

Pregnant women should not be drinking alcohol, nor should they use naltrexone or numerous other medications.

If you have an addiction to an opiate such as heroin, morphine, or any synthetic opiate such as oxycodone, you should inform your prescribing physician because you could precipitate an opiate withdrawal reaction if you take naltrexone. This is critical because precipitating opiate withdrawal could be fatal. Do not take naltrexone if you are physiologically dependent on opiates.

If you are currently abstinent, unless you are relapsing, there is no valid reason for you to start the treatment. You are to be commended—stay with your current treatment if it is working for you. The Sinclair Method is intended for those who are *currently* drinking excessively, whether frequently or infrequently, or wish to prevent an escalation of the drinking. Naltrexone does not cause withdrawal reactions from alcohol.

Compulsive Drinking Is Not Your Fault

It is now widely accepted that about 10 percent of the normal population inherit the genetic potential for alcoholism. Even though you may have the genetic predisposition for alcoholism, you will only develop the addiction if you begin drinking. At this stage, you are able to choose whether or not to drink. Most people are not genetically predisposed to alcoholism. When they start social drinking, they generally do not get enough reinforcement from endorphins to go on to compulsive addictive drinking.[*]

However, if you are genetically predisposed to alcoholism *and* you begin drinking, the compulsion creeps up, gradually becoming programmed into your brain. As this programming becomes more firmly entrenched over several years, you drink increasing amounts. You may notice that two or three drinks are not enough, so you drink more. Even though you might not set out to become intoxicated, you find this happening way too often.

Your craving for alcohol, the conscious and unconscious thoughts, feelings, and sensations telling you that you really need a drink, starts building to higher and higher levels. Whether you notice it depends on your style of drinking. If you drink in a Mediterranean style, that is, drinking every day, along with meals, you may never feel the craving until you try to stop drinking. For many people, the motivation for alcohol is all a matter of scheduling. It is a product of the Alcohol Deprivation Effect and Mediterranean-style alcoholics may never feel the overpowering craving until they have been deprived of alcohol for a few days or more.

At this stage in the learning of the addiction, you may realize that alcohol is interfering with your life and try to limit the amount you drink. After one too many hangovers, perhaps after doing and saying regrettable things, you swear that you will never touch another drop of alcohol again...until, of course, the next time.

By this time, you have lost control over alcohol, and drinking has become a powerful *unconscious biological reflex*. It is as though in addition to the normal drive for food and water, a new drive has been installed into your body, in this case for alcohol. Once this has occurred, the drive for alcohol becomes permanently entrenched as a physiological addiction, and you begin to "need" alcohol as though it were water.

You no longer drink out of choice. Just as your brain is wired to instruct you to drink water when you are thirsty, you drink because your brain has become wired to crave and drink alcohol—the choice is no longer yours. Instead, your addicted brain makes the choice for you. You are ensnared and enslaved because

---

* This is a bit of a simplification. The risk for alcoholism is affected by many genes, so there is no sharp division between those who are at risk and those who are not. Instead, there is a continuum. At one end are individuals who, once they start drinking, progress to alcoholism in only a few years. At the other end are a few people who are protected by genetic factors from developing alcoholism. In between are the majority of people, who become addicted only when the environment is conducive to drinking large amounts of alcohol.

drinking has now become an unconscious, automatic, uncontrollable "learned reflex."

You probably did not realize you carried the genetic potential for compulsive drinking when you took the first drink of your life. But years later, by the time you had lost control, taking a drink for you was different than it was when you first began your journey. You find yourself unable to stop at your second or third drink, which have now become just like throwing gasoline on a fire. Your drinking flares up uncontrollably, with a single drink being enough to ignite a serious bout of drinking. In chapter 13, we'll see how recovered alcoholic David, a telecom programmer, explained how he considered his own alcoholism in terms of computer programming. The hardware is like the addictive wiring—the neural circuitry in your brain causing craving and drinking—and the software programming is the repeated learning to drink with endorphin reinforcement from alcohol over many sessions.

As you proceed through the Sinclair Method, remember not to be hard on yourself—as so many alcoholics tend to be—for your addiction. You are not a weak, immoral person. No amount of self-recrimination can de-addict you. Like millions of others, you are no more responsible for compulsive drinking than you are for any other inherited illness. But, just as a diabetic is responsible for regularly taking insulin—or the use of a condom is absolutely necessary to practice safer sex—you are responsible for your own cure. Always take your medication before drinking alcohol.

By now, you should appreciate that the Sinclair Method works by blocking reinforcement (which is not the same as pleasure) from the endorphins released by alcohol in your brain. You were programmed to crave alcohol through repeated reinforcement from endorphins over many drinking sessions. More precisely, the neural pathways that cause you to think about alcohol, to want it, and to drink it, became progressively more powerful each time they were used and then bathed in endorphins.

Opioidergic System

Certain neurons in the brain release substances similar to morphine and other opiates. These substances are called endorphins and enkephalins. They fit into the same receptors as morphine and heroin. The release of such substances also occurs in the most primitive organisms. Even some bacteria release an opiate-like substance, apparently as a signal to other bacteria that something has disturbed the integrity of the community. In higher organisms, the natural opiates play a role in intestinal contraction. They also can block the transmission of pain, such as from injury or childbirth. This is why morphine is effective as a painkiller.

In the brain, the endorphins are generally released into the open space between neurons, rather than being confined to a small space within a synapse. Thus, one neuron releasing endorphins is able to affect hundreds or thousands of neurons in its vicinity. Endorphins, therefore, do not act like synaptic transmitters such as glutamate, serotonin, or acetylcholine and might instead be called local hormones. Both external opiates and natural endorphins provide reinforcement. That is, they strengthen the connections within the pathway of neurons that have just recently been used; therefore, whatever behavior occurred just before the opiates or endorphins appear becomes more likely to occur again in the future. (Some researchers have speculated that endorphins produce reinforcement by releasing dopamine, but it now seems more likely that the endorphins have a direct reinforcing ability themselves.) In other words, each time you use a pathway that produces a behavior that, in turn, releases endorphins, the endorphins make that pathway stronger by reinforcing it. As a result, it will take less stimulation to get that pathway activated again in the future, and it will be harder for some other pathway to inhibit it and prevent the behavior from occurring (illustrated in Appendix B).

The opioid system has evolved the function of reinforcing behaviors particularly on the basis of sensory input. For example, putting a drop of sugar or saccharin on the tongue causes sensory neurons to fire and eventually produces a release of endorphins in the brain. This provides a very useful survival function from an evolutionary perspective. Instead of having to wait until after a food has been digested to reinforce the behavior that produced the food, we have developed an instant chemical dipstick—our tongue. We stick it into a food. It analyses the amount of sugar present. If there is a lot, endorphins are released, and we quickly and efficiently learn to eat ripe fruit with the nutrients we need rather than unripe, unhealthy fruit. The endorphin reinforcement requires only the sensory input, rather than the actual ingestion of the nutritious substances. Consequently, although it is a useful shortcut for learning, it can be fooled, for example, with saccharin that produces the sweet sensation—and the endorphin release—but no nutrition.

What Happens When You Drink on Naltrexone

Injesting sugar, saccharin, and alcohol causes endorphin release in the brain. Naltrexone has the ability to completely block the effects of the endorphins diffusing around the brain—which would otherwise be activating billions of opioid receptors resulting in reinforcement or strengthening of the pathways or circuitry producing craving and the drinking.

However, *each time you drink while on naltrexone, the reinforcement from endorphins will be blocked in your brain.* Taking naltrexone will not only prevent the opioid pathways in your brain from being reinforced and strengthened, but each time you have a drink while on naltrexone, you will be weakening the endorphin-reinforced pathways—the super-highways that became hard-wired into your brain and now control your drinking and your life. The Sinclair Method progressively reverses your addiction, ultimately removing it from your brain by trimming back the super-highways so that they are restored to their original condition as the narrow pathways you started out with *before* you began drinking.

The solution to your problem is not through abstinence—it is through Naltrexone + Continued Drinking.

Step Two:
Self-Assessment—
Do I Need Help?

It's a Disease: That's Why There's a Cure

In its policy statement on Alcoholism as a Disease, the American Medical Association (AMA) states that it "urges change in federal laws and regulations to require that the Veterans Administration determine benefits eligibility on the basis that alcoholism is a disease."[50] The issue of whether or not "alcoholism is a disease" is most relevant in terms of funding. If patients have "a disease," then it is easier to obtain paid access to treatment through private and public health insurance programs. The American Medical Association considers alcoholism to be an "illness characterized by significant impairment that is directly associated with persistent and excessive use of alcohol. Impairment may involve physiological, psychological or social dysfunction." The amount you drink is not the crucial issue—it is a question of what happens when you do and that is why it is said, "If you have problems when you drink, you have a drinking problem." One of the problems is simply the impairment produced by intoxication. Other problems are caused by the fact that alcohol tends to accentuate whatever we are feeling at the time we drink it. If we are feeling happy and talkative, we may feel more intensely elated and talkative. But it can also accentuate feelings of depression and despair. And if we are angry and aggressive, alcohol can exaggerate those feelings while interfering with the good judgment needed to keep out of a fight. On the other hand, much of what distinguishes alcoholics is what happens when they do *not* drink. How severe does craving become? Some of the Mediterranean-style alcoholics do not know they are alcoholics until they try stopping and find it is impossible. This is probably the most important sign of alcoholism: the inability to remain abstinent.

Alcoholism is a "progressive disease" that has been described in stages.[51] Do any of these stages apply to you? Are you in the early or middle stages? Do you have a loved one or friend to whom any of these apply? Begin thinking about your drinking in terms of these stages:

Early Stage:
1. You are beginning to experience problems with your drinking. You become preoccupied with drinking, start sneaking drinks, and feel some guilt about your drinking behavior.
2. You sometimes become intoxicated, and may have had blackouts—not remembering what you said or did while drunk.
3. You look forward to drinking sessions, associate with other heavy drinkers, and are less interested in activities that do not involve drinking.
4. Friends and family are concerned about your drinking, and drinking interferes with your work—for instance, you begin calling in sick because of a hangover.
5. You experience withdrawal symptoms such as tremors, depression, and anxiety when you stop drinking.

Middle Stage:

1. You may or may not openly acknowledge it, but drinking has become a problem for you.
2. You are unable to manage your drinking. Even though you wish that you could drink less, you find yourself drinking compulsively.
3. You begin to use alcohol as an antidepressant but find that drinking results in hangovers, which make you even more depressed.
4. You begin to have health problems, and your doctor may recommend you drink less or stop altogether.
5. You may miss workdays and lose your job, get convicted of drunk driving, or get into alcohol-related conflicts with loved ones and friends. You start having alcohol-related medical problems such as liver inflammation, heart disease, or diabetes.
6. Withdrawal symptoms—tremors, depression, and anxiety—as the alcohol wears off are now a regular part of your life.

Late Stage:

1. Your life is now totally unmanageable.
2. You may have hepatitis, cirrhosis, pancreatitis, high blood pressure, and internal bleeding.
3. Deep depression, sleep disorders, and memory problems are prominent. If you have been drinking for many years, your memory may become impaired by Wernicke-Korsakoff Syndrome, a condition that results in permanent brain damage. In *The man Who mistook His Wife for a Hat*, Oliver Sacks describes how one of his patients thought he was living decades earlier because years of drinking had erased entire portions of his memory.
4. You may experience hallucinations, convulsions, and have brain seizures known as delirium tremens (DTs) when you stop drinking. This can be fatal and you need medical attention urgently.

Is the Cure Right for Me?

Do you identify with any of the stages described here? Do you agree with the statement: "If you have problems when you drink, you have a drinking problem"? Does alcohol control you? Would you like to regain control over your drinking? Do you want to stop altogether? Has drinking interfered in your family, social, or work life? Has your health suffered? Have you had any bruises, falls, or accidents while drunk? Have you experienced "blackouts" as a result of heavy drinking? Have you encountered legal problems as a result of your drinking?

If you answer affirmatively to any of these questions, then you should definitely consider the Sinclair Method because it is grounded in mainstream science and offers the most hopeful, effective, and clinically proven plan to break the cycle of compulsive drinking—without the demands of going cold turkey or abstinence. It is especially worth considering if you have tried and failed with other therapies.

In its original form, the Method involved close supervision over eight sessions with a physician and psychologist. However, the research now proves that it is possible to proceed on your own with minimal therapy, as long as you are medically fit to receive a prescription for naltrexone.

Your Mental Health

You can benefit from the Sinclair Method even if you have a psychological or psychiatric condition in addition to alcoholism. For instance, if you suffer from clinical depression distinct from your drinking problem, the treatment can help you with compulsive drinking. However, if you have been diagnosed with a psychiatric condition, you should always consult with a trusted physician before beginning the Sinclair Method.

One of Sinclair's findings from an analysis of the Finnish alcoholics was that the treatment produced a very large decrease in depression. The patients took a test for depression (the Beck Depression Inventory) before treatment and again after about three months of being treated with naltrexone. Naltrexone itself does not have any antidepressant effects, but the depression was dissipated because the drinking had decreased. This helps to answer an old puzzle in the alcoholism field: does depression cause people to drink excessively or does excessive drinking cause people to feel depressed? The fact that it was possible to reduce depression to normal levels in the vast majority of patients with naltrexone shows that usually it is the drinking causing the depression. There were, however, exceptions: patients with a primary problem of depression remained depressed even after their drinking was well under control.

The Cure Does Not Judge You

The Sinclair Method advocates a non-judgmental position with respect to addiction. From a philosophical and practical point of view, it is imperative that you try to avoid the stigma, taboo, and shame so often associated with the label addict, alcoholic, or drunk. You should not consider yourself morally degenerate, weak, or inferior because you have a drinking problem.

From a Sinclairian perspective, you would most certainly not be labeled in a negative way. In any event, labeling does not help with treatment. Nevertheless, it is useful to ask yourself important questions about your drinking patterns. The questionnaires and tools in the next parts of this chapter can help with that.

In the past, a great deal of effort has been expended trying to draw a demarcation line between alcoholics and people who are not alcoholics. In fact, alcoholism exists on a continuum—some are more badly affected than others—and there is no split between the two. It is like trying to define a boundary between red and yellow: it is impossible to say at which shade of orange that red stops and yellow begins.

The effort would be worthwhile if the treatment given to alcoholics were different from what should be done with heavy drinkers, or if the treatment were so dangerous, painful, or expensive that it should only be given to alcoholics. None of these conditions are true, however, for the Sinclair Method. It will cure the alcoholic, but it also is useful for the heavy drinker as a preventative against developing alcoholism. It is safe, painless, and cost-effective.

On the positive side, diagnosing someone as being an alcoholic can be useful in helping the person get into treatment. The self-diagnostic tools here may be useful for getting yourself into treatment. If you have found that you do fit the following criteria, then by all means get help. The Sinclair Method, however, is also for people who simply want more control over their drinking or want to prevent future problems with alcohol. You do not need to have the scarlet letter "A for Alcoholism" branded on your forehead.

Questionnaires and Tools to Help with Self-Assessment

Please consider the following questions for yourself right now:

1. Do you have a blood relative who has had a drinking problem?
   Yes _____   No _____

2. Has anyone ever told you that you drink too much?
   Yes _____   No _____

3. Do other people have different opinions about your drinking style than you do?
   Yes _____   No _____

4. Do you sometimes think that drinking causes problems in your life?
   Yes _____   No _____

If you answered yes to question 1, you should consider the possibility that you *may* be at risk of alcoholism if you ever start drinking. If you answer yes to questions 2 through 4, consider the relevance of your answer. Others might be wrong, but sometimes they can tell if you are harming yourself, even before you recognize it yourself.

CAGE

The CAGE questionnaire, which was developed in 1970 by Dr. John Ewing, founding director of the Bowles Center for Alcohol Studies for family practitioners and alcohol treatment professionals, consists of four powerful questions:

1. Ever felt you ought to Cut down on your drinking?
2. Have people Annoyed you by criticizing your drinking?
3. Ever felt bad or Guilty about your drinking?
4. Ever had an Eye-opener to steady your nerves first thing in the morning?

Interpretation of CAGE Questions

These questions are significant if your affirmative answers apply within the past twelve months. Answering yes to two questions is considered a strong indication of an addictive drinking problem; answering yes to three questions is said to confirm an addictive drinking problem. These questionnaires are not intended as a formal diagnosis; they are included to help you begin thinking about your drinking style.

 Step Three:
Your Prescription
for Naltrexone

Obtaining Your Prescription—Drinking on Naltrexone Is "Good Medicine"

Chapter 1 described how naltrexone was approved for the treatment of drinking problems by the FDA in 1994 in the United States and subsequently by medical authorities in many other countries. Back then, the World Health Organization endorsed naltrexone, and the NIAAA confirmed that it was the first truly effective medication to help in the battle with addictive drinking.* But it took another twelve years for the American Medical Association (AMA) to acknowledge that naltrexone should be widely used for alcoholism in general medical settings with its May 2006 publication of the results of Project COMBINE, the largest multicenter clinical trial in the history of addiction research.

---

* See Appendix D for the letter by Enoch Gordis, MD, past director of National Institute on Alcohol Abuse and Alcoholism, "Letter to Colleagues," dated February 6, 1995–that's twelve years ago as this is written!

Unfortunately, the fact that naltrexone is not a sufficient ingredient in itself generally remains underreported. In other words, it will not work on its own together with abstinence. Most doctors and patients assume that medications are taken for specific illnesses or conditions. Thus, aspirin helps reduce pain, antibiotics cure bacterial infections, and insulin controls diabetes. Doctors write out prescriptions for medications. Patients follow doctors' orders and take the medications, which are presumed to have inherent healing properties. While most medications—antibiotics, antihypertensives, or antidepressants—may work like magic, the patient need do little apart from taking the medication.

This is not the case with naltrexone for alcohol addiction. The medication is only part of the treatment. Active drinking is required in combination with the medication to produce results. As we have seen, the scientific evidence from more than seventy published clinical trials confirms that the medication only works with concurrent drinking—according to the formula of Naltrexone + Drinking = Cure.*

Although pharmaceutical companies list every conceivable drug side effect for legal reasons, they characterize naltrexone as a well-tolerated, safe, nonabusable medication. Naltrexone (50 mg) was first branded as ReVia™ in the United States and in several other countries. In the United Kingdom, it is branded as Nalorex®. It is also sold under the brand name Depade® in the United States. Other brand names for naltrexone include Naltima and Nodict (India), Narpan (Malaysia), Antaxone and Celupan (Spain), and Narcoral (Italy). The long-acting monthly injectable form of naltrexone is branded as Vivitrol® in the United States.†

Naltrexone is available in time-release formulations that ensure it is released slowly and continuously into the bloodstream, and is always in the body. When this happens, the opioid receptors are blocked continually for a month or more. This procedure offers some advantages over taking pills orally, and nice results have been obtained with the monthly sustained release Vivitrol®

---

* See the annotated bibliography on the clinical trials in Appendix A.

† More information is available from the manufacturer, Alkermes, at www.alkermes.com.

injection. However, the long-term effects of the slow-release preparations have not been fully examined.[52] Continual administration also prevents the use of naltrexone selectively to weaken only alcohol drinking and not other behaviors (discussed in chapter 9), as well as preventing pharmacologically enhanced learning of healthy alternative behaviors.

During Step Three, you begin thinking of drinking alcohol while on naltrexone as being "good for me" or at least "necessary for me to get better." At first, it may feel strange, but you will soon get used to it. Remember, the combination of the two—Naltrexone + Drinking—*is* your medicine, your ultimate cure and freedom from your addiction. But doing either alone—drinking without taking naltrexone or taking naltrexone without drinking—will do nothing to help reduce the craving and break your addiction.

Here are some reminders. Naltrexone + Drinking alcohol over three to four months produces:

- Decreased craving for alcohol without having to stop cold turkey.
- Reduced interest in and obsessive thoughts about drinking.
- Drinking reduced to within normal safety limits—no more than twenty-four drinks per week for men and no more than five drinks on a single occasion or no more than sixteen drinks per week for women or four drinks on one occasion. (Upper limits are set by different agencies; these limits are derived from the World Health Organization.)
- The ability to choose to abstain totally—but only after an average of three to four months on the Sinclair Method.
- Automatic and gradual withdrawal and detoxification from alcohol.
- Setting your own goals—total abstinence or drinking within safe limits.

What Does It Feel Like to Drink While Taking Naltrexone?

If you took naltrexone without drinking, you would *feel* about as much as you would if you took a multivitamin—virtually nothing.

Fewer than 10 percent of patients reported temporary nausea in clinical trials in which it was given to abstinent patients. It produced even fewer side effects in patients who were still drinking. The medication is not psychoactive, and it will not make you feel high or low. Naltrexone does not bring relief from alcohol craving like a painkiller relieves a headache. Some patients report they do not get a "buzz" from the first drink when they begin drinking while taking naltrexone. However, even when you do take it together with alcohol, you do not *subjectively feel* it working in your system.

One of the nice features of naltrexone and other opioid antagonists is that the endorphin system they block is relatively unimportant most of the time. Endorphins are involved in many forms of reinforcement, but usually as just a backup or shortcut system. Their role as painkillers may be important in the wild, where animals often have to function despite severe injury in order to survive, but in our modern world, we are seldom faced with such challenges. Other neurochemicals that modulate behavior, such as dopamine, serotonin, and epinephrine, are critically involved in the regulation of vast numbers of activities, and one must be very careful with drugs that alter these systems. With the endorphin system, however, most people can't even tell if it has been blocked by an antagonist such as naltrexone. Indeed, that has been tested in some of the double-blind clinical trials in order to demonstrate that the patients really could not tell if they had been given an opioid antagonist or a placebo.[53]

Remember, naltrexone by itself will not reduce the craving or de-addict you in fifteen minutes, fifteen days, or fifteen years. You should **be aware of false claims on the Internet that naltrexone can abolish your craving within fifteen minutes.** As we saw in chapter 3 on the scientific evidence behind the Sinclair Method, naltrexone is only effective if combined with drinking over the course of at least three to four months. **Extinction takes time and requires active drinking together with naltrexone before full de-addiction can happen.**

Alcohol Abuse and Addiction Are Not Rational

Some people have questioned whether patients would actually take naltrexone. If naltrexone blocks the "pleasure" from drinking, a rational patient would simply stop taking the medication in order to get pleasure again from drinking.

First, let's start with an established fact. Compliance has been extraordinarily good with the Sinclair Method. More than 85 percent of the alcoholics being treated with naltrexone do indeed take their medication, even though they have been told that it blocks initial euphoria from alcohol.

That is not rational, you might complain. No, it is not, and the reason is that alcohol abuse is not a rational behavior chosen logically for its ability to produce euphoria. Studies of human social drinkers show that euphoria is only occasionally increased by alcohol.[54] If you are in a melancholy mood, red wine will make you bluer. If you are in a party mood, you will fly through the air on bubbles of champagne. If you are feeling frustrated, you may become aggressive—hence, the violence associated with drinking and crime. If you are in a hospital gown in a stainless steel laboratory at nine o'clock in the morning with nothing to eat or drink, alcohol will not produce euphoria—as was demonstrated in one PET brain scan study in Finland on the effects of alcohol.[55] The study demonstrated nicely some of the immediate effects of alcohol on the brain, and it showed that an opioid antagonist blocked these effects. The researchers had hoped to measure if it was blocking euphoria as well, but failed because the alcohol did not produce any significant increases in euphoria under stark laboratory conditions.

Among alcoholics, there is very little—if any—pleasure obtained from drinking, and certainly not enough pleasure to compensate for all the pain they get from their continued abuse of alcohol.[56] Alcoholics drink because they have become wired to drink. There is no rational reason for choosing to drink because they do not "choose" to drink, any more than you choose to lift your leg when the doctor taps your knee. You are wired to produce

the knee-jerk reflex, and the alcoholic has become wired to produce the drinking reflex.

So, yes, naltrexone may partially block the pleasure—if any—
from drinking. But pleasure is not why alcoholics continue drinking. Consequently, the blocking of pleasure from alcohol has
stopped few patients from taking their naltrexone. If they had
been told to abstain from drinking, compliance would have been
much more difficult. Alcoholism, by definition, is difficulty in abstaining from alcohol. And clinical trials that have instructed patients to abstain have met with more problems with compliance.
However, being told to take a pill before drinking is an easy com-
mand to obey.

The pleasure from alcohol may be unimportant for the alcoholic, but the overall pleasures in life are important. Many behaviors are reinforced by endorphins, and we would not want to lose
these other joys in life. As a solution for this problem, the Sinclair
Method uses a process called *selective extinction* that removes
the behaviors related to alcohol craving and abuse but supports
and strengthens the other behaviors reinforced by endorphins.
(This will be discussed in chapter 9 in the section titled *Selective
Extinction: How to Maximize Your Results.*)

Your subjective sensations, feelings, and emotions hardly
change when you drink while taking naltrexone. However, the
pathways controlling your drinking are incrementally weakened
each time you do it. This occurs at the microscopic level of tril-
lions of connections between neurons in the brain.* Just as you
cannot *feel* the metabolic processes in your liver or kidneys, you
do not *feel* the de-addiction process as your nervous system is
restored to normal.

As you drink on naltrexone, you will not be aware of the neural
super-highways being weakened and cut back into their original
condition. The process amounts to the gradual but steady weakening of the addictive circuitry wired throughout your brain and

---

* To appreciate the scale of the wiring and pathway system in the human brain, consider this:
the human brain contains approximately 1,000 billion (1 trillion) nerve cells or neurons,
which are wired in pathways at junctions called synapses. Each neuron has, on average, 7,000
synaptic connections to other neurons–7,000 trillion connections. Receptors are even smaller,
with each connection containing large numbers of them.

nervous system. As you proceed to drink while taking naltrexone, your brain is no longer being reinforced by endorphins. This produces pharmacological extinction—Sinclair's amazing discovery—which automatically weakens the wiring causing your addiction. De-addiction happens slowly but surely with *the research showing that the more often you drink on naltrexone, the more you weaken your addiction.** One could not ask for an easier, more elegant, or dignified solution to addictive drinking—you literally "Drink Your Way Sober."

Working with Your Doctor Toward Your Cure

Regaining control over your drinking means taking the initiative as soon as possible. You need to enlist the support of a physician to prescribe naltrexone.† Your main objective in Step Three is to obtain your prescription for naltrexone so you can follow the simple yet powerful formula of Naltrexone + Drinking over three to four months = Cure in Step Four.

Your physician does not have to instruct you to carry on drinking while on the medication. He or she simply instructs you that, if you are going to drink, always take your medication before you do. An additional instruction would be "Do not take your medication on days when you are not drinking" because naltrexone has no de-addictive action on its own.‡

The question of whether it is unethical for physicians to tell you formally to drink, especially if you are addicted to alcohol, is easily resolved. If you already have an addictive drinking problem, you will drink anyway, no matter what anyone, including yourself, tells you to do. In this way, your doctor can safely say, "I do not

---

* Sinclair insists: "We want to be clear that we are not encouraging patients to drink very large quantities at one time. Large volumes of alcohol do not help (do not hasten the de-addiction process) and can be dangerous. But drinking frequently while on naltrexone is beneficial since each time drinking is an extinction session." N. B. My parentheses.

† Because they are so safe, naltrexone and nalmefene, like many other prescription-only medications, could become over-the-counter (OTC) medications in the future. Just like many countries made the anti-cholesterol drugs known as statins OTC drugs, it is a question of both regulation and demand.

‡ Please refer to chapter 9 and the section titled *Selective Extinction: How to Maximize Your Results*.

advise you to drink but, if and when you do drink, make sure you take naltrexone beforehand."

The aim of the Sinclair Method is to reduce craving and drinking to safe levels. Because withholding an effective treatment is not in the patient's best interests, in light of the research supporting extinction treatment, it may also be argued that it is *unethical* to instruct patients to take the medication in the wrong way—together with abstinence. Success is accomplished by drinking while taking the medication in order to reset the wiring in your brain, driving the craving and addiction back toward zero. Remember, as we saw in chapter 3, the research on the opioid antagonist medications (naltrexone, nalmefene, naloxone) proves that the addictive wiring, acquired over many years of drinking, is restored functionally to the state it was in *before* the addiction took root.

If you have a trusting relationship with your doctor, you might wish to refer him or her to chapter 17 ("For Medical Professionals") and to the research articles listed in this book—especially if your physician is unfamiliar with the way naltrexone works with the Sinclair Method. You might also want to inform your physician that pharmacological extinction is part of mainstream medicine and that it has been scientifically substantiated over the past thirty years. Now it has the backing of more than seventy published clinical trials (listed in the annotated bibliography). You may also wish to inform your doctor that naltrexone was approved by the FDA in 1994, and endorsed for use in alcoholism by the WHO (1994) and by more than twenty leading alcohol researchers in the United States, who published their findings of Project COMBINE in the *Journal of the American Medical Association* in 2006 (Anton, O'Malley et al., 2006).

Because naltrexone is an opioid antagonist, it cannot be abused. You cannot get high from it as you can with tranquilizers or many other prescription drugs. Naltrexone poses no addictive risks. Therefore, physicians can feel safe about prescribing it in general medical settings.

The normal dose is 50 mg to be taken an hour before drinking alcohol. Some doctors recommend that you begin treatment with half the normal dose (25 mg) by breaking your tablet in half. This is recommended to help you get used to taking the medication and may be done on the first two or three drinking sessions.

Your doctor will require a blood test before prescribing naltrexone to check for cases of existing liver damage. The reason for this is that one study using massive doses of naltrexone (300 mg daily) found they were stressful to the liver. There is no evidence that any lower doses of naltrexone stress the liver. Moreover, one of the common measures showing the effectiveness of naltrexone is that the same measures of liver damage improve as a result of the treatment. Nevertheless, it was felt that naltrexone should not be given to people who already had severe damage to their livers, so a liver function test is needed, and a small percentage of patients will not be able to start naltrexone. Although 100–150 mg doses are *occasionally* prescribed in special cases, you must stay within the recommended dosage and not take more than the usual 50 mg dose of naltrexone without consulting your physician—taking a higher dose will not speed up your three to four month de-addiction process. A dose of 50 mg should block 100 percent of the opioid receptors for most people; doses of 100 or 150 mg still only block 100 percent of the receptors, and thus do not accelerate the treatment.

One of the advantages of nalmefene, the sister compound to naltrexone, is that it is not metabolized in the liver, so doctors will not require liver function tests before prescribing it.[57]

If you are a weekend drinker, only take your medication on weekends. Do not take it during the week, unless of course you find yourself drinking during the week. If you drink every day, take your medication every day. If you drink six days a week, take it six times during the week, one hour before you have a drink. If you find you have the urge to drink and have accidentally had a drink without taking your medication, take your tablet immediately. *Always keep the medication with you.* Some people keep their medication on their person for years, even after choosing to abstain completely—just in case.

Naltrexone + Drinking = Cure

Don't be alarmed if you come across misconceptions about taking the medication. Many people assume that naltrexone should be used with abstinence. Such misconceptions are often understandable. While they may be unscientific, they seem to make good common sense—"Take this pill for that problem" is the way in which we have become accustomed to thinking about medication in general. Most of us are taught to think of tablet-taking as a passive process. We take tablets for headaches and the headaches go away—there is nothing more we have to do. They work magically to kill pain, put us to sleep, cure infections, and restore normal heart rhythms—all by themselves.

The administration of naltrexone is a profoundly different procedure. It requires continued drinking on the medication. Your de-addiction is an *active* process. You *actively* take naltrexone and then you *actively* drink alcohol. Remember, your de-addiction is not instantaneous. It takes time to de-addict yourself. But if you follow the formula of Naltrexone + Drinking = Cure, your chances of beating the bottle—of regaining control over alcohol—are in the region of 80 percent.

The main objective of Step Three is to secure your prescription for naltrexone. In practice, most physicians in the United States will be pleased to write you a prescription for naltrexone—especially because the AMA published the results of Project COMBINE in May 2006 endorsing the use of naltrexone for alcoholism in general medical settings.

However, if for some reason your doctor feels that the Sinclair Method is beyond his or her expertise, do not be disheartened. Your doctor may refer you to another physician or you can be proactive and find one who is more open-minded, someone who will take the time to consider the solid science behind the Sinclair Method. Please refer to chapter 17 ("For Medical Professionals") and to www.cthreefoundation.org for updates.

Step Four:
Charting Reduced
Craving and Drinking

Beginning Your De-Addiction with Naltrexone + Drinking

Now that you have your prescription for the medication, you can actively and enthusiastically begin your de-addiction treatment. The science behind the treatment proves that you have every reason to be optimistic. You continue drinking as you normally do except that now, you are sure to take naltrexone an hour before every drinking session.

You must decide for yourself if you feel comfortable about telling others that you are in treatment. This is a matter of personal choice and judgment. For instance, you might feel secure telling people close to you—loved ones or close friends—that you are following the Sinclair Method. They should not be concerned if they see you drinking because now you are taking naltrexone, and Naltrexone + Drinking will break your addiction in about three to four months. At the same time, you might feel better keeping your treatment to yourself with people with whom you aren't as close—employers, colleagues, or acquaintances. Cultural differences should also be considered. In some cultures, one's health is a completely personal matter. In others, it is the concern of the family or the whole community.

Drinking habits and styles vary enormously from person to person. Some of you may be drinking heavily on a daily basis, starting your day with an alcoholic drink early in the morning or with one at noon. Others might begin at 6 p.m. and drink steadily throughout the rest of the evening. Some of you may be bingeing only on weekends or only after a period of days or weeks when the craving has built to a breaking point. Drinking problems come in many shapes and forms and there are probably as many triggers for drinking as there are varieties of alcoholic beverages.

It's Like Learning to Use a Parachute

By now, you should know that the end of your craving and addiction won't come from trying to abstain. If you are unable to control or stop your drinking through normal psychological or faith-based treatments, you actually have *to start using the Sinclair Method.*

Starting treatment can feel like attending preparatory classes for skydiving. Your instructor may use instructional videos to show you how to jump out of the plane, how to overcome your initial fear of heights, how to use your safety parachute if your main one malfunctions. The instructor may be repetitive and even very boring. Of course, you understand the reasoning behind your instructor's repetition—doing things properly can make your trip from an altitude of 15,000 feet back to earth smooth and enjoyable. Above all, doing things properly can save your life. The Sinclair Method is similar.

Now, as the urges arise, you permit yourself to drink—but only if you have already taken your medication. Each drink on naltrexone is part of your curative curve as you start the first of many Naltrexone + Drinking sessions to break free of your addiction. Remember, the cure occurs incrementally—drink by drink—as the microscopic yet densely wired system driving the addiction in your brain is dismantled, weakened, and ultimately broken through extinction.

Drinking Measures

Starting with the first application of the Sinclair Method, the usual practice has been to have patients record their drinking in a diary. However, the benefits from Naltrexone + Drinking are not dependent on keeping the diary. (The rats never kept drinking diaries and it worked for them.) On the other hand, diligently keeping the records probably is beneficial to your progress and being able to look back and see the progress you have made often helps maintain motivation. Therefore, keeping a Drinking Diary is strongly recommended.

Before you begin taking your medication and start your Drinking Diary, you should familiarize yourself with drinking measures, which indicate the number of alcohol units in a beer, a shot of vodka, or a glass of wine. Many people think that there is a difference between drinking beer, wine, and spirits, but it's all the same as far as your brain is concerned—alcohol is alcohol. The following Drinking Diary lists the alcohol content of each drink. Although restaurants, bars, and pubs measure alcohol by standardized servings, it has been found that when people drink on their own, they tend to pour larger quantities. *Research shows that people underestimate how much and how frequently they drink.* Please keep a Drinking Diary using the following format and be aware of the safe drinking levels outlined below.

Drinking Diary

Sinclair recommends the following format for your Drinking Diary. Use a small diary you can easily carry with you.

Drinking Session Number	Day	Date	Naltrexone Dose	Alcohol— Number of Drink Units
	Mon.			
	Tues.			
	Wed.			
	Thurs.			
	Fri.			
	Sat.			
	Sun.			
	Week total			
	Mon.			
	Tues.			
	Wed.			
	Thurs.			
	Fri.			
	Sat.			
	Sun.			
	Week total			

Comments: _____

Drinking Measures

In the United States, one drink unit is defined as having one-half ounce of pure alcohol, such as the following:[58]

10–12 oz of beer (4–5% alcohol)	= 1 drink
8–12 oz of wine cooler (4–6% alcohol)	= 1 drink
4–5 oz of table wine (9–12% alcohol)	= 1 drink
2.5 oz of fortified wine (20% alcohol)	= 1 drink
1.25 oz of 80 proof distilled spirits (40% alcohol)	= 1 drink
1 oz of 100 proof distilled spirits (50% alcohol)	= 1 drink

International measures:

1 bottle (330 ml) beer (4.7% alcohol content)	= 1 drink
1 mug of beer (4.7% alcohol)	= 1.5 drinks
1 bottle strong beer (6% alcohol)	= 1.3 drinks
1 mug strong beer (10% alcohol)	= 2 drinks
1 glass (12 cl) wine (10% alcohol)	= 1 drink
1 bottle (75 cl) wine (10% alcohol)	= 6.5 drinks
1 glass (8 cl) fortified wine (20% alcohol)	= 1 drink
1 bottle (75 cl) fortified wine (20% alcohol)	= 9.5 drinks
1 shot (4 cl) spirits (40% alcohol)	= 1 drink
1 small bottle (50 cl) spirits (40% alcohol)	= 12 drinks
1 bottle (70 cl) spirits (40% alcohol)	= 17.5 drinks

Wines include champagne.
Fortified wines include sherry, port, and vermouth.
Spirits include vodka, gin, whiskey, rum, cognac, and liquors.

Upper Limits of Moderate Drinking[59]

Men: Twenty-four units per week or five units during any single drinking session

Women: Eighteen units per week or four units during any single drinking session

For assistance in counting drink units, visit this Web site: *www. knowyourlimits.info.*

Measuring Your Cravings

Craving goes hand in hand with excessive drinking and addiction. You should assess your craving levels on a weekly basis. The Visual Analog Scale of Alcohol Craving (VAS) is a simple instrument to help you chart your craving levels as they decline over the course of treatment. You will actually be able to plot the reduction in craving over the next few weeks and months. If you are working with a trained counselor, you may wish to share your weekly VAS results with him or her as you progress through treatment.

Visual Analog Scale of Alcohol Craving (VAS)

Imagine that you are in a situation where you would typically be drinking. How badly would you want to drink? Determine the point on the line below that best describes your level of craving for alcohol and draw a clear vertical line at that point.

Date: _____

If alcohol were available,
I would not want it   I could not resist drinking it

◄──►

Begin Your Drinking Diary

Now that you have your supply of naltrexone, what do you do? You should immediately begin your Drinking Diary and continue drinking on naltrexone. One patient aptly described this process when she said, "I no longer simply go drinking. I go Nal-drinking so that I can Null my drinking."

Begin by taking half the normal dose, 25 mg, for the first two drinking sessions. You can break your 50 mg tablet in half or ask your pharmacist to do this for you. After the first two doses, you move to the full dose of 50 mg, which is the official recommended dose.

The Drinking Diary is an integral part of your treatment plan. It serves as your roadmap, guiding you toward the cure. If you drink only on weekends, that is fine—you will be able to plot your weekend drinking. If you drink every day, you will be able to plot your daily drinking pattern as it declines. At first, you might not notice much of a difference, but as time passes, you will experience a steady decline in your consumption. Most people notice an observable reduction in craving and the actual number of drink units per week within the first six weeks.

When you begin treatment, you should not be perturbed if you find yourself drinking well over the safety limit or even far more than you would like. After all, this is why you are on the Sinclair Method. Some people drink many times over the safety limit—twenty-four units per week for men and no more than five units on one occasion and eighteen drinks per week for women and no more than four units on one occasion—every week. knowing how much you drink is essential. (Please note that many restaurants serve "a drink" equivalent to two or more units.) This way you can accurately plot how much you are drinking and thus monitor your progress on a weekly basis. *Clinics have found that the Sinclair method brings drinking down to an average of fewer than nine units per week after three or four months.*[*]

A couple of cautions are in order. First, you must be particularly careful not to drink and drive or use machinery. Naltrexone can actually increase some aspects of intoxication. Sinclair found an increase in motor impairment from alcohol in rats.[60] Later research found increased problems from alcohol related to the divided attention needed in driving.[61] Second, do not drink more in a session than you are used to. Naltrexone will not block alcohol poisoning.

What Should You Expect to Happen?

The answer is that no two people are alike. Some people respond to treatment more quickly than others. Generally, naltrexone side effects are rare and include symptoms like mild itchiness or transient nausea. Compared with the side effects of addictive drinking, most patients report they are both minor and temporary—well worth the effort. The majority of patients taking naltrexone report few or no side effects.

Be alert that, even very early in your treatment, you may occasionally experience a surprising ability to stop after only a couple drinks. However, this decrease in drinking and craving is merely an artifact of the treatment. The naltrexone is blocking some of the effects from the first drink and from stimuli that have become conditioned to release endorphins; this helps block the "first-drink effect." It is a beneficial but weak effect. The powerful effects from

---

* Sinclair reports on a large follow-up of the first Finnish naltrexone patients that these benefits were still in effect three years after the start of treatment.

pharmacological extinction develop much more slowly and cannot cure you in a week or two. It took you a long time to reach your current craving and drinking levels, and it will take *at least* three to four months to reverse the addiction. Some people take longer before the neurological scaffolding—the addictive wiring in the brain—is brought down, reduced, and restored to its normal, healthy, pre-addicted state.

Of course, each of you will be progressing through treatment at your own pace. But everyone has to follow the formula: Naltrexone + Drinking = Cure to be successful. You should expect success—like the seventy-five patients in Figure 8 who showed reduced craving over three to four months.

You can also expect your actual drinking to go down to about fifteen drinks per week within three to four months and eventually down to nine drinks per week, as shown in Figure 9 (page 120).

You set your own treatment goals. Only 3 percent of the patients originally treated by Sinclair's group chose total abstinence as their original goal, but about a quarter of them were abstinent after three months of treatment. Before treatment, it may be difficult to imagine a life without alcohol, but by the end of treatment, your craving will have decreased so noticeably and dramatically that total abstinence becomes a matter of personal choice. You will no longer fear alcohol. You will not be in its vise; you will not be its servant or puppet. You will find that you no longer obsess or think about it and it will become more or less irrelevant in your life. However, the ultimate goal is to break the addiction so that you control your drinking instead of it controlling you.

Some people may wish to drink two or three times a year—for instance, at Christmas or on New Year's Eve. This is fine as long as you always take your medication before you do so. The point is that the Sinclair Method allows you to cut back or stop altogether without the nagging feelings of deprivation and threat of relapse associated with traditional abstinence-based treatments. You will not have to attend regular support groups—unless you choose to do so.

If you choose to continue drinking, the treatment will result in a massive decrease in your desire for alcohol and also the actual

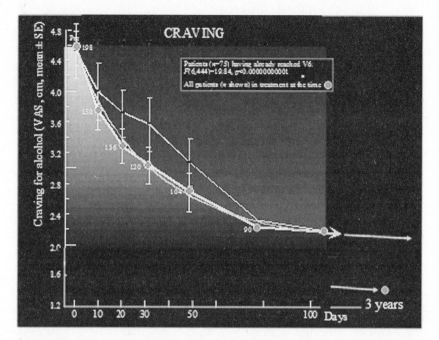

Figure 8. Redrawn from Sinclair, JD. (2001). Evidence about the use of naltrexone and for different ways of using it in the treatment of alcoholism. *Alcohol and Alcoholism*, 36: 2–10, 2001.[62]

amounts you drink when you do. You will find yourself simply losing interest in alcohol without losing interest in the party.* Because de-addiction occurs at the microscopic level of opioid (endorphin) receptors and synapses in the brain, you will not know why the voice in your head suggesting "I could do with a drink" or "I need a drink" simply seems to have disappeared. Your rescue from the bottle happens as if by magic. It is not magic, of course, but the fruits of the Sinclair Method are astonishing indeed.

Most likely, others will also notice positive changes—you no longer get drunk, depressed, hung over, out of hand, or aggressive, and you don't lose your judgment and control. Drinking + Naltrexone produces a state of permanent physiological de-addiction.

---

* Some patients benefit from brief counseling or coaching as they adjust to social situations in which they mistakenly think they need alcohol as a "social lubricant."

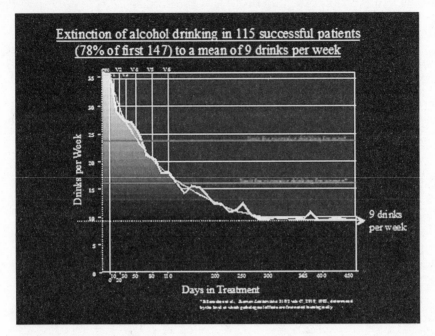

Figure 9. Setting your goals

Selective Extinction: How to Maximize Your Results

Selective extinction is a technique you can use to enhance your resistance to alcohol while encouraging competing positive, desirable behaviors. After a month or two of treatment, you will find that your craving for alcohol has progressively decreased with each Naltrexone + Drinking session, so there are days when you will simply not want to drink. *Selective extinction means that on these days you do not take naltrexone or drink but instead do things that you normally find rewarding.*

If possible, before you start taking naltrexone, you should make a list of healthy, positive behaviors that you find rewarding—or found rewarding before alcohol began negatively interfering in your life. Typically, in clinics, the physician will point out which of these behaviors are probably reinforced by endorphins, but you can do it yourself. For instance, you may include sex or some vigorous exercise such as hiking, sailing, jogging, tennis, yoga, or aerobics on your list of pleasurable activities. Maternal and paternal activities, such as the warm "Ooh! The baby!" feeling you get from cuddling children or pets, almost certainly produce endorphins. So do thrilling behaviors (for example, amusement park rides), novel experiences, eating highly flavored foods, especially sweets and spicy meals. Sensual pleasures usually involve endorphins. Performing, singing, presenting, and acting all involve endorphins.

In general, activities that are stimulated by a little alcohol, such as an appetizer before eating, are opioidergic, that is, they are reinforced by endorphins. On the other hand, behaviors that involve long periods of high attention and holding still, like target practice, are probably not opioidergic. Of course, there are unhealthy opioidergic behaviors like high-risk behaviors, gambling, or taking opiates and other drugs, which obviously should not be on your list.

Make sure you do not participate in the healthy opioidergic activities while you are on naltrexone—save them for your "No Drinking—No Naltrexone" days.

On naltrexone- and drinking-free days, the opioid system in your brain will be more sensitive to reinforcement from endorphin release because of a phenomenon known as *receptor upregulation,* which causes *receptor supersensitivity.* The naltrexone causes the upregulation, but so long as it is in the brain and blocking the receptors, there is no effect. When you stop taking naltrexone for a while, however, there is a period of a few days when the naltrexone is gone and the extraordinary large number of opioid receptors are now free, producing more reinforcement whenever endorphins are released. You can take advantage of opioid receptor supersensitivity because endorphin-related activities are more rewarding than normal. In this way, you begin replacing "bad" endorphin activities such as drinking with "good" ones such as vigorous exercise. You will find your interest and enjoyment will increase progressively for the healthy activities, helping to fill the vacuum as drinking decreases.

Naltrexone offers a window of opportunity for pharmacologically enhanced learning of healthy behaviors. If you last took naltrexone on a Friday afternoon, Saturday is a washout day, when the medication is being removed from your body. Starting Sunday afternoon, roughly two days since your last dose of naltrexone, you are in a state where patients report that doing those alternative behaviors is especially reinforcing. A highly flavored meal tastes great. Even the first bite of chocolate is fantastic. Sex is more rewarding. Exercise feels marvelous. The supersensitivity gradually disappears over the next few days, so it is wise to make an effort to engage in the healthy activities during this window while you get more reinforcement.

At any time, you can return to drinking; just make sure you take naltrexone an hour before you take the first sip of alcohol. Typically, patients start by having only a weekend without naltrexone and drinking—and with practicing a healthy behavior on Sunday afternoon and evening—then return to Naltrexone + Drinking, and avoiding the other opioidergic behaviors. Subsequent periods without alcohol and naltrexone become progressively longer. Eventually, drinking while on naltrexone was occurring only once a week or less often, and the periods without alcohol and naltrexone were six days or longer.

For more on selective extinction, see Richard's story in chapter 12.

Follow Up, Follow Through, and Therapy

You should see your physician from time to time—at least once a month—even if you have a renewable prescription that does not require regular visits. However, in situations where it is not feasible to see your doctor more frequently or you simply do not wish to, you can still be successful on your own. You can follow the Sinclair Method as privately or as publicly as you choose. But you must follow the Golden Rule now and after you complete the program: always take naltrexone before you drink.

The Sinclair Method requires personal motivation to take your medication consistently before drinking. You do this for the rest of your life—but only when you drink. Once you have started the program, there is absolutely no point in stopping and starting.

Stay with It; It Takes Time to Work

Research shows that the minimum time for obtaining most of the benefits from the Sinclair Method is three to four months' worth of treatment. While most people regain control over their drinking in three to four months, in some cases the treatment may require nine or ten months. Don't fool yourself—the addictive wiring in your brain became super-strengthened over years, not overnight. The addictive circuitry will not be sufficiently de-activated after a month or two of the Sinclair Method. If you do not complete the minimum three to four month treatment period, you will be like a half-baked cake—a cheesecake without the cheese—and because your treatment will be incomplete, you will still be addicted to alcohol.

Actually, the treatment never stops, although after the three or four months, most of the time it consists of only carrying the naltrexone around with you. There never comes a time, however, when you drink without taking the medication. If you did, even after you are cured, you would start relearning the addiction to alcohol. Being cured does not mean you cannot develop the disease again.

10 Step Five: The Golden Step— Staying Cured

How Do I Know I'm Cured?

You will know you are cured when your craving for alcohol is noticeably reduced. Because de-addiction is automatic and integral to the Naltrexone + Drinking formula, you will become increasingly aware that you are less preoccupied with getting the next drink and that you are drinking less as you progress through treatment. Your interest in alcohol will wane. You no longer need it. You can take it or leave it.

In summary, these are the main indicators of success:

- You are drinking within the safety limits or not drinking at all.
- Your craving levels are way down or nonexistent.
- Your mood has improved and you feel better physically and emotionally.
- Hangovers are history.

- Others notice that you are drinking less.
- Alcohol no longer dominates your thoughts or rules your life, and you have stopped obsessing about the next drink.
- You have simply lost interest in drinking—you can take it or leave it.
- Your confidence and self-esteem have improved.
- Your relationships no longer suffer as a result of your drinking.
- Your psychological and physical health has improved. Your depression has lifted. Your liver function is improved.

You are cured because your brain has been restored to the condition it was in before you began to drink. This means that the reflexive addictive wiring is no longer connected in your body. Based on the empirically tested discovery of pharmacological extinction, the treatment has proved to be the most powerful alcohol de-addiction tool in the arsenal of weapons against alcoholism. Indeed, prior treatments were like using bows and arrows against addiction. The Sinclair Method presages a new era in treatment, not only for alcohol, but for many other substances (for example, heroin,[63] cocaine,[64] amphetamine[65]) and non-substance addictions (for example, gambling).*

You did not need lengthy, expensive, and unpleasant detox and costly hospitalizations. You did not have to experience *delirium tremens* (the shakes) or seizures. There was no need to break promises that you would never drink again. De-addiction did not have to be difficult or painful. You did not need to embrace a new ideology, religion, or rigid treatment regime. You did not have to suffer needlessly. You no longer end up disappointing yourself and others. Now you are drinking—if you have chosen to continue drinking—within safe limits. Or because, for the first time in years, you are easily able to choose not to drink at all.

Once you have successfully completed the full course of pharmacological extinction, your brain is restored to the state it was in *before* you had your first drink, before you learned the craving

---

* Please see chapter 15: The Sinclair Method as a Blueprint for Treating Other Addictions (Heroin, Cocaine, Amphetamine, Sex, Gambling, Chocolates, Smoking, Computer Hacking, and Pathological Thrill-Seeking).

and the addiction. The little voice in your head asking for a drink is either dulled or simply gone.

The Golden Rule of the Cure

If you are a patient following the Sinclair Method you have only one absolute rule: take naltrexone before drinking. You must take your medication for the rest of your life—but only when you drink alcohol. Following this Golden Rule is easy to do. Always take your medication before drinking.

If you begin to drink without the medication, you will undo the gains you have made. If you drink without your medication, even though you have completed the full course of treatment and are "cured," one can predict with a high degree of confidence that you will eventually return to where you began. On average, it will take you roughly three to six months to reach your original craving and drinking levels and become re-addicted—re-wired—if you drink without naltrexone.

Of course, a single drinking session without naltrexone will not re-addict you after completing the Sinclair Method. However, before you ever contemplate drinking without naltrexone, ask yourself if it is worth taking the first step back on the road to addiction again. Remember, extinguished behaviors can be relearned if they are made while reinforcement is not blocked, and the relearning is faster than the original learning. Naltrexone is your insurance policy against relearning the addiction, and therefore against relapse. Always take your medication before drinking—if you drink.

"Recovering" versus "Recovered"

If you follow the Five-Step Plan meticulously for at least three to four months, the wiring controlling the craving and drinking in your brain will be weakened to the point where your nervous system will be *restored* to virtually the same state it was in *before* you began to drink, *before* you learned how to crave alcohol, and before you lost control. This is what is meant by being cured of your addiction, and why the Sinclair Method is such a profound breakthrough in psychological medicine. Over months of treatment, the primary cause of the alcoholism—the super-strengthened system—is destroyed. The connections between neurons in your brain that had been reinforced so often and so well by endorphins when you drank have now been weakened and silenced. No other treatment has ever been able to claim that it can remove an addiction from your nervous system so that you are cured by the treatment. Being de-addicted means that your opioid-reinforced brain has been returned to essentially the state it was in *before* you had your first drink (and the thousands that followed it), which led to Learned Alcohol Addiction.

In other words, once you have completed extinction treatment, you will be cured. Therefore, you will *not*, as you would with every other traditional rehab, be in a state of ongoing perpetual recovery. You will not be a recovering alcoholic who is always at risk of relapsing and slipping back into benders or bouts of heavy drinking.

In biology, the term *metamorphosis* means "a profound change in form from one stage to the next in the life history of an organism, as from the caterpillar to the pupa and from the pupa to the adult butterfly."[66] The Sinclair Method allows you to become that adult butterfly.

Once you have successfully been through the Sinclair Method, you will be de-addicted. Now you are a former alcoholic—a recovered alcoholic—and will remain so as long as you follow the Golden Rule.

Congratulations! You have beaten your addiction to alcohol.

SECTION THREE

Real Stories of Real Cures

If this book has struck a chord with you, I hope the following testimonials will help you realize you aren't alone, and you too can cure your dependence on alcohol.

11

Julia's Story: Sinclair "Deluxe" Treatment

"The most astonishing thing about miracles is that they happen."
—G. K. CHESTERTON (1874–1936)

ALTHOUGH INTENSIVE PSYCHOTHERAPY is not a requirement for successful treatment, Julia's story has been included because it provides an insight into both the theory and practice of the Sinclair Method and, at the same time, illustrates how the treatment can be enhanced through close, one-to-one contact with competent, caring professionals.

Julia, a thirty-eight-year-old woman, and her devoted husband, James, have been married for eighteen years. They live in a beautiful lakeside house in the Pacific Northwest together with their two adolescent daughters. A little more than two years ago, Julia lost her ability to control her drinking. Although she could sustain periods of abstinence, she frequently found herself craving alcohol, especially by the end of the week. The family became

131

accustomed to Julia getting drunk at parties and on Friday and Saturday nights. But when episodes of severe intoxication spilled into the week as well, her features thickened and her delicate, luminous complexion turned rough and pallid. She began taking "hair of the dog" drinks on Monday mornings after everyone had left the house.

A gifted potter, Julia once ran a successful small pottery business from a studio at her home. But her studio was now a mess, and she no longer used it. James, a highly respected lawyer and a passionate conservationist whom everyone thought of as a gentle soul, could not stop himself from quarrelling with her over her drinking. He had always adored her, but their once near-idyllic life had come to resemble a war zone. Horrified to find himself contemplating divorce, he implored her to seek professional help, but she angrily refused.

"I just have to drink," she told him. "I don't know why. You can all leave me if you want to; I just can't stop it."

A few days later, James read a newspaper article about the Sinclair Method. He nervously contacted a clinic in Florida that was offering this new treatment. He explained that his wife was terrified because she had heard that addicts were hospitalized, forced to stop drinking and attend group meetings, and go through the torture of detoxification. She had also heard that many people who had gone to rehabilitation were often not only unsuccessful, roller-coasting between abstinence and relapse, but were often left feeling even more desperate after treatment. The trained receptionist explained that the Sinclair Method was different, a completely new approach that did not demand total abstinence, and she sent James an information packet describing the treatment.*

The skillfully worded packet went a long way toward persuading Julia to see a doctor at the clinic. "No one is born an alcoholic," one brochure in the packet explained. "Drinking is gradually learned. Each time you drink, alcohol causes the release of endorphins or morphine-like substances in the brain." Endorphins are the body's "molecules of emotion" and can suppress pain. The

---

* This treatment was conducted at a private clinic in Finland.

endorphins strengthen or reinforce the drinking and everything that goes along with it—thinking about alcohol, going to the bar, wanting a drink, ordering it, waiting for it, and finally, drinking it. This happens to everyone but some people, because of their genetic make-up, receive more powerful jolts of reinforcement from the endorphins. Over time, alcohol begins to dominate their lives, and they end up out of control—totally addicted to alcohol. But, the brochure explained, the vicious cycle can be broken or weakened through the "natural process of extinction using the medicine naltrexone to block the endorphins and the reinforcement they produce in the brain."

The entire family read the information packet. They learned that the treatment did not require hospitalization. This was especially encouraging to Julia, who hated anything to do with hospitals. She read that her goals would be "reduction, control or abstinence" and that she need not abstain before beginning treatment. The treatment would reduce her desire to drink while she continued to drink! The clinic's brochure explained that the drinking would decrease, not because of external demands or threats, but because the patient would simply lose interest in it. Using an approach that is entirely compatible with that of Alcoholics Anonymous, the Sinclair Method "works well for both people who are severely addicted, and for those who merely drink more than they would like."

This seemed too good to be true to Julia, but she was encouraged by the fact that she would not be given strong medications, such as barbiturates or benzodiazepines, which can be addictive. Julia also learned that the World Health Organization and the FDA had already reported that naltrexone was safe and did not produce lasting or serious side effects when it was used together with alcohol. The treatment, which normally takes between three and four months, was not to be undertaken without a doctor's prescription. Individual therapy was not always required, but could be helpful as part of a comprehensive treatment program. Julia and her family agreed that she should make an appointment at the clinic.

Her first appointment was not what she expected. The staff at the clinic treated Julia with dignity and did not label her as a "weak-willed alcoholic." Julia was told that she would be seen by a team consisting of a physician, Dr. Anderson, and a counseling psychologist, Dr. Simon. Having two primary caregivers, she was informed, was not necessary but could be helpful.

At Julia's first screening session, Dr. Anderson explained how she had become addicted to alcohol. He decided to accept her for treatment, saying, "The Sinclair Method is not for those who are currently abstinent."

"You mean to say that if I were in A.A. already for a few months and not drinking at all, I would *not* be able to have this treatment?" Julia asked, astonished.

"That's right," Dr. Anderson smiled, "The treatment is only for those who are currently drinking. *It only works if you take the medication an hour before you have your first drink.* We do not prescribe this treatment for those who are abstinent."

"Well, it's a good thing I *am* drinking, isn't it?"

"Until I saw Dr. Sinclair's research data, I never would have thought this possible," Dr. Anderson replied. "We've treated a few hundred cases, and the results are excellent!"

In addition to the standard psychotherapeutic approach of "inspiring hope," Dr. Anderson made certain that Julia was not pregnant, did not have a medical condition that would make her unsuitable for treatment, and was not taking other opiates, such as heroin. As a final precautionary measure, Julia was scheduled for lab work to test for any undiagnosed medical problems.

From the start, Julia was impressed by the nonjudgmental approach of her doctor. She felt a faint flutter of hope. "These people really care," she thought. "They really are trying to help me." She was also impressed by the visual aids Dr. Anderson showed her, detailing the connections and pathways in her brain that had become strengthened over years of drinking. Julia said later that she felt better knowing that there was "something physically wrong in my brain and nerves and not me as a person. The way my drinking had become worse over the years suddenly made sense to me. After all, I didn't start out with this craving. I certainly never drank in the mornings or binged. Before I became addicted, I used to drink quite moderately."

Julia took James to her next appointment with Dr. Anderson. He checked the Drinking Diary he had given her at their first meeting and conducted a medical examination. Julia had not been drinking every day since her initial screening visit, but her diary did show bingeing: well over sixty drinks per week, with most of it concentrated over the weekend. "I just can't stop after the first drink. Why, doctor? Why?" She then saw some biological drawings depicting how addiction had been "burned" into her brain over years of drinking through the mechanism of reinforced learning.

(Please see the images and explanation in Appendix B.)

The biological or "Purple Rain" drawings—as Dr. David Sinclair calls them—showed how alcohol causes endorphins to reinforce drinking, so that the nerve pathways become stronger. The next set of drawings showed how taking naltrexone before drinking would ultimately extinguish her addiction. For Julia, these drawings placed things in perspective, and she was relieved and thankful that the cause of her problem was not personal weakness but "brain biology." Her genetic predisposition for alcoholism and many drinking sessions over the years had combined to make her an alcoholic.

The learning was connected to stimuli. She learned to drink in response to various external or internal stimuli. These stimuli thus gained the ability to make her crave and drink alcohol. One set of stimuli always present with every drink except the first one of the day are the sensations produced by the alcohol already consumed, including the taste, smell, and feel, and the stimulatory effect produced by low doses of alcohol. Julia learned that was why the first drink made it almost impossible to stop. Her drinking was learned, and much of it had been learned as a response to the stimuli produced by the previous drink.

"I was just better than others at learning drinking," Julia exclaimed.

Dr. Anderson said that the situation could be corrected in a matter of months—without willpower or even trying to stop drinking. "All I had to do to beat this thing was to take one of those white tablets before having a drink," she thought to herself later on.

To James, it seemed a dangerous contradiction to encourage an alcoholic to carry on drinking—even after taking naltrexone. Emotionally, he still reacted by hating the fact that his wife had become an alcoholic, that alcohol was destroying their lives. Surely Julia should stop drinking immediately? But James finally grasped the theory. He was even more optimistic when he was shown the reduced craving and drinking results compiled from other successful patients.

Dr. Anderson gave Julia her prescription for naltrexone, and he informed her that this was not a "get sober" medication—she should not operate machinery or drive while drinking. Looking at the tablets in her hand, Julia still wondered if they could actually help her. As directed, Julia started out by taking her first dose (25 mg) an hour before taking her first drink. Two days later, an hour before her next drinking session, she took the full (50 mg) dose.

"I didn't really notice anything much," she told her psychologist, Dr. Simon, at the next meeting. "Perhaps there was a bit less of a buzz, but I can't be sure."

Dr. Simon was supportive. "There are no right or wrong reactions," he said.

She handed in her Drinking Diary and the Visual Analog Scale (VAS) form, which tracked her craving on a scale from 0 (no craving) to 10 (highest craving). Drinking was slightly down at forty-six drinks for that week and her craving was in the high range—naltrexone was not a "magic pill" and did not work overnight. Julia was still seriously addicted to alcohol.

"The Golden Rule," her psychologist repeated, "is that you *always* take the medication an hour before drinking. The fact that you reduced your drinking by a few drinks this week is because, by blocking the effects of endorphins, the naltrexone reduced the stimulatory or first-drink effects of alcohol. Extinction has started, but you still have a way to go. You have just begun treatment. Keep going."

Julia was thrilled that she had had less to drink because it gave her more than just a flutter of hope. The session involved an explanation of stimuli or triggers that elicit craving and drinking. When asked about her drinking history and the situations that set off her drinking, Julia explained, "I found that I started as a way to enjoy myself or relax on weekends. I loved it when the kids were small, tucked up in bed, and James and I could be alone. It was so romantic to be in front of the fire with a bottle of red wine. Red wine, that's my favorite. Drinking seemed to improve our lovemaking and took the inhibitions out of me. And that's when I started drinking socially, which is interesting because I didn't drink as a teenager. Now I don't even need an excuse; I drink out of habit."

Julia told Dr. Simon that when she first began drinking, parties were major triggers for getting drunk. James dreaded them. He thought Julia was being selfish when she drank too much. He didn't know that her brain biology would not allow her to keep her promise not to drink. It was during this session that Julia learned about the specific triggers that caused her to drink. Over several years, she had come to associate drinking with many situations. The therapy would require that Julia drink while on the medication in all the situations in which she normally drank—privately at home, in social situations, through all seasons, in the morning, afternoon, and evening—whenever she was accustomed to drinking. She had to use naltrexone to extinguish her addiction with every drinking situation.

"Just wait till I tell the family about all this," she told Dr. Simon. "My drinking had become a secretive, private matter. It was like a love affair, taking precedence over the things I most treasured. I am beginning to understand why my drinking was more important to me than my wonderful family. It was because my brain took over and ran the show."

"Once we have your drinking under control or you have reached your goal in a few months, we will still want you to keep your medication with you at all times—just in case your craving returns and you have the urge to drink. But, for the moment, let's proceed with you taking your medication and drinking. Go home, take your medication, and drink as usual. Remember to keep up with your Drinking Diary. We can discuss options of where and when to drink at your next session. Though before we meet, you will have a short meeting with Dr. Anderson."

The next meeting with Dr. Anderson lasted only ten minutes.

Julia was asked if the medication had any side effects, but there were none to report. She handed in her Drinking Diary and her subjective craving level was assessed. The number of drinks per week and her craving levels were still high. She was also given standard research questionnaires. The Beck Depression Inventory evaluated depression. The Obsessive Compulsive Drinking Scale assessed her thought patterns related to drinking.

Her next counseling session two weeks later with Dr. Simon was designed to help her prepare for the future. Julia's drinking habits were explored. "Everyone has their unique triggers," Dr. Simon said. "I see from your diary that your drinking is down a bit, from forty-six to thirty-eight drinks this week. Normal progress."

Julia still found that she wanted to drink on her own as well as on social occasions. "I am so grateful that my family understands that I have to drink to be cured," she said to Dr. Simon. "It was a hard one for my daughters to understand. Now they are even pleased when they see me with a glass in my hand! They know how the medication and treatment works."

"Be alert for the festive season, for emotional triggers, for any situation in which you normally would drink," Dr. Simon reminded her. "And above all, remember our golden rule—*never drink without first taking naltrexone!*"

The session ended with Dr. Simon saying that a support group for patients had started and that Julia was welcome to join it. Julia did not feel this was for her.

By the end of the eighth week, Julia's drinking had dropped to twenty-three drinks per week. This was good progress, but still a bit above the safety limit for women. She told Dr. Anderson what had been happening in her life: "James and I are getting on better already. We actually made love for the first time in ages! I no longer stumble into things. For one thing, my knees are better because I'm not bumping into the glass coffee table. My hangovers have lessened. I am actually enjoying my non-drinking days. Last weekend we all went for a picnic. I had my naltrexone and a bottle of nice California red wine with me. But I didn't open it. The girls were amazed, and James said I was being strong. The amazing, wonderful thing is that I was *not* being strong. My urge to drink simply was not there. I wonder if it really is possible to stop altogether. I can see how it might be."

Dr. Anderson noted that Julia still had three instances over the past two weeks where she had consumed more than five drinks in a single drinking session. He explained that she was doing well, but still had much of the neural circuitry that caused craving and drinking in line with her binge-style drinking. "Focus on enjoyable activities on your non-drinking, non-medication days," Dr. Anderson advised. "Your social drinking has diminished already, but I see that you are still drinking on your own—drinking less, but you still took more than five drinks one after the other on your own."

Julia felt positive. She had begun to sense that control over alcohol was within her reach. Her mood improved. She was optimistic and, for the first time in years, had a sense of purpose.

When she arrived home, the first thing she did was to go into her disused pottery studio at the end of her garden. She stood by the lake under a bright blue sky. The air was crisp and blazing fall colors reflected on the water. Julia felt happy and with that feeling came a sudden urge for a drink. Because, although she was happy, she was also sad. Sad that more than six years had gone by without doing much pottery. Sad because of what her drinking had done to her marriage and to her family. She looked at the disused trays, the dusty objects she had so lovingly crafted, painted, and fired. Then she reacted the way she did automatically under stress. She rushed to the kitchen and poured a stiff vodka. She knocked it back neat without having taken her medication.

In a state of panic, she called Dr. Anderson.

"Am I relapsing?" she asked urgently.

"When did you have the drink?"

"About fifteen minutes ago."

"Take your medication as soon as you hang up. It will still have the chance to do some good. Don't worry, Julia. The worst thing is for you to punish yourself. You will get there in the end."

Julia followed his advice and took the medication. She returned to her studio carrying the bottle of vodka and her portable CD player. "What the hell," she thought. "I may as well. I've taken my medication." She spent the next three hours listening to music while she cleaned the studio and threw out broken pieces of pottery.

Julia was startled when her eldest daughter, Sonia walked in.

"What are you doing here, Mom?" Sonia asked anxiously.

"Oh, nothing much. I thought I would clean the studio. I guess I'd better lock up, and get some dinner ready." It was then that she noticed the bottle of vodka. She had not touched it—not once since the first drink. The thought of drinking had not entered her mind. Surprised and delighted, she told Sonia about it.

"You are coming back to us, Mom, you are coming back!" Sonia said, "Let's tell Dad."

Julia's next appointment was with Dr. Simon, who had asked if James would be able to attend part of that session. The idea was to go over the treatment with James because he was so intimately involved with Julia.

"I can't believe it, Doctor, I am getting my wife back," James said. "She drinks, but not as much. She doesn't get crazy. Her moods are better, right, Julia?"

Julia smiled and said, "I'm sure it's working. But I still somehow think I need time. I don't crave as much. I'm not fixated on getting my next drink."

After four months, the Drinking Diary showed that Julia was drinking within safe limits—less than eighteen drinks per week and no more than four on any single occasion. Dr. Simon was cautiously optimistic. "You've come a long, long way, Julia," he said. "We expected this. The great thing is that *you wanted* to stay on track. It would be best for you to continue with our therapy sessions. We can explore whether you wish to continue drinking with naltrexone or to abstain altogether."

Six months later, Julia realized that her life was no longer being controlled by her drinking. "Why then should I continue to drink?" she asked herself. She came to the conclusion that drinking was not for her. She was able to attend parties without drinking. She was happy to tell people that, after her Sinclair Method treatment, she thought it best for her to avoid alcohol. "By all means, you go ahead," she told others at a party. "Most people can handle alcohol. I can't."

Julia keeps her naltrexone pills with her at all times, just in case the urge creeps up on her. Even now, after five years of complete abstinence, she is never without her naltrexone.

12

Richard's Story: The Sinclair "Lite" Method—Same Great Success, Less Intensive

"Miracles don't just happen, people make them happen."
—MISATA KATSURAGI[67]

RICHARD'S CASE demonstrates that the Cure is successful with minimal intervention from doctors and therapists.

While I was on sabbatical in South Africa, I traveled to a lovely oasis town set among oak-lined streets in a valley surrounded by mountains. The people in South Africa are particularly friendly and hospitable, and it wasn't long after we checked into our guest-house that we were invited to a party given by a local family we had met at one of the town's bars.

It was a perfect summer evening. At the party, we got around to discussing Nelson Mandela's brilliant achievements, other beautiful places to visit, and of course the wonderful South African wines. The conversation veered to the high levels of intoxication I had observed throughout South Africa. Alcoholism is also a problem in South Africa. At the party, I met Margaret, an attractive, friendly woman with a bold, direct gaze. As soon as she heard that I was a psychologist with an interest in addictions, she told me that her husband, Richard, was a severe alcoholic. "I didn't know he was when I married him. I probably would never have married him if I had known," she sighed. "I thought he simply liked his drink."

"Have you been married long?" I asked.

"Five years and three months," she replied. "This is my second marriage, but his first. I already had two kids when we married. My late husband was a great father. He died quite suddenly of cancer. I decided to leave the city and move to a small country town. The school here is good, and I wanted my kids brought up in a clean and healthy environment. Then I met Richard and we fell in love. He's been fantastic to my kids." She clutched her necklace. "I didn't know he was an alcoholic," she said again.

"What do you mean by alcoholic?" I asked.

"He wakes up at 3 a.m. to start drinking again," she replied. "It's physically amazing. I wouldn't have believed it unless I'd seen it for myself. He simply can't stop. A real addiction."

I noticed her twelve-year-old daughter Alice nodding in agreement. "Yes, he drinks all the time," Alice said. "It's terrible."

"He's a great guy," Margaret said. "We all love him. He's not like the other alcoholics I know. His personality barely changes when he drinks. He doesn't become violent or nasty like so many others I've met."

A short while later, when Alice had gone, Margaret spoke more openly. "Richard simply drinks all day long. I'm worried about his health. Our sex life is zero. There's nothing we can do about it. I wish there was. He's had seizures, and I've had to rush him to the hospital. A few years ago, he managed to stay clean for six months. He's been to the local A.A. and for meetings in other places. But he always goes back to drinking. Our doctor is a great guy but says he can't help."

At this point, I mentioned Sinclair's work: "Thousands of alcoholics have already been successfully treated for this addiction," I told her.

"I beg you, I *implore* you, please tell us if there is anything like this out here. Personally, I find it hard to believe that *anything* can help, but I'm ready to try anything. You see, I think Richard is dying." Her voice dropped to a whisper. "I'm sure that if he goes on like this, he'll die."

I quickly explained how the Sinclair Method works, how the patient must be medically evaluated before treated with naltrexone. I made it clear to her that the method works only by combining the medication with drinking alcohol, and that there were dozens of published clinical studies in support of the treatment. I told her that Richard would need to keep a record of his craving, as well as a Drinking Diary. I ended by assuring her that there was every reason to be hopeful.

"Please, will you meet my husband?" she asked.

Richard was forty-five years old, yet looked much older. He had a ruddy complexion, was somewhat underweight, but otherwise looked healthy. He appeared to have a great deal of energy and was very friendly. He certainly believed he was well able to handle his drink.

"A bottle of wine is nothing for me," he said. "Lots of guys lose their judgment after only a few drinks. I remember virtually everything that happens—except if I've had a blackout. I *am* an alcoholic. No question about it. I don't deny it. If I try to stop, I get the shakes. Margaret says you have something that might help. I'm curious. As I've said a million times, I'll try anything. I get up at 2 or 3 a.m. and start with my first drink. I hardly eat or sleep. My job is great because I run a pub so I can drink as much as I like, and I don't have to worry about being fired."

Richard and I arranged to meet the next day at his pub so we could discuss his situation in private. I met with Richard, and Margaret joined us after about an hour.

Richard had been able to stay sober for periods of about three months before relapsing. "I've been to A.A. I've done my ninety-day-every-day meetings. It's a great idea and works for some guys. But I *always* end up relapsing. It's those one or two drinks. The devil gets into me and I'm on a roll again. Of course I don't like it." A worried look settled on his face. "I love hiking in the mountains around here. I used to ride horses, take tourists on three-day trails. It's been years since I last went out. I'm dying to see more wildlife. There are leopards and other amazing cats around here." He stared moodily at his drink. "But I'm in the grip of this stuff. Then of course there's Margaret. I love her kids as my own. I know I'm harming them, too."

I began with the standard explanation of how the Sinclair Method is being used to great effect in the United States, Europe, and Australia. It is well known that inspiring realistic hope is a powerful therapeutic tool. So I went through a basic explanation about the scientific basis of how the treatment works. "You have an 80 percent chance of being successful, but you have to be conscientious about keeping accurate records, as well as always taking your naltrexone before you drink," I said. "Besides all that, the fact that you really *want* help will go a long way toward being successful."

I went on to explain that naltrexone was available in many countries, and that it was now available in South Africa as an import under the name ReVia™. Richard was eager to give it a proper try, and I suggested I speak with his doctor about the treatment.

Richard's physician, Dr. Gordon, was very friendly and open. He grasped the fundamentals of the Sinclair Method within minutes. He even made fun of my repeating myself about how the medication should only be taken if the patient drinks, that it should not be taken during periods when the patient is not drinking.

"It seems odd to me, but if you say the studies show it works this way, let's go with it," he said. He asked me to e-mail some medical publications on extinction to him and agreed to examine Richard, order blood tests, and provide a prescription.

I offered to support Richard by telephone and to see him again after about a month. In the past, he had been given diazepam (Valium) to calm his withdrawal symptoms, and his doctor was aware of this. Both Richard and his doctor knew that this treatment would require at least three to four months—perhaps even longer.

Margaret was especially supportive and involved, but was afraid of hoping too much. "If you can help us, I don't know how I'll ever be able to thank you," she said repeatedly. "We'll do exactly as you say. I only hope and pray it works."

I informed her that it was up to Richard to be proactive, but that her involvement would be crucial. She was the most supportive of partners. Her love for Richard was obvious.

Prior to seeing Dr. Gordon to begin treatment, Richard kept a Drinking Diary. His drinking level was clearly way over the top; he took the equivalent of more than fifteen drinks per day—that's more than 100 drinks per week—the equivalent of three bottles of 12.5 percent wine every day. Yet despite this, his liver tests showed relatively mild elevations. Dr. Gordon found that his blood pressure was high enough to prescribe an antihypertensive medication.

Richard started out on half the dose of naltrexone—25 mg for the first two days. He then moved onto the recommended dose of 50 mg per day and experienced slight nausea over the next few days. After a week, Richard said, "I'm doing exactly as you say. I am taking the medication an hour before I have my first drink at around 3 a.m. I'm drinking about the same amount, perhaps a few drinks less per day. I feel less nauseated, though. May I call you next week?"

By the end of the second week, Richard reported, "I'm drinking less. In fact, on Wednesday and Thursday I didn't drink anything." He laughed suddenly. "No, I didn't take my medication as you said not to take it unless I was drinking."

"That's exactly how extinction works. It doesn't happen overnight," I replied.

However, Richard's journey was not entirely smooth. I received a frantic call from Margaret late one night about a month into treatment, "Richard's hands are trembling, and he's shaking all over. What if he has another seizure?"

"Call Dr. Gordon and explain that the symptoms may be related to his detoxification," I said. "You see, he is gradually detoxifying. Even though he's down to almost half his usual number of drinks, because of the sheer amount he has been drinking, he may be experiencing some withdrawal symptoms. If he were to stop abruptly—go cold turkey—we would probably have to hospitalize him. But the Sinclair Method allows for a gradual reduction in drinking."

Dr. Gordon concluded that the symptoms were related to withdrawal, and said that he could offer medication for that but would prefer not to. Richard was slowly going through withdrawal. Because his drinking levels had been so high, it was both normal and expected that he would experience some withdrawal symptoms as he began reducing the amount he consumed. But because the Sinclair Method allowed for gradual withdrawal by continuing to drink while taking naltrexone, Richard's symptoms were far less severe than if he had suddenly gone cold turkey. This is a major advantage of the Sinclair Method. By the end of the seventh week, Richard was drinking less than thirty drinks per week and had had several alcohol-free days.

"Don't for one minute let yourself think that you are cured," I said to him over the phone. Richard understood the idea behind selective extinction—that he should avoid hiking in the mountains while on naltrexone. Because endorphins are also released during vigorous exercise, he should not hike or ride on the same days that he takes his naltrexone. So he should save hiking and other positive activities for the days he's not drinking (and, subsequently, not the taking the medication).

By the end of the twelfth week, Richard was drinking well within accepted safety limits—less than twenty-four drinks per week, and no more than four drinks in a single drinking session.

"I just don't feel like it," he said. "I'm sleeping much better. My appetite has returned; just ask Margaret. I'm eating like a horse. I feel like I have begun a new life. The main thing is that my craving is far lower than it has ever been."

After five months Richard felt that alcohol was not the major feature of his life.

"I can easily serve customers in my pub without having the least desire to drink," he said, "I thought I might be less funny and entertaining, but that has not been a problem. The kids are pleased, and so is my fantastic Margaret."

At seven months, Richard was hardly drinking at all. Yet he felt he was the kind of person who might occasionally want to have a drink in the future. "Yes, I know what you are going to say—never, ever, take another drink without first taking my medication."

When I next saw him about a year later, Richard showed me a gold cylindrical pendant made by a local jeweler. He wore it around his neck. He opened the cylinder to expose two naltrexone tablets. He laughed. "I know what you are going to say next."

"What's that?" I said.

"Never leave home without it," he replied.

One of the main points about Richard's case is that his treatment was successful with a limited number of one-on-one sessions. Richard also did not receive any conventional psychotherapy. At that time, the results of Project COMBINE, published in the *Journal of the American Medical Association* in May 2006, had not yet been published. It confirmed that patients could be treated with naltrexone in primary care settings without intensive psychotherapy. Nevertheless, it should be pointed out that this "lite" version is not always suitable for patients who have psychological problems in addition to alcoholism. Such patients may require additional psychotherapeutic support. Yet if Richard had not tried this way, he would most certainly have been left untreated in his idyllic country town. He would still be struggling with his drinking. He would still be reflexively waking up at 3 a.m. for a drink, his family would still be unhappy, and his health would still be deteriorating. Instead, he is healthy and enjoying the countryside on long hikes.

13

David's Story:
A Relapsing Patient
Is Successful

"Every patient carries her or his own doctor inside."
—Albert Schweitzer (1875–1965)

Davidʼs STORY shows how the Sinclair Method can be an effective self-help treatment as long as the patient receives basic medical care and understands the proven fundamental formula: Naltrexone + Drinking = Cure.

David, a thirty-year-old Silicon Valley computer expert, seemed to have everything going for him as a well-paid consultant for an international cellular telephone company. However, his excessive drinking gradually got worse, and he began to skip work on Monday mornings. Then, because of his increased drinking, he eventually lost his contract with the cellular phone company.

David's excessive binge-style drinking was out of control. However, he maintained that because he did not drink during the week he was "not an alcoholic." As predicted by the Alcohol

151

Deprivation Effect (chapter 2—The Genesis of the Cure for Alcoholism) and in line with all the research, David managed to go for weeks without drinking, like many alcoholics.

It was only after a drunken boating accident during which he came very close to drowning that he acknowledged that he had a serious problem. His girlfriend threatened to leave him if he continued along this suicidal path. David then entered an outpatient program along the lines of A.A. However, the craving would always get the better of him, and he would relapse after a month or two of abstinence.

Finally, his girlfriend left him. David was absolutely distraught. He vowed to find a solution and began to search the Internet, where he started learning about naltrexone.

David found a sympathetic psychiatrist willing to listen to him. "I was amazed how little the doctor seemed to know about learning and extinction," he told me. "But he was great—like he was very kind, didn't mind hearing my opinion. He read the scientific papers I gave him and seemed happy to give it a go. He had no problem prescribing naltrexone and was thorough medically. First, he took blood samples himself, and made me see an internist for a general physical exam." It took about two months for David to notice significant reductions in craving and actual drinking. But he persevered with the treatment.

David's natural love of computer hardware and the software that made it function tied in to his treatment. He observed, "The brain is like the hardware. When we are born it is like a half-full—or half-empty—computer hard drive. It has less software on it. Installing software is like learning in the brain. But as soon as you start adding new programs to the hardware there is a risk of viruses creeping in. Drinking alcohol for me was as though I had a glitch in my brain, a preinstalled program, which allowed me to learn a new program—craving alcohol. Maybe I inherited it. My uncle was an alcoholic and a compulsive gambler. Who knows? What I do know is that I had no 'antivirus' software in my brain. The naltrexone acts as a sort of slow virus removal tool. Each time I drank with naltrexone in my system, it was as though I was removing the virus—the craving and the addiction—bit by bit. I definitely noticed my craving was going down. Drinking on naltrexone was, in a weird sort of way, *good for me*."

"I started leaving my drinks and not finishing them. After a while, I became aware that I even stopped thinking about and planning my drinking sessions. I stopped seeing a long happy hour as a reward after working hard. I'll say this—not drinking was very new to me! I used to look forward to having a good drinking session, especially at the weekend. Alcohol was entrenched in my early social life. It gave me Dutch courage with dating. It changed my personality. I became a clown and loved the feeling. I wondered how I could live without it. Would it dampen my personality? But this hasn't been a problem. I have found I have more time for my work. People say I'm easier, nicer to be with, which in a way came as a surprise because I thought I needed to be a bit sozzled to get going socially. If anything, I am maybe too obsessive about my job now. But it's well worth it."

After a full six months of on-off drinking and occasionally still getting drunk even with naltrexone, David chose to be mostly abstinent. He drinks occasionally, but reports that the whole concept of drinking has taken on a different dimension. It no longer holds much significance for him. He likens drinking without naltrexone to turning on his computer without antivirus software running as protection in the background—he would leave himself open to the virus to reinstall the craving and addiction.

14

Pete's Story: A Troubled, Relapsed Alcohol and Cocaine Addict Until He Got a Prescription for Naltrexone

"The future is here. It's just not widely distributed yet."
—WILLIAM GIBSON (1948–)

THE FOLLOWING CASE is based on the experiences of Pete, an acquaintance of mine who suffered from severe alcoholism. As his drinking problem grew further out of control, he also began to abuse cocaine. Then Pete hit rock bottom.

Pete is a humorous, friendly, well-liked, exuberant thirty-eight-year-old, Irish-born hairdresser living in London. "My parents have always been afraid of alcohol because my grandfather was a committed alcoholic!" he told me. "He drowned before I was born. People said he was blind drunk at the time. And what did I do? Well, I went and followed in grandfather's footsteps. I disappointed everyone with my cocaine and boozing. I am totally useless and a mess—not at all like my brother who has a mortgage and has helped my parents out ever since my father had a stroke."

Pete started drinking when he was about sixteen. "It was the usual. I would go to city pubs with a group of guys, and would spend summer afternoons, especially Saturdays and Sundays, drinking beer. I loved the feeling of beer. I was shy talking to girls, but when I had a few beers in me, my inhibitions flew out the window. I could talk to anyone and didn't care what they thought."

When Pete came home after a night out and vomited, was hung over and depressed the next day, his family put it down to growing pains and typical teenage behavior. Time went on, and Pete regularly got wasted on weekends. He left school early because he was somewhat dyslexic and teachers said that he could not concentrate in class, and to compensate, he had become the class joker. "One thing I think alcohol did for me was to help me ease up, let go of being uptight. And I found I had confidence even when I was not drunk." He left school when he was seventeen and had the good fortune to find work apprenticed to a celebrity stylist at a famous hairdressing salon in London's West End. He did well because his clients found that he was not only a talented hairdresser but had a way of making them laugh at themselves. "I became a sort of therapist to my clients and earned huge amounts for doing their hair at home. I went to the Caribbean on movie shoots, and I met lots of models and stars. I even had a client who was a major star, and I traveled on set with her."

Having a "good time" for Pete meant parties, sex, and above all, drinking. Because many of his clients were the wives and girlfriends of bankers and lawyers, as well as successful business people, Pete had more than his fair share of the champagne life. He frequented many of London's exclusive nightclubs, restaurants, and bars. By his early thirties, Pete found that he could "wake up on a Sunday morning not knowing where I was or who I had slept with. I sometimes couldn't remember where I had been or what I had done the night before. That was when I started having serious blackouts. Maybe the blackouts started before. I just don't know. It was about that time that I started using cocaine—not regularly though—only on weekends."

Pete found that cocaine took him to new levels of confidence. It seemed to take care of his depression temporarily, which in part was exacerbated by his heavy drinking. He began to call in sick on Monday mornings and found that the best solution was to have a drink and go back to bed. Although Pete was earning enough to rent his own place, he still lived with his parents. On days when he was unable to make it into work, he would get his parents or his girlfriend to "call in sick" on his behalf. In the language of traditional addiction treatment, they would be known as "co-dependents"—people who help the addict continue drinking. Inevitably, Pete lost his job with the celebrity hairdressing salon. He was thirty-two.

He then drifted from one salon to the next. His private clients began to abandon him, he said, "because of my drinking and cocaine use, my styling deteriorated. Also, I sometimes forgot to go to appointments or cancelled them because of a hangover." A year later, Pete fell in love with Moriko, a successful fashion designer. "We were so in love. I could make her laugh and feel good about herself. She knew I had a drinking problem, but I hid my cocaine use from her. I can't believe what a fool I was. She backed me by giving me $50,000 to start my own salon. What did I do? I got swindled by a guy who said he would become my partner, and I blew the rest of it on trips to Thailand and the United States." Much of the money also "went up my nose and on impressing good-time friends." Heartbroken, Moriko abandoned him as a totally lost cause.

Pete then made a determined effort to go straight. He managed to get a full-time job working for a large company as an in-house hairdresser. He was able to hold the job for several months but eventually relapsed badly. On impulse, he confessed his predicament to the salon manager. "I came in one Monday morning and in front of everyone, including clients, just blurted out that I was depressed and I had a drink-drug problem." After this, he stopped drinking for a while. Like many addicts, he was able to withstand a few weeks without drinking or taking drugs. But as the Alcohol Deprivation Effect (see chapter 2—The Genesis of the Cure for Alcoholism) steadily increased, and the craving for a drink tormented him, he lost his resolve. "All it took was one drink and I was off. My personality changed totally. I became reckless and also craved cocaine. I couldn't stop. About two years ago, I got in with a bad crowd, and the rest is history."

Pete found himself visiting seedy crack-cocaine houses. His car, along with all of his hairdressing equipment, was stolen. By then he had run up credit card debts of more than $30,000. His boss lost patience and made no attempt to hide his feelings of contempt.

Fortunately, the company policy compelled the manager to refer him to the company doctor. "I was very lucky," Pete said later, "because this doctor was only staying at the company for another two weeks. He was a kind man. If he had left the company before I met him, I don't know if I would have gotten into treatment because I saw him going out of his way to make all sorts of calls, and pulling as many strings as he could to get my treatment covered by the company's health insurance."

Pete then entered the $30,000 twenty-eight-day inpatient treatment, which was run along the lines of the Minnesota Model, where Alcoholics Anonymous (A.A.) and the Twelve Steps are used. Pete was prescribed medication to help him with withdrawal, together with a new antidepressant. He participated in group therapy sessions and saw both a psychiatrist and an addiction counselor. In addition, his parents and brother attended family therapy sessions. Pete learned that "my drug of choice was alcohol, not cocaine." He was told that he had an "incurable disease," which meant that he would simply have to deal with the craving and addiction for the rest of his life. He also learned that he could relapse, but that A.A. meetings would help him. "I had to get a new mobile phone number because dealers and the old crowd still called me. I went through hell in the clinic."

When Pete had called me to say, "Guess where I am," I had not been all that surprised. When I saw him during Sunday visiting hours a few weeks later, he showed me his room, which could not be locked. I met several patients ranging in age from teenagers to the elderly. Some told me that they had been through the treatment more than once.

Because I was writing this book on the Sinclair Method, I was interested in following Pete's progress. Pete's therapy had provided him with an understanding of how and why he became addicted.

He had also learned that his addiction was not only dangerous but far more powerful than his conscious will. He would have to surrender to a Higher Power.

Just as we saw in chapter 2, as a result of the Alcohol Deprivation Effect, Pete found that, despite attending the twenty-eight-day inpatient treatment, his persistent craving for alcohol had not abated. But there were those rare moments, those brief precious periods, when he felt free of the craving. He attended his A.A. meetings and did everything prescribed by his counseling team.

Three months after his discharge from the rehabilitation program, I called Pete to see how he was getting on. "I'm doing fine," he said, "But it's hard every time I walk past a wine store. I crave red wine—especially when I go past a good French restaurant. So I don't go out anymore. I stay at home on Saturday nights and watch DVDs or use the Internet. My girlfriend says that if I touch even a drop of wine she will leave me for good."

Pete managed to get a part-time job at a salon in London, but barely made ends meet. His days as a celebrity hairdresser were long over. He declared bankruptcy. After six months, he had still not touched a drop of alcohol.

Seven months after his discharge, I again called him to ask how things were going. He said, "Good so far as drinking goes. But I am totally depressed. I often feel like crying. I still want a drink. I don't know how I am going to handle Christmas with my girlfriend's family." Pete's treatment had helped him to white-knuckle it through the craving thus far, but he was still in the grip of severe Alcohol Deprivation Effect. It transpired that of the twenty-seven patients in the group who started treatment with him, seventeen had already relapsed. One in his group had died of an overdose (alcohol combined with other drugs). He was only thirty-five years old. Pete desperately craved a drink but remained clean.

When I next heard from Pete, about a year after he had begun his inpatient treatment, he said, "I have relapsed five times and lost my driver's license. I found myself in a pub near home. My craving was going bananas. I just couldn't resist. The cops were sneaky. They were in plain clothes and in the pub with me. They just followed me out to my car and let me drive off until I was stopped and breathalyzed. I asked for a blood test. I ended up spending the night in a cell with a seriously heavy guy. My fault. But I couldn't help it. I was just stupid and weak."

Enthusiastic about the Sinclair Method results and the clinical trials on naltrexone and nalmefene combined with drinking alcohol, I explained how I thought Pete might benefit—if, and only if, he found that the craving continuously led to heavy drinking and relapse. In line with the Sinclair Method, I could never suggest that a successfully abstinent alcoholic start drinking again just so he or she could start on the Sinclair Method. Yet I could see that Pete was headed for more serious bouts of drinking, self-recrimination, guilt, and depression. And I knew that the craving would always be with him.

I briefly described how the Sinclair Method worked, explaining that it meant taking naltrexone before drinking and that treatment had to be conducted under proper medical supervision. "Great, so it means I can drink again!" Pete joked.

"Listen, Pete, we all know that alcohol abuse is no laughing matter, especially when it reaches the levels it has for you," I responded indignantly.

"I'm just joking," he replied. "I don't know how my parents would react. My girlfriend, I can tell you, will say a huge no. But if I tell them that naltrexone blocks the pleasure from alcohol they might be more open. Also, if I have proof like scientific papers that it really works…"

I explained that naltrexone certainly did not block the intoxication from alcohol. It is not a "get sober pill." I told him, "You will still get drunk and feel the effects of alcohol. It may prevent the initial euphoric high that some people, especially those who have not had a drink for a while, tend to experience. And, to begin with, it will still produce inebriation. In fact, you may 'feel drunker' when you take it together with alcohol. And you certainly cannot safely operate a vehicle when drinking just because you've taken the medication. What will happen is that over time, usually within four to six weeks, you will notice your craving going down and the amount you drink will decrease, which is why you have to be meticulous about recording exactly how much you drink and crave. That's why it is best to work with people who know how the Sinclair Method works. Simply giving you a pill without understanding how it works won't help. It's not that complicated but you will need professional guidance to know how to use it properly."

Even though Pete was attending A.A. meetings, he continued to relapse. He could abstain for a few days but soon found himself bingeing. It was a vicious cycle. Pete called me to ask about starting on naltrexone. He pleaded, "Let me try naltrexone anyway. Could you write to my doctor and tell him about it? He's given me antidepressants before. Why not naltrexone? You say it's not possible to abuse it, right?"

I wrote to Pete's doctor, enclosing additional supporting scientific papers presenting several clinical trials, news articles, and other papers describing how naltrexone had been approved in 1994 by the FDA in the United States specifically for alcohol abuse, and that it was also approved for this use in many European countries. I also attached a copy of an open letter to colleagues from Dr. Enoch Gordis (1995, see Appendix D), former director of the National Institute on Alcohol Abuse and Alcoholism in the United States, which described how naltrexone is a safe medication that could help alcoholics deal with their craving. Dr. Gordis wrote, "One million Americans seek alcoholism treatment each year, many more than once. Of treated patients, approximately 50 percent relapse within the first few months of treatment. While not a 'magic bullet,' naltrexone nevertheless promises to aid many of these patients in their struggle to overcome a chronic relapsing disease." Pete's family doctor refused to contemplate prescribing naltrexone for alcohol addiction because it has only been approved in the United Kingdom as a treatment for narcotic (heroin, morphine, other opiates) addiction. In the United Kingdom, doctors cannot prescribe a medication for use outside the scope of that drug as approved by the United Kingdom's National Health Service (NHS) using public funds. The NHS provides all British citizens with free medical treatment but is very cautious about prescribing medication because of the high costs of most drugs.

There was no government-sponsored program Pete could turn to for naltrexone treatment. He certainly could not afford a private psychiatrist outside the National Health Service (private psychiatry fees in London can cost up to $300 to $600 per consultation). Unlike Richard's open-minded doctor in the United States who readily prescribed naltrexone, Pete's physician would have had to comply with National Health Service rules and regulations. Therefore, unless he could get into a special program—an unlikely prospect—there would be no naltrexone for Pete.

Mercifully, a gift from a family friend enabled Pete to see a private physician. While naltrexone is approved for treating opiate addiction in the United Kingdom, and it is easily available by prescription from any pharmacy, it is not on the government's approved list of medications for alcoholism. Although the government will not pay for it, any licensed physician can legally and ethically prescribe it for alcoholism. I referred Pete to a private physician who worked with addictions and who was well-versed in using naltrexone in line with the Sinclair Method.

Within four months, Pete said, "I am a new man with this treatment. I am drinking far less and when I walk past a restaurant the glass of red wine sitting on the table doesn't grab me deep down in the gut like it used to. I am so grateful for finally getting this treatment. It's exactly as you said it would be. My plan is to go completely abstinent. My craving is way down and I am hardly drinking at all."

A Sober, Happier Future

15

The Sinclair Method as a Blueprint for Treating Other Addictions

(Heroin, Cocaine, Amphetamine, Sex, Gambling, Chocolates, Smoking, Computer Hacking, and Pathological Thrill-Seeking)

THIS CHAPTER EXPLORES the important implications of the Sinclair Method for other addictions. Sinclair's concept of pharmacological extinction for alcoholism is similar to Jenner's first vaccination against smallpox. Both serve as blueprints to extend basic scientific discoveries.

Just as Jenner's smallpox vaccination eventually led to vaccinations against many other infectious diseases such as rabies, polio, and tuberculosis, so may Sinclair's pharmacological extinction for alcohol addiction lead to the cure for many other addictions. Sinclair proved that the formula of Naltrexone + Drinking was 100 percent successful in alcoholic laboratory animals. Similar success rates were achieved for animals addicted to sweets (saccharin) and methadone, which is closely related to morphine and heroin. Clinics treating human alcoholics with pharmacological extinction produced success rates of around 80 percent—that is, patients had either stopped drinking completely, or if they still were drinking, their consumption had fallen to less than half of their pretreatment level or to less than the amount producing tissue damage.

Preliminary research indicates that naltrexone is promising in the treatment of addiction to opiates, cocaine, amphetamine, and some other drugs. Used with selective extinction, opioid antagonists may be helpful in treating certain eating disorders. Non-substance addictions such as compulsive gambling, kleptomania, self-mutilation, computer hacking, extreme sports, and sexual compulsions, where no actual substances are introduced into the body, may also benefit from pharmacological extinction. All of these probably involve jolts of endorphin reinforcement to the brain. However, not all addictions are primarily mediated through the endorphin or opioid system. Tobacco addiction, for example, is probably mediated through the nicotinic receptor system. Nevertheless, the scope for using naltrexone or nalmefene for pharmacological extinction of various addictions is both promising and wide open.

Opiates—Morphine, Heroin, and Synthetic Opiates Like Oxycodone

The most obvious application for extinction produced with opioid antagonists such as naltrexone is the treatment of addiction to heroin, morphine, oxycodone, or other opiates. Indeed, there is already considerable evidence that extinction can cure opiate addiction.

Animal studies show that treatment with opioid antagonists extinguishes self-administration of both methadone and morphine. Similarly, as was already discussed in chapter 4, a major study sponsored by the National Institute on Drug Abuse (NIDA) demonstrated that naltrexone was effective in treating heroin addiction, but only in the subgroup of patients who took opiates while on the medication, thus making extinction possible.[68] That subgroup consisted of patients who actually disobeyed instructions not to use opiates while in treatment.

Recently, the Sinclair Method was tested intentionally in a double-blind, placebo-controlled trial with heroin (opiate) addicts.[69] The results showed naltrexone offered excellent benefits when compared with placebo. There also have been reports from several groups that are giving slow-release naltrexone implants or injections to detoxified opiate addicts.* Clearly, there is potential for both treatment and prevention. Nevertheless, treating addiction to heroin and morphine is more complex and dangerous than treating alcoholism. The primary reason is that naltrexone and other opioid antagonists cause an immediate withdrawal in opiate-dependent patients, which can even be fatal. Consequently, detoxification is a necessary first step in treating opiate addicts with naltrexone, even though it is not needed in the case of alcohol. In addition, powerful opiates can kill more quickly and easily than alcohol. In other words, it is easier to take an overdose of an opiate than of alcohol. Therefore, great care must be taken in working with opioid antagonists and opiates. Legal problems also arise when working with addiction to heroin or other illegal opiates.

In most countries, a doctor cannot advise a patient to take heroin while on naltrexone because taking heroin is illegal. One way around this is for the physician to tell the patient, "Don't take opiates, but if you ever do decide to take one, take naltrexone first."

Another potential solution to this problem is to switch the patients to a legal opiate, such as methadone or buprenorphine, and then extinguish the use of the legal opiate with naltrexone or nalmefene. The procedure is effective in animal models and should also work in humans addicted to opiates.

Do not confuse extinction treatments of opiate addiction with the "rapid detoxification" methods being promoted commercially in many countries, where heroin addicts are anesthetized and then given naltrexone. This concentrates all of the effects of opiate withdrawal into a short but very intense session. Clinics using rapid detoxification are advised to have emergency resuscitation equipment on hand. The safety of such procedures is debatable and serious caution is advised before seeking this treatment. The

---

* Vivitrol® injections have been approved in the U.S. and most recently, in Russia. More research is needed on the implants.

treatment does remove physiological dependence, just as a few days without opiates would, but it does not remove the learned behavior of opiate self-administration and the craving for the drugs.

Cocaine

Powdered cocaine and crack, the solid smokeable version of the same drug, had once been thought to work primarily through the dopamine neurochemical system. However, the accumulating evidence already suggests it should be possible to treat cocaine addiction with naltrexone too.

First experiments indicated that cocaine self-administration by rats was learned through reinforcement from the opioidergic system.[70] Naltrexone was found to suppress cocaine self-administration in cocaine-addicted rats.[71] Then a clinical trial in Texas obtained results similar to those in Figure 6 from the Finnish trial with alcohol addiction. Patients using naltrexone with a protocol that allowed extinction were completely free of cocaine during the last third of the trial.[72] In contrast, the results from patients who used naltrexone with traditional procedures that demand abstinence tended to be worse than results from patients given a placebo.

Xenova, the biotechnology company, is in the early phases of testing a vaccine called TA-CD 82 μg for cocaine addiction. The vaccine may work by producing antibodies to cocaine, thus activating a form of pharmacological extinction by blocking reinforcement in the brain from cocaine each time the addict uses it. More clinical trials are needed.

Amphetamine—Speed, Uppers, TIK

Although amphetamine also affects the dopamine system in the brain, addiction to amphetamine may be driven primarily through the opioid system in the brain. One of the most convincing and groundbreaking studies proving that naltrexone attenuates or cuts craving and that it significantly reduces amphetamine addiction was conducted by Nitya Jayaram-Lindström (2007) of the

Department of Clinical Neuroscience at the Karolinska Institute in Stockholm.*

Jayaram-Lindström points out there are an estimated 35 million amphetamine abusers—more than the total number of heroin and cocaine abusers combined.† In its final phase, the study used a double-blind, placebo-controlled design—the gold standard in clinical trials—and obtained results showing that naltrexone was effective in treating amphetamine addiction.

Phase 1 of the study involved nineteen drug-naïve (non-addicted) individuals, concluding that "pretreatment with naltrexone significantly reduces the subjective effects of amphetamine." Phase 2 involved twenty amphetamine-dependent patients. Again, naltrexone "significantly attenuated the subjective effects of amphetamine" and "craving for amphetamine was blunted by naltrexone." The data "provide proof-of-concept that naltrexone not only dampens the subjective effect of amphetamine in the event of drug use, but also decreases the likelihood of additional drug consumption" in already addicted patients. Nitya Jayaram-Lindström concluded the following:

> Thereafter, we investigated the effect of chronic treatment with naltrexone in amphetamine dependent individuals, in an open-label design. The aim was to assess the tolerability and compliance to naltrexone in this new population. Twelve weeks of treatment with naltrexone led to a reduction in both frequency and quantity of drug consumption. Overall, the results showed that naltrexone was well tolerated with minimal side effects.
>
> Finally, we investigated naltrexone for the treatment of amphetamine dependence in a randomized placebo-controlled trial. Patients either received 12-weeks of treatment with naltrexone or placebo. Twice-weekly urine toxicology tests were performed and in addition patients received weekly relapse prevention therapy.

---

* Congratulations to Nitya Jayaram-Lindström for producing a superlative dissertation. Download the dissertation at http://diss.kib.ki.se/2007/978-91-7357-449-5/thesis.pdf. Retrieved February 26, 2008.

† Amphetamine is cheap to make in illicit laboratories around the world—it is less expensive than cocaine or heroin on the street.

The results indicate that treatment with naltrexone reduced the percentage of amphetamine positive urine samples in patients with chronic amphetamine dependence. Continued treatment with naltrexone also led to a reduction in craving as compared to placebo. In addition, the medical safety of naltrexone was further confirmed in this population.

In conclusion, naltrexone pharmacotherapy significantly reduces the reinforcing effects of amphetamine in acute and chronic dosing models. Taken together, this thesis provides support for the potential use of naltrexone as a treatment for amphetamine dependence... The results of the clinical trial further consolidate the finding that chronic treatment with naltrexone leads to a sustained effect on the behavioural and subjective correlates of reward, i.e., sustained reduction in amphetamine consumption and craving.

This four-phase study represents the beginning of a new era in the battle against amphetamine addiction with major implications for solving the massive problem in the United States, EU, and in emerging countries such as India and post-apartheid South Africa. In countries where amphetamine or "TIK" addiction has run unchecked, it has caused untold misery, by leading to increases in the numbers of crimes, murders, bankruptcies, and suicides. Although the study does not speculate on the mechanism of action—how and why naltrexone works—it does suggest that amphetamine addiction is mediated through the opioid system.[73]

In conclusion, amphetamine or speed addiction might eventually be dealt with via one of three routes of administration of opioid antagonists: 1) A short-acting nasal spray comprising naloxone. In this case, the amphetamine addict would gradually "cut" the addiction by inhaling naloxone sprayed into the nostrils before snorting, swallowing, smoking, or injecting amphetamine. The medication would rapidly block the opioid receptors in the brain to produce extinction of amphetamine addiction; 2) Naltrexone or the longer-acting, more potent nalmefene (it has the strongest opioid receptor binding or blocking effects of all three of the opioid antagonists currently available) would be taken by tablet at least thirty minutes before drug use to produce extinction; and

3) sustained-release once-a-month injections of naltrexone (e.g., Vivitrol®)[74] or nalmefene (e.g., REVEX®)[75] or implants. More research is needed to validate this treatment for cocaine and amphetamine addiction—especially in indigent, hard-to-reach, and noncompliant populations. This line of research might well turn out to be most effective, for example, by starting a course of one to three months of long-acting naltrexone or nalmefene depot injections, followed by naltrexone or nalmefene tablets post de-addiction treatment—just in case the patient feels he or she is about to relapse.

Even after de-addiction, patients may encounter stimuli they associate with alcohol or drug use—and these stimuli or associations are so powerful that they may trigger relapse even after years of abstinence. Therefore, all Sinclair Method patients—whether they abused alcohol or (in the future) cocaine or amphetamines—with or without cross-addiction to alcohol—should carry naltrexone or nalmefene tablets on their persons at all times. As already emphasized, great caution should be exercised with opiate addicts—especially heroin addicts—when administering opioid antagonists such as naloxone, naltrexone, or nalmefene because withdrawal from this particular class of drugs may be life threatening; careful medical management is vital in these cases.

Nalmefene has the advantage over naltrexone in that it is not stressful to the liver. In doses six times higher than those normally prescribed for alcoholism, naltrexone caused liver damage. Therefore, there is a contraindication against using naltrexone in patients who already are suffering from severe liver damage. Nalmefene does not have this problem, so it can be prescribed without first doing a blood test for liver damage. Therefore, it may become the treatment of choice for a variety of addictions. A great deal of preliminary research points to a bright future for the treatment of amphetamine, cocaine, and—with great medical precaution—even heroin addiction. Now, as described in chapter 4, all we need do is get society to turn the supertanker around and begin to use pharmacological extinction.

Sexual Compulsions

The rise of the Internet through the 1990s has seen an increase in reported "Internet sex addiction." "Naltrexone in the Treatment of Adolescent Sexual Offenders," published in the *Journal of Clinical Psychiatry*, reported the results of a small 2004 trial that concluded that naltrexone was beneficial in treating sexual compulsions but at higher doses than normally used in alcohol treatment: "Fifteen of twenty-one patients were considered to have a positive result and continued to respond for at least four months to an average dose of 160 mg per day with decreased sexual fantasies and masturbation...Naltrexone at dosages of 100 to 200 mg per day provides a safe first step in treating adolescent sexual offenders."[76] It is possible that the benefits observed here will generalize to the larger population of non-socially deviant hypersexual patients or "sexual addicts."

The fact that benefits were observed in this small sample points to the role of the opioidergic system in sexual addiction. In other words, various sexual compulsions may well be mediated through endorphin release. If so, the social ramifications have far-reaching consequences in terms of cost (prosecuting and imprisoning offenders) and prevention of re-offending. For instance, it is well known that rapists and pedophiles usually re-offend when released from prison. The pattern is similar to that for alcoholics or heroin addicts who, though severely punished (through imprisonment, frostbite, or accidents) or treated (through various group, insight, and self-help methods) simply fail to remain abstinent after prison or treatment. Compulsive sexual addicts might be able to impose self-restraint or self-deprivation through iron willpower temporarily, but in the end, most invariably relapse. Society often insists that they are depraved and weak-willed individuals who deserve to be locked away. However, when prison sentences end, most offenders re-offend upon release. Newspapers abound with stories depicting people set free only to re-offend.

How might pharmacological extinction be used to treat sex offenders? I recall an ethics committee meeting I attended in 1982 at a California state psychiatric prison facility called Atascadero

State Hospital. The committee was considering the options of castration versus a trial using a long-acting "anti-sex" hormonal drug (Depo-Provera®) in the treatment of rapists. The researcher in favor of the treatment recounted how one rapist really wanted to be castrated. The rapist said that if released he just knew he would re-offend. He said, "I am plagued by sexual thoughts of raping women. I try not to have them. The more I try the harder it gets. I can go for a few days without release (imagining the rape fantasy), but I always fail. I want castration. I would rather have no balls and be free, than have big balls and be in San Quentin." He was, of course, referring to the notorious California prison at San Quentin, and was certain that, if released from Atascadero, he would be caught raping again and sentenced to San Quentin for life. The ethics committee, caught up in the politically correct winds of the era, refused even to hear the proposal through. The researcher was cut short. There were not going to be state-sanctioned castrations in California—the "politicians would not hear of it." In any event, castration might not be effective because sex hormones are produced not only by the testes but also by the adrenals. It was also shown that men who had their testes removed due to medical reasons could still have a sexual drive. At the time, no one seemed aware that the compulsive components of sexuality might well be mediated through the opioidergic system. How then might a sex offender be treated using extinction?

Treatment would not be much more complex than extinction of alcoholism. The patient would be given naltrexone or nalmefene to block the opioid receptors in the brain. He would then be instructed to become aroused to the deviant fantasy. This would be carried out in controlled conditions, in a special private booth where stimuli (video) of the rapist's chosen fantasy would be presented. The patient would spend a period of several months attending these treatment sessions. His craving and behavior would be actively extinguished. Treatment would then focus on selective extinction, where he would be instructed to masturbate to socially acceptable fantasy and stimuli without taking the medication. The treatment would of course be conducted under careful supervision, and the patient monitored after release. All of this is a matter of legislation and funding for more research. It is worth considering that many sex offenders will get out of prison anyway. Left untreated for the sexual addiction—as they usually are when released—they are at high risk for re-offending.[77] The government claims to protect society. Offering or even mandating pharmacological extinction of sex offenders at least a year prior to their prerelease dates could help reduce re-offense rates.

Gambling

About 2 to 3 percent of Americans are said to have a gambling problem, and 1 percent have a pathological addiction to gambling. One report suggests that 86 percent of Americans have gambled at least once in their lives and about 60 percent gamble during any given year. The prevalence of gambling has increased in America, partly from online gambling and partly from the spread of casinos. Gambling in the form of lotteries, new casinos, online betting, and racing in many emerging countries is thought to exert a profound economic drain on these societies, as well.

"Gambling addiction blamed as mother of three shoots herself after allegations that she stole vast sums from her company to fund her habit"—*Sunday Times* (South Africa), October 28, 2001.[78] This headline refers to Ronell Poverello, who suffered from a severe gambling addiction and finally committed suicide as a result of her addiction. Ronell held a highly paid job at Eurocopter, from which she eventually stole more than $5 million to fund her habit. She became addicted to gambling and whatever she did on her own to stop was futile. It is of course tragic that she took her own life—to avoid shame, stigma, and prison—because by all accounts she was a fine mother and otherwise healthy. Her three children now have no mother.

The outcome might not have been so tragic if Ronell had had access to naltrexone treatment like Beth Irvin, whose story follows, did. It may be something of a surprise, but it is highly likely that endorphins, the body's natural morphine-like hormones, produce powerful reinforcement in the brains of those with the genetic predisposition for gambling addiction. If this were not the case, it is unlikely that opioid blockers, such as naltrexone or nalmefene, would be effective in controlling gambling.

In the United States, the National Center for Responsible Gaming funds studies and cites the following:[79]

The drug Naltrexone has been found to significantly reduce gambling urges and behaviors among pathological gamblers, according to a University of Minnesota study reported in the June 1, 2001, issue of *Biological Psychiatry*.

The clinical trial, funded by a $54,000 grant from the National Center for Responsible Gaming (NCRG), found that 75 percent of the patients receiving Naltrexone improved in terms of their urges to gamble. Because of Naltrexone's actions in the brain areas that process pleasure and urges, the study's lead investigator, Suck Won Kim, M.D., had theorized that this drug would be useful for treating pathological gambling. Naltrexone has been effective in the treatment of alcoholism and bulimia.

"Gambling has taken control of my life," said Beth Irvin, who is now being treated with Naltrexone. "I've tried to control this addiction in hundreds of other ways and I believe what I'm experiencing today is a miracle of science."

The publication of the Naltrexone trial follows on the heels of the release of another NCRG-funded study of the brain's reward circuitry. A grant of $175,000 from the NCRG to Massachusetts General Hospital (MGH) helped support a study, published in last week's issue of *Neuron*, examining how the human brain responds to the anticipation and reward of money.

The researchers, led by Hans Breiter, M.D., co-director of the Motivation and Emotion Neuroscience Center at MGH, used the neuroimaging process called functional magnetic resonance imaging to monitor the brain activity of volunteers participating in a game of chance. "This is the first demonstration that a monetary reward in a gambling-like experiment produces brain activation very similar to that observed in a cocaine addict receiving an infusion of cocaine," Breiter said.

"We are very proud to have supported cutting-edge research that will help us understand and treat gambling disorders," said Maj.

Gen. Paul A. Harvey (Ret.), chairman of the NCRG. "Furthermore, we are gratified that two of the most prestigious academic journals have confirmed the rigorous review process that we used to select these projects for funding."

The NCRG has awarded $3.7 million in research grants since 1996 and an additional $2.3 million to establish the Institute for Research on Pathological Gambling and Related Disorders at Harvard Medical School's Division on Addictions. A landmark 1997 Harvard study, funded by the NCRG, estimated that approximately 1 percent of the adult population can be classified as pathological gamblers. This estimate is now widely accepted as the most reliable statistic about the prevalence of gambling disorders.

It is well established that alcohol drinking is controlled through reinforcement from endorphins released by alcohol. But how do we explain the role of the opioidergic system in terms of non-substance behaviors such as addictive gambling?

The reason naltrexone might be effective with compulsive gambling is that, as with alcoholism, this behavior is also most likely mediated and learned through reinforcement from endorphins. It could be that the gambler who wins is receiving an internal shot or dose of powerful endorphin to the brain. Or it could be simply the situation of placing a risky bet causes endorphins to be released, regardless of whether the person wins or loses.* In either case, the gambling is powerfully reinforcing for some people, and the addiction is probably influenced through genetic predisposition.

The internal shot of endorphin can be problematic for those who have inherited the genetic predisposition that puts them at risk of developing a gambling addiction. These people may have been born with a brain that is uniquely sensitive to endorphins—unlike the majority who gamble but never have the strength of the behavior increase to compulsive or pathological levels.

---

*The one-armed bandit machine is a classic example of "variable ratio reinforcement": you never know when or how much reinforcement you will receive. Time intervals may be long or short and amounts vary. This form of learning is most resistant to extinction, which would bode poorly for an extinction treatment if the reinforcement for pathological gambling actually came from the money winnings. In fact, compulsive gamblers appear to get reinforcement regardless of whether they win.

In addition to open-label and placebo-controlled trials showing that naltrexone is effective in treating pathological gambling, a large clinical trial has now been published showing that nalmefene also works for gambling.[80] It is likely that the benefits from the opioid antagonists in treating gambling come from pharmacological extinction—just as they do for treating alcoholism and drug addiction. Thus far, however, no clinical tests of the mechanism involved have been conducted.

Further research into the application of pharmacological extinction is required in gambling and other non-substance disorders such as sexual addictions and kleptomania. In the latter case, it may turn out that the high risk associated with kleptomania and the excitement of stealing cause powerful reinforcement from internal shots of endorphins in a manner similar to that produced by gambling. The same mechanism may also apply to self-mutilation or compulsions such as computer hacking and Internet addiction. All these may be similarly reinforced through the opioidergic system.

The story of rogue trader Nick Leeson caught the attention of the media in the early 1990s. Working in Singapore for Barings Bank as a derivatives trader, Leeson caused an unprecedented collapse when he illegally ran up a debt of more than 1 billion U.S. dollars. Primed on the thrill of high risk, Leeson kept on plowing funds into the Asian markets in the hope that his gambling would pay off. It never did. After fleeing, being caught, and sentenced to six years in a Singapore prison, Leeson was eventually released. He wrote a direct account of what happened in his exciting yet sad book, *Rogue Trader: How I Brought Down Barings Bank and Shook the Financial World* (Leeson, 1997).

The account introduced readers to the high-rolling life of traders in early 1990s Singapore, where compulsive deal-making produced exhilaration and thrills. It got traders high—similar to the thrill-seeking, endorphin-like highs described by Kevin Mitnick in his account of master computer hackers in *The Art of Deception*. One wonders if naltrexone or nalmefene, used with pharmacological extinction, might play a potent role in treating other compulsive business gamblers. How would we put this to the test?

Give them naltrexone or nalmefene and say, "Off you go, gamble away while on the medication"? Obviously, this has some practical limitations.

Chocolate, Sweets, Obesity

No doubt about it, we all know how chocolate can be addictive. Chocolate contains fats, theobromines, and sugar—the addiction is probably more complex and may involve more systems than the endorphin release in the brain. Nevertheless, it is likely that the opioid system is the most important for most of us. For others, there is no strong compulsion, and they can take one or two squares of chocolate every day without bingeing. But others can't stop once they have started, clearly showing craving and addiction profiles. Much like "just one drink at the bar" can become two bottles of vodka for an alcoholic, so can one square of chocolate lead to bingeing on the entire chocolate bar—and then some. Chocolate and sweet flavors in general release endorphins in the brain. In fact, Sinclair's laboratory experiments on selective extinction used the drinking of saccharin solution as the alternative behavior that was strengthened with pharmacologically enhanced learning during breaks in naltrexone or nalmefene treatment.

AA line of rats bred for high alcohol drinking show an exceptionally high liking for sweets, particularly for extremely strong sweet solutions that other rats, including the alcohol-hating ANA rats, avoid. To make sure this was related to alcohol drinking and was not just a coincidence, Sinclair went to the Alcohol Research Center at Purdue University in Indianapolis and tested their alcohol-preferring P rats and the non-preferring NP rats; the same relationship was found.[81] A large number of studies since then have indicated that alcoholics and the children of alcoholics also have a higher preference for strong sweet flavors. It also has been shown that the opioid antagonists—naloxone, naltrexone, and nalmefene—extinguish saccharin drinking in the same way they do alcohol drinking. We will see later how a special Sweet Test has been used in Finland for predicting how well patients might respond to the Sinclair Method before they begin. Finally, alcoholics trying to abstain often use sweets as a form of substitute for alcohol, with some success.

The relationship between alcohol and sweets is the result of both of them causing a release of endorphins. This prompts one to ask a rather exciting question: can we use pharmacological extinction for a "sweet addiction"? The answer is probably yes, at least to some extent. Again, more clinical trials are needed.

Although single trials do not qualify as scientific proof, an interesting anecdote is worth mentioning. When starting to write this book, I discussed the concept of naltrexone and pharmacological extinction with a friend of mine, Dominique, an American writer living in London. She told me she was a secret chocolate addict. No one knew about her addiction. Every night after putting her son to bed, she would, without fail, ceremoniously sit down and eat two large bars of English chocolate. If Dominique did not have her chocolate for more than two days, her craving for it would soar. She regularly exercised at the nearby gym every day and otherwise watched her weight. "I would rather not eat anything else if it meant I couldn't have *my chocolate*," Dominique stated categorically. "I want naltrexone. Now!" "It's on prescription, and I doubt your doctor would give it to you—for *chocolate addiction* no less! If she read the official prescribing information in England, it would say that naltrexone is only approved for narcotic addiction like heroin or morphine—not anything else," I informed her. Nevertheless, she managed to get a prescription from a friendly doctor for two packs (or two months' worth) of 50 mg naltrexone tablets and called me, saying, "I've got it and I'm going ahead—whatever you say."

I explained how *in theory* she might proceed, but warned that no trials had yet taken place specifically for chocolate or sweet craving and addiction. "Hypothetically, this is how someone might try it. They would take naltrexone an hour before their chocolate binge. This would ensure opioid blockade of endorphin release when the chocolate was eaten. They would record the amount eaten every day and see what happens." I also warned her about extinction of other behaviors, that she could theoretically extinguish her love of exercise if the medication were in her system the next day when she went for her daily workout.

"I'll eat at 5 P.M. It should be pretty much out of my system by the next afternoon from what I can gather." I replied that it might be better to selectively extinguish her chocolate addiction—one day eating chocolate with naltrexone, the other working out but with no naltrexone.

Dominique carefully weighed her chocolate every day. After six weeks, Dominique said, "It definitely works. I'm eating less. Instead of two bars, I'm down to half. It seems to happen automatically. I'm simply not that interested. It's not on my mind so much. No doubt this works for me!" Although proper scientific research is needed to confirm our hunch that pharmacological extinction can help with bingeing on sweets, this little story informs us how opioid antagonists may well reach beyond alcohol treatment.

In fact, several tests of naltrexone in the treatment of eating disorders have been conducted. For example, there was an experiment on the combined effects of naltrexone with a tricyclic antidepressant medication. In an eight-week, double-blind, placebo-controlled study of thirty-three obese bingers, Alger (1991) and associates found that naltrexone (100–150 mg per day) produced significant reduction in the duration and frequency of bingeing in bulimic patients.[82] The study was published in the *American Journal of Clinical Nutrition* and concluded "that naltrexone and imipramine may be useful agents in the treatment of binge eating." In 2011, research was conducted in a Phase 2 double-blind placebo controlled FDA-approved clinical trial by Lightlake Therapeutics using naloxone nasal spray to treat Binge Eating Disorder (BED). The results were highly significant among 127 obese binge eaters.*

It is certain that mechanisms responsible for excessive eating and the bingeing of carbohydrates, fats, and sweets are highly complex, involving far more than just the opioidergic system. If the opioidergic system—endorphins—were the main mechanism involved in the drive to eat these foods, we would probably

---

* http://finance.yahoo.com/news/lightlake-therapeutics-inc-announces-positive-123000013.html

have seen noticeable weight reductions among the tens of thousands who successfully used naltrexone to curb their drinking in Finland. There were individuals being treated for alcoholism there with naltrexone who did lose considerable weight, but most people did not. One possible explanation, Sinclair has suggested, is that endorphins reinforce many different actions related to eating. In the laboratory, one can isolate these actions and show in one study that naltrexone reduces eating and in another that it increases eating. These opposing effects cancel out each other in a real-life setting. He has suggested using selective extinction in order to separate the various actions. This idea, however, remains to be tested clinically.

Nicotine and Smoking

"Will it work for smoking?" Many people eagerly ask this question. On the basis of the data, it seems likely that extinction with opioid antagonists will not work for tobacco smoking. For example, one clinical trial in Texas gave naltrexone to patients who were both heavy drinkers and heavy smokers. The drinking decreased with a classical extinction curve, but the smoking remained at the same high level. Similarly, there is no evidence from the clinical trials of naltrexone for alcoholics that smoking decreased. As mentioned earlier, the reason for this failure probably is that the reinforcement from nicotine does not involve the opioid system. The data are not yet clear about the specific system providing the reinforcement, but the first step in the process must be the activation of nicotinic receptors for the neurotransmitter acetylcholine.

I address the controversial problem of nicotine addiction because it is highly likely that pharmacological extinction will prove an effective route to removing the pathways controlling nicotine addiction in the brain—but probably not through the opioid system and naltrexone. Smoking is highly complex in terms of the effects nicotine has on hormones and neurotransmission in the brain. The case for the use of naltrexone or nalmefene for nicotine addiction is still open, but so far there are no convincing data that the medicines are helpful for this application.[83]

Nevertheless, the Sinclair Method may answer the challenge of nicotine addiction. Instead of using naltrexone or nalmefene, the treatment would need to use specific nicotinic blocking drugs, such as mecamylamine, varenicline, and/or erysodine. This has been demonstrated in laboratory studies by Xiu Liu and associates (2006).[84] The de-addictive principle is identical: give the smoker the blocking agent before he or she smokes, which should produce a reduction in craving and actual smoking.

Along these lines, Dr. Jed Rose, Chief of the Nicotine Research Program at the VA Medical Center, Durham, North Carolina, says this about mecamylamine and extinguishing tobacco addiction:

Mecamylamine is an old drug that used to be used to treat high blood pressure many years ago, but it actually blocks receptors that respond to nicotine. In the brain and the rest of the nervous system, there are receptors that nicotine acts upon to stimulate events that produce this addictive pleasure, and mecamylamine blocks most, if not all, of the actions of nicotine.

So what we have found in several studies is that when we put smokers on mecamylamine treatment before they quit smoking, that they then experience the act of smoking cigarette after cigarette for, let's say, two weeks without enjoying the usual nicotine effect. And going through a behavior without enjoying the ultimate chemical reward extinguishes, if you'll pardon the pun, but in psychological jargon you'd call that extinguishing a behavior when you take away the reward for it.

And what we find, is that smokers start to lose their craving for tobacco and that their success rates are boosted again by a factor of two. But in our studies this is now doubling success over and above the level of the nicotine patch, because we actually give the nicotine patch after they quit smoking and find that they still get the benefits of relief of withdrawal symptoms from the nicotine patch, but that the smoking cigarettes is less enjoyable because of the mecamylamine blocking its effect, so that the combination, instead of totally canceling out, we tend to get the best of both worlds.

The mecamylamine blocks many of the rewarding effects of smoking. The nicotine patch can still produce some relief of withdrawal symptoms. And between the two drugs in this combination, the smoker is kept comfortable and yet cigarettes are not nearly as tempting.

The implications are astounding. If mecamylamine is the effective nicotine blocker it is said to be, then millions of smokers may be able to reverse their addiction in much the same way as alcoholics can with naltrexone. The formula would be: Mecamylamine + Smoking = Cure. This would be a great boost to the whole world because smoking is known to be the most preventable cause of death.*

Jed Rose correctly suggests that nicotine addicts be taken through an extinction program using mecamylamine as the blocking agent. Unfortunately, he suggests that, after extinction treatment, the smokers be put onto nicotine skin replacement patches—without continued nicotine blockade from mecamylamine. This would cause patients to learn a new behavior reinforced by nicotine—the use of the nicotine patch.

Wearing nicotine replacement patches or chewing nicotine gum is certainly not the same as quitting smoking. It is in fact the same as smoking, though the method of drug delivery—gum or patch instead of inhaling nicotine through tobacco smoke—is different. Instead of taking the nicotine into the body via the lungs, the drug simply passes through the skin or mouth. These alternative administration routes are probably of some use in quitting smoking, but they only satisfy the underlying craving and addiction and do not remove it. Years later, the former smokers who quit with these substitutes may still feel the desire for a cigarette.

To act in accordance with the Sinclair Method, smokers would have to smoke while on the medication if they wished to extinguish the craving and behavior. If they were to abstain, as many

---

* More effective nicotinic blocking agents might soon be developed. Of course, a smokable herb having nicotinic blocking action, if mixed with tobacco and smoked, might also prove effective.

smokers can for long periods between relapses, and take the medication while abstinent, there would be no effect, no extinction.

In fact, this was demonstrated in 1987 by Pomerleau, who showed that acute administration of mecamylamine actually increases smoking if smokers were pre-treated with mecamylamine (as opposed to placebo) without simultaneously smoking while on the medication.[85]

Pomerleau attributed "the observed increases in nicotine intake to compensatory behavior designed to overcome mecamylamine blocking effects." If, however, this were true—that mecamylamine was still active when the subjects were smoking—then the conditions are identical to those in experiments showing decreases in smoking while on mecamylamine. It seems more likely that this result is similar to the findings with both alcohol (see Figure 6) and cocaine—that the subjects taking naltrexone during abstinence tended to do worse than the placebo patients because they had enhanced learning of drinking or cocaine use right after the end of naltrexone administration at the time when there is pharmacologically enhanced reinforcement from endorphins.

Finally, as Alcoholics Anonymous warns, "Once an alcoholic, always an alcoholic," Smokers Anonymous might say, "Once a smoker, always a smoker." Alcoholics and smokers who manage to stop drinking and smoking always remain at risk of relapse, especially if they have "just one drink" or "just one puff."

The reason for this is that the neural pathways associated with the particular addiction have, over time and practice, become transformed into neural super-highways. These neural networks in the brain are primed and ready to fire if the addict takes "just the one."

The point about extinction is that once treatment is fully accomplished, the smoker would almost be back to the biological condition he or she was in before taking the first puff and smoking the first few hundred cigarettes that slowly created the addiction in the first place.

The amount of research on extinction for smoking is miniscule—nowhere near as extensive as it is on alcoholism. Much, much more needs to be done before we know for sure that it will work. The research needs to be done properly, without re-addicting smokers through the use of nicotine patches or gum after they have been through de-addiction treatment. Also, there are qualitative differences between smoking and alcoholism because they operate on different neural systems in the brain.

Despite this, patients may still find physicians willing to prescribe mecamylamine for smoking addiction even though the medication has not received FDA approval for nicotine addiction. For instance, Dr. Gabe Mirkin explains the reason pharmaceutical companies have not spent "the 10 to 20 million dollars necessary to prove that mecamylamine cures nicotine addiction was that the drug had run out of its patent. Even if a researcher proved that mecamylamine cured smoking addiction, anybody could profit by marketing the drug. It has been four years since Merck stopped making mecamylamine, but I am delighted that another company called Layton Bioscience will market mecamylamine under the trade name Inversine to treat Tourette syndrome, a condition in which a person shakes or moves uncontrollably. Nobody has done the necessary research to show that mecamylamine helps to cure nicotine addiction, but I will be prescribing 2.5 mg two or three times a day to help my patients stop smoking."[86]

Computer Hacking, Internet Addiction, and Thrill-Seeking

Computer hacking exhibits the classic signs of craving and addiction. In fact, efforts are under way to include "Internet Addiction" in the American Psychiatric Association's diagnostic manual.[87] In his compelling book *The Art of Deception*, renowned former Internet hacker Kevin Mitnick (2002)—once on the FBI's Most Wanted List but now a sought-after Internet security consultant—describes the experience of compulsive hacking.* Mitnick suggests that computer hacking can be much like a drug addiction.

---

* Kevin Mitnick spent almost five years in the late 1990s locked up in a federal detention center in Los Angeles—without trial for five years and with one year spent in solitary confinement. Now he is *paid* by large corporations for his services—finally achieving personal triumph over the zealous prosecution and judge in his case (see see www.mitnicksecurity.com).

Mitnick, now a very successful security consultant and author, describes a hacker who was intent on cracking the system to get secret files out of a company's computer:[88]

> Danny was moving closer and closer, and his excitement was building. He was anticipating the rush, the great high he always felt when he succeeded at something he knew only a very limited number of people could accomplish. Still, he wasn't home free yet. For the rest of the weekend he'd be able to get into the company's network whenever he wanted to, thanks to that cooperative computer center manager.... The next step took nerve: Danny called back to Kowalski in Computer Operations and complained, "My server won't let me connect," and told the IT guy, "I need you to set me up with an account on one of the computers in your department so I can use Telnet to connect to my system." Once logged into the temporary account, Danny was able to connect over the network to the Secure Communications Group's computer systems. After an hour of online searching for a technical vulnerability that would give him access to a main development server, he hit the jackpot. Apparently the system or network administrator wasn't vigilant in keeping up with the latest news on security bugs in the operating system that allowed remote access. But Danny was. Within a short time he had located the source code files that he was after and was transferring them remotely to an e-commerce site that offered free storage space. On this site, even if the files were ever discovered, they would never be traced back to him. He had one final step before signing off: the methodical process of erasing his tracks. He finished before the Jay Leno show had gone off the air for the night. Danny figured this had been one very good weekend's work. And he had never had to put himself personally at risk. It was an intoxicating thrill, even better than snowboarding or skydiving. Danny got drunk that night, not on scotch, gin, beer, or sake, but on his sense of power and accomplishment as he poured through the files he had stolen, closing in on the elusive, extremely secret radio software.

Although he would not be consciously aware of it, Danny most likely got his buzz that night from an internal shot of endorphins being released in his brain. Computer hacking, feeling the "rush" when he cracked the system, is similar to gambling or thrill-seeking, or perhaps even deal-making in big business. Like a cocaine rush, the high is short-lived. Soon the craving for more and more and more takes root, building up like the deprivation effects first described by Sinclair in terms of alcohol addiction. Could Danny be treated with the Sinclair Method? The answer is that if his thrill seeking is mediated by endorphins—which most likely it is—then probably the answer is yes. However, we would have to give him naltrexone or nalmefene and then get him to hack away.

Hacking is illegal, which presents a catch-22 treatment situation for the clinician. Clinicians can't tell their patients to go and hack into someone's system; however, they can tell a patient, "Hacking is illegal. But if you find yourself unable to control your behavior, then at least make sure you take naltrexone before you do."

We have seen how various addictions are gradually learned over time. This is not mere speculation. In the case history section, we saw how Julia and Richard progressively learned to crave alcohol, and how Pete developed his addiction to both cocaine and alcohol. We also saw how successful Julia and Richard were with the Sinclair Method and, despite periods of abstinence, how Pete continued to crave his red wine and relapse many times after completing standard twenty-eight-day detox and ongoing A.A. meetings. It seems increasingly likely that the same problem may apply to compulsive computer hacking and Internet sex addiction if they are primarily mediated via the release of endorphins in the brain. It is also probable that naltrexone or nalmefene combined with actively performing the unwanted behavior will extinguish new addictions that have begun to emerge with the introduction of new technology.

Extreme Sports, Excessive Exercise

So far, we have been interested in treating dangerous, stigmatizing addictions like alcohol, cocaine, gambling, and new technology addictions. But can we become addicted to healthy activities, like running, bodybuilding, and working out? And what about thrill-seeking like bungee jumping or kite-surfing? On the face of it, we most certainly can.

Millions of people are physiologically *addicted* to running, to the gym, to thrill-seeking. John, age 68, is a retired university professor. He says, "I am addicted to extreme sports. I used to be an obsessive surfer and windsurfer. Now I am a kite-surfer. If there is no wind for my kite-surfing I get depressed. I have to get out there at least once a day. I am obsessed. It doesn't matter how cold the sea or outside temperature is. I put on my wetsuit and go for it. When there is no wind during the winter, I go to Hawaii or Mauritius and I plan these trips well in advance. I must be crazy to do such a dangerous sport, a sport for twenty-year-olds, at my age."

John exhibits signs of addiction to kite-surfing. He thinks about kite-surfing obsessively, especially if he has not had his fix for a while. It is most likely his brain is reinforced by a shot of endorphin release while he is out on the water, and that he inherited genes for strong opioid reinforcement and perhaps even for endorphin release triggered specifically by extreme sport situations. If he had never done any extreme sport, he would not have developed his "addiction."

The main point here is that John actually does no real harm to himself. But he might one day throw chance to the wind, overcome by the urge to go out onto the open sea in dangerous conditions. In this case, John would be putting himself at risk and his addiction could be said to be harmful. Could he be cured using the Sinclair Method? Most probably he could. If he were to take naltrexone and then kite-surf, John would not experience the effects of endorphins released by his thrilling activity. In theory, John's kite-surfing could be extinguished by taking naltrexone—that is why, during the alcohol treatment, patients are taught about selective extinction. In practice, John's kite-surfing is under control. He still has time for family and friends and is living a healthy life. We could be treading a fine line here—best leave John alone with his extreme sport. But in Judy's case, exercising to excess has clearly become a problem.

Judy is an attractive nurse, a little over forty-five years old, and married to a well-known orthopedic surgeon, Simon. The couple started a family and subsequently moved from the East Coast to Southern California when Simon was offered an excellent academic post while also pursuing a clinical practice.

Soon after moving to San Diego, Judy gained weight after giving birth to two children. The family was affluent, and Judy really did not have to work. She spent her time raising her children and began to gain a great deal of weight. When her eldest child was ten, Judy attempted to lose weight. Her program consisted of diet and exercise. Diet and exercise. Diet and exercise. Judy has lost more than thirty pounds but has become addicted to working out in the process. She spends mornings, afternoons, and many evenings at the gym. "I have to go. I become sad if I am sick and cannot go. Even my trainer thinks I am overdoing it. Simon is so caring and understanding, I know that he loves me. But I also feel that my marriage is suffering. I am often too tired at night to make love. I even work out on Sundays."

The point here is that Judy's exercising is out of control—it controls her, she doesn't control it. She thinks about working out incessantly, looking forward to her next fix. Judy literally gets "high" off her own endorphins every time she exercises to excess. In this case, compulsive excessive exercise is detrimental to her health, to her family, and to her marriage. If nothing else works, Judy could be a candidate for extinction treatment using naltrexone.

Naltrexone has not been approved by the FDA for "exercise addiction" and could only be offered as a special treatment for this kind of compulsive behavior. It is safe to say that there are reasonable grounds for using naltrexone to cut back her exercise addiction to appropriate levels—if the situation were to get out of hand, if she wanted to reduce or stop exercising excessively, and if her marriage were threatened. The Sinclair Method would be appropriate in this case.

Is there any behavior that is reinforced by endorphins that does not, in some individuals, become a harmful addiction? Sinclair tells me that once he and Dr. Marc Shinderman were thinking about this question. They went down the list of the many different behaviors that are probably opioidergically reinforced, and finally settled on maternal nurturing behavior.

It is known that endorphins control the response of female rats retrieving their pups in response to their ultrasonic cries. "Surely, there cannot be too much motherhood?" When they thought about it further, however, they realized that there may be an example of it becoming an addiction—in the case of daughters of alcoholics. Marc immediately thought of women he knew from his clinical experience who spend nearly all their lives taking care of an alcoholic father. And when he dies, she marries another alcoholic and devotes her life to taking care of him... The nurturing behavior, so essential in moderation, becomes so powerful in these women that it dominates their entire lives. It dominates their thinking. They become nervous if deprived of the chance to nurture. At least from our external perspective, their addiction to maternal behavior appears to have become detrimental to the women.

It might be mentioned in passing that both the Finnish high-drinking AA rats and the Indianapolis high-drinking P rats are excellent mothers, but both programs have had problems in breeding the low-drinking lines.

16 | The Human Costs of Alcoholism

"My alcohol abuse, though dangerous, was not unprecedented. You can find girls who abuse alcohol anywhere. We are everywhere. Of the girls I've known over the past nine years, the ones who took shots, did keg stands, toppled down stairs, passed out on sidewalks, and got sick in the backseats of cabs, there have been overachievers, athletes, dropouts, artists, snobs, nerds, runway models, plain-Janes, and so-called free-thinkers."

—KOREN ZAILCKAS,
in *Smashed: Story of a Drunken Girlhood, 2005*[89]

THE MAJORITY OF PEOPLE who drink alcohol do not go on to become alcoholics. This is fortunate because the World Health Organization (WHO) states that 2 billion people—a third of humanity—routinely consume alcoholic beverages. Of this number, 76.3 million or 3.8 percent are diagnosable with serious alcoholism.[90] The WHO also reports a worldwide loss

of 1.8 million lives every year as a direct result of excessive drinking. To put this figure in perspective, the WHO states that HIV-
AIDS takes 3 million lives worldwide every year.

Unfortunately, alcoholism is responsible for more than just
death. Unintentional injuries alone account for about one-third of
the 1.8 million deaths worldwide. Alcoholism spreads paralyzing
illnesses, heart disease, diabetes, and cancers. Through no choice
of their own, alcoholic parents abandon their children in favor of
the bottle. They often lose the ability to be providers, which leads
to family breakdown. All this can only suggest the unspeakable
pain and suffering experienced by millions—especially children.
The increased impulsiveness and poor judgment caused by heavy
drinking also contribute to suicides, depression, violence, crime,
car accidents, drownings, the use of other drugs (such as cocaine,
amphetamine, and opiates), and non-substance addictions such as
compulsive gambling.

Given the choice, most alcoholics would rather not be alcoholic. Perhaps this is one reason 5 million people attend Twelve-Step
A.A. meetings worldwide. But A.A. is not the only treatment. In
a 1995 "Letter to Colleagues," Enoch Gordis, former director of
the National Institute on Alcohol Abuse and Alcoholism (NIAAA)
wrote that "Approximately 1 million Americans seek alcoholism
treatment each year, many more than once." According to NIAAA,
however, there are 17 to 18 million Americans with serious drinking problems with 8 million fitting the diagnosis for full-blown
alcoholism.[91] A National Household Survey puts the U.S. total for
underage binge drinkers—more than five units in one sitting—at
a staggering 46 million. Problems from alcohol are worldwide. The
British Medical Association (BMA) estimates that one in twenty-
five adults in the United Kingdom is "alcohol dependent." The
Center for Public Health at John Moores University in Liverpool in
England found that 18.2 percent of British adults binge drink more
than double the daily recommended limit at least once a week. The
UK office for population censuses and surveys claims that 7.5 percent of men and 2.1 percent of women are "dependent on alcohol."
The societal costs in the United Kingdom are £2.3 billion ($4.6 bil-
lion) a year, with a £1.4 billion ($2.8 billion) loss to industry from

alcohol-related absenteeism and £207 million ($414 billion) for the annual cost to the National Health Service.[92] While figures vary among reports, the general trend shows unacceptably high rates of drinking in both the United States and the United Kingdom.

In European Union countries, excessive drinking accounts for more than 20 million cases and nearly 10 percent of "ill-health and deaths."[93] The 2006 European School Survey Project on Alcohol and Other Drugs discovered that the European Union has "the highest proportion of drinkers and the highest level of alcohol consumption" in the world.

In America, the NIAAA also found that alcoholism is the costliest disease, draining U.S. society of $187 billion annually; that is almost half the entire Pentagon budget for 2003. Alcohol abuse accounts for 9 percent of the "disease burden" in developed countries, causing accidents and compounding illnesses like hepatitis, cirrhosis, cancers, heart disease, and stroke. According to the American Medical Association, alcoholism accounts for 3.5 percent of all annual deaths—105,000—in the United States.[94] Alcoholism is clearly a world problem. Apart from lost lives and financial losses, alcoholism contributes to violent crime and the highest per capita incarceration rate in the world.

Because alcohol addiction is the result of having the right genetic predisposition and learning to drink through practice, many teenagers now get a head start on the road to alcoholism with the launch of sweet and tasty alcohol-laced "soft drinks" known as *alcopops*. The overall number of alcoholics is increasing, and we can expect more accidents, lost workdays, illness, broken lives, crime, and premature deaths.

Unfortunately, the research shows that average failure rates for standard alcohol treatments like psychotherapy, A.A.'s Twelve Steps, and various inpatient detoxification regimes range upward from 85 percent. Until now—until the arrival of the Sinclair Method—the outlook has been particularly bleak.* Ask any

---

* It's even worse than the outlook for cocaine and heroin addiction. For instance, a congressionally mandated study revealed that more than 50 percent of cocaine addicts and more than 66 percent of cocaine and heroin addicts were using within a year. ("Staying Clean," February 10, 2002, Peggy Orenstein, New York Times.)

experienced general practice physician what he or she thinks, and you will hear a dismal prognosis on alcohol addiction.

Facts and Figures

The facts and figures as reported by various agencies do not always match each other exactly. Nevertheless, they reflect a similar overall pattern. Figures from the U.S. Centers for Disease Control and Prevention (CDC), the National Institute on Alcohol Abuse and Alcoholism (NIAAA), the National Institute on Drug Abuse (NIDA), the Substance Abuse and Mental Health Services Administration's Office of Applied Studies (SAMHSA—OAS), and others summarize the trouble as follows:[95]

- Approximately 7 percent of Americans aged eighteen years and older—17.8 million—have a drinking problem. Of these, 8.1 million are alcoholics.
- Despite extraordinary high failure rates, every year more than 3 million Americans (approximately 1.4 percent of the population aged twelve and older) receive some form of treatment for alcoholism.
- Studies of suicides in the general population show that 20 percent were alcoholic.
- Two-thirds of the population consumes alcohol, but 10 percent of drinkers drink half of all alcohol consumed.
- Alcohol accounts for 105,000 deaths annually, making it the third leading cause of preventable death in the United States.
- In 2004, 22.5 million Americans aged twelve or older were classified as having substance dependence or abuse problems (9.4 percent of the population), about the same number as in 2002 and 2003. Of these, 3.4 million were classified with dependence on or abuse of both alcohol and illicit drugs, 3.9 million were dependent on or abused illicit drugs but not alcohol, and 15.2 million were dependent on or abused alcohol but not illicit drugs.
- In 2004, 19.9 percent of unemployed adults aged eighteen or older were classified with dependence or abuse, while 10.5

percent of full-time employed adults and 11.9 percent of part-time employed adults were classified as such. However, most adults with substance dependence or abuse were employed either full or part time. Of the 20.3 million adults classified with dependence or abuse, 15.7 million (77.6 percent) were employed.

- In 2004, 3.8 million people aged twelve or older (1.6 percent of the population) received treatment in the past twelve months for a drug or alcohol use problem. Of these, 2.3 million received treatment at a specialty facility for substance use treatment, including 1.7 million at a rehabilitation facility as an outpatient, 947,000 at a rehabilitation facility as an inpatient, 775,000 at a hospital as an inpatient, and 982,000 at a mental health center as an outpatient. Non-specialty treatment locations were self-help groups (2.1 million people), private doctors' offices (490,000 people), emergency rooms (453,000 people), and prisons or jails (310,000 people). (Note that the estimates of treatment by location include people reporting more than one location.)

- The number of people over the age of eleven who were dependent on or abusing a substance in the past twelve months or who received specialty treatment for a substance use problem within the past twelve months (i.e., the people classified as needing treatment for an alcohol or illicit drug use problem) was 23.48 million (9.8 percent) in 2004. Of these, 2.33 million received treatment at a specialty facility in the past year. Thus, 21.15 million people needed but did not receive treatment at a specialty facility in 2004. The number needing but not receiving treatment did not change significantly from 2002 to 2004.

- Of the 21.15 million people who needed but did not receive treatment in 2004, an estimated 1.2 million (5.8 percent) reported that they felt they needed treatment for their alcohol or drug use problem. Of these, 441,000 (35.8 percent) reported that they made an effort but were unable to get treatment, and 792,000 (64.2 percent) reported making no effort to get treatment.

- Among people who needed but did not receive treatment and felt they needed treatment for a substance use problem, the most often reported reasons for not receiving treatment were not being ready to stop using (40.0 percent) and cost or insurance barriers (34.5 percent). However, among the people who made an effort but were unable to get treatment, 42.5 percent reported cost or insurance barriers, and only 25.3 percent reported that they were not ready to stop using. These results are based on 2003 and 2004 combined data.
- The number of people needing treatment for an illicit drug use problem in 2004 (8.1 million) was higher than the number needing treatment in 2003 (7.3 million); similarly, the number of people receiving treatment for drug use at a specialty facility was higher in 2004 (1.4 million) than in 2003 (1.1 million). These 2004 estimates were similar to the corresponding estimates in 2002 (7.7 million needing treatment, 1.4 million receiving treatment).
- In 2004, 6.6 million people needed but did not receive treatment for an illicit drug use problem. Of these, 598,000 (9.0 percent) felt they needed treatment. This number increased from 362,000 in 2002 and from 426,000 in 2003. Of the 598,000 persons who felt they needed treatment in 2004, 194,000 (32.4 percent) reported that they made an effort but were unable to get treatment, and 404,000 (67.6 percent) reported making no effort to get treatment.

Driving under the influence of alcohol is highly representative of alcohol abuse in developed countries. The numbers for the United States are represented graphically in Figure 10: Substance Abuse and Mental Health Services Administration's Office of Applied Studies (SAMHSA—OAS) Results from the 2004 National Survey on Drug Use and Health: National Findings—Driving Under the Influence of Alcohol in the Past Year, by Age: 2003.

The Center on Alcohol Marketing and Youth at Georgetown University reports the following:[96]

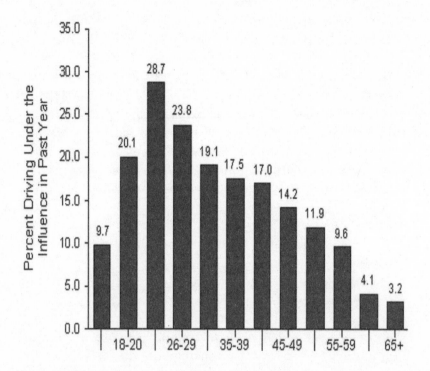

Figure 10. Males were nearly twice as likely as females (18.2 vs. 9.3 percent, respectively) to drive under the influence of alcohol.

- Alcohol use among young people under the age of twenty-one is the leading drug problem in the United States.
- Underage drinking cost the United States $53 billion in 1996 and $62 billion in 2001, the most recent year for which estimates are available.
- More youth in the United States drink alcohol than smoke tobacco or marijuana, making it the drug most used by young Americans.
- Every day, 5,400 young people under the age of sixteen take their first drink of alcohol.
- In 2005, one out of six eighth graders, one in three tenth graders, and nearly one out of two twelfth graders were currently drinkers.
- More than 7 million underage youth, ages twelve to twenty, reported binge drinking—having five or more drinks on at

least one occasion in the past thirty days—in 2004 according
to data released in September 2005.

Girls are binge drinking and getting drunk more according
to federal surveys reported by the Office of Applied Statistics
(OAS) of the Substance Abuse and Mental Health Administration
(SAMSHSA) (see www.samhsa.gov/ and www.oas.samhsa.gov):[*]

- Girls are binge drinking more, while boys are bingeing less
  or increasing their bingeing at a slower rate than their female
  peers.
- At the same time, twelfth-grade female drinkers and binge
  drinkers are now more likely to drink distilled spirits than
  beer.
- The new "alcopops" are particularly attractive to girls and
  most popular with the youngest drinkers.
- Surveys conducted till 2006 by SAMHSA and the OAS suggest that boys' and girls' binge drinking is increasing, but the
  girls' rate is increasing faster than that of the boys.[†]
- At the same time, girls' beverage preferences appear to have
  changed: the favorite beverage of twelfth-grade female drinkers and binge drinkers (the only grade for which data are
  available) has shifted from beer to distilled spirits in the past
  ten years.

Underage drinking has serious consequences:

- Every day, three teens die from drinking and driving.
- At least six more youth under the age of twenty-one die each
  day of non-driving alcohol-related causes, such as homicide,
  suicide, and drowning.
- More than seventy thousand college students are victims of
  alcohol-related sexual assault or date rape each year.

---

[*] http://www.oas.samhsa.gov/nsduh/2k6nsduh/2k6results.cfm.

[†] See http://www.oas.samhsa.gov/p0000016.htm#Standard.

- Recent studies have found that heavy exposure of the adolescent brain to alcohol may interfere with brain development, causing loss of memory and other skills.

Underage youth continue to find alcohol easily accessible:

- According to a national study released in 2005, more than 60 percent of eighth graders and more than 80 percent of tenth graders said it was fairly easy or very easy to obtain alcohol.
- A 2005 study conducted for the American Medical Association found that nearly half of all teens surveyed said they in fact had obtained alcohol.

Youth exposure to alcohol advertising is substantial:

- For instance, on television from 2001 to 2004, the average number of alcohol ads seen by young people from ages twelve to twenty grew from 209 to 276, an increase of 32 percent.
- The fifteen television shows in 2004 with the largest audiences of teens from ages twelve to seventeen all had alcohol ads.

Long-term studies have shown that youth who see, hear, and read more alcohol ads are more likely to drink and drink more heavily than their peers:

- The first national long-term study of youth throughout the United States, funded by the National Institute on Alcohol Abuse and Alcoholism, found that for underage youth, exposure to an additional alcohol ad was correlated with a 1 percent increase in drinking, and that youth drank 3 percent more for every additional dollar per capita spent on alcohol advertising in a local market.
- This study comes on the heels of two other long-term federally funded studies, as well as a variety of studies from other countries, that taken together, present an increasingly

compelling picture that alcohol marketing has an effect on young people's drinking.

- Nearly 11 million underage youth, ages twelve to twenty, reported drinking in the previous thirty days in 2004, according to the National Survey on Drug Use and Health (NSDUH) released in September 2005.
- In 2005, the national Monitoring the Future (MTF) study found that one out of six eighth graders (17 percent), one in three tenth graders (33 percent), and nearly one out of two twelfth graders (47 percent) were current (in the past thirty days) drinkers.
- Six percent of eighth graders, nearly 18 percent of tenth graders, and more than 30 percent of twelfth graders had been drunk at least once in the past month.
- More than 7 million underage youth, ages twelve to twenty, reported binge drinking in the past thirty days in 2004, which is defined as having five or more drinks on a single occasion (that is, within two hours).
- Although available data suggest that the percentage of adolescents who had five or more drinks in a row in the previous two weeks declined dramatically from 1983 to 1992, only the eighth graders are currently substantially below 1992 levels, according to the 2005 MTF study.
- Data from the National Survey on Drug Use and Health (NSDUH) found that overall rates of binge drinking increased among twelve-to-twenty-year-olds between 1991 and 2003, from 15.2 percent to 18.9 percent.
- By age fourteen, more than half of children who reported using any alcohol in the past month also reported binge drinking in that same month.
- Ninety-two percent of the alcohol consumed by twelve-to-fourteen-year-olds is consumed when binge drinking.

Young people drink more heavily on individual occasions than do adults:

- In comparison with adults twenty-six years and older, young people drink less frequently but consume more when they drink, according to a 2005 analysis by the National Institute on Alcohol Abuse and Alcoholism (NIAAA). While adults drink alcohol an average of nine days per month, young people ages twelve to seventeen do so about five days per month. However, whereas adults average fewer than three drinks per occasion, youth consume about five drinks at a time.

The Sinclair Method offers a cost-effective, practical, and positive solution to addictive and problem drinking. Sinclair's discoveries produce more than mere palliative care—they offer a real cure for alcoholism.

17 | For Medical Professionals

THIS CHAPTER is intended for the medical doctors who will be prescribing naltrexone. Naltrexone was originally approved by the FDA as an adjunct for use within comprehensive programs of alcoholism treatment. This situation has now changed. The COMBINE Study[97]—the largest controlled clinical trial in the field of alcohol dependence—found that naltrexone was effective even without intensive counseling.* It worked with only minimal medical supervision, similar to what can be provided by general practitioners. This confirmed similar results from Australia[98] and Finland.[99]

As a result, naltrexone can now be prescribed not only by large alcoholism clinics and hospitals with comprehensive programs but also by individual doctors.

---

* When these results were presented at the RSA (Reserach Society on Alcoholism) meeting (Chicago, 2007), Dr. Sinclair commented that he was not surprised naltrexone worked without counseling because it had worked well with his rats and they had never paid any attention to what he said to them.

The information about how to use naltrexone can be obtained by surveying the dozens of clinical trials but, unfortunately, not from the package inserts. They are generally accurate about contraindications and precautions, but to varying degrees in different countries, the package inserts have failed to specify the requirements necessary for positive results.[100] They also do not reflect what has been learned since naltrexone was first approved. A copy of the insert used with Depade® brand of naltrexone is included at the end of this chapter, with notes added to correct such omission. First, however, the chapter summarizes what a medical doctor needs to know for safe and effective use of naltrexone.

Eligibility for Treatment

- Naltrexone can be used for patients wishing to have more control over their alcohol consumption, including not only those meeting the criteria for alcohol dependence but also heavy drinkers who would like to reduce their intake to healthier levels to prevent development of alcoholism. It can be used not only for patients aiming for eventual abstinence but also for ones whose goal is moderate social drinking.
- People who currently or recently have been using opiates (e.g., heroin, opiate-based pain-control medication) are not suitable candidates for naltrexone treatment.
- People with acute hepatitis or liver failure are not suitable candidates. A blood sample should be taken prior to treatment and a liver function test (LFT) performed. The practice of putting patients with elevated values on forced abstinence for a couple of weeks to bring levels down to acceptable limits is not recommended: a short period of abstinence may lower the measure, but it does not correct the underlying liver damage. Nalmefene, if approved, would probably eliminate this limitation.
- Patients who are actively drinking are better candidates for naltrexone than ones who have been abstinent for more than a week.

- Patients whose goal is not abstinence but reduced drinking and/or more control over drinking are particularly good candidates for naltrexone. Treatment with naltrexone is the only method in which controlled drinking is an acceptable goal. The placebo groups in the clinical trials demonstrate, however, that controlled drinking procedures produce especially poor results when naltrexone is not being administered.
- Preliminary studies indicate that patients with a positive family history for alcoholism, and perhaps also ones with a high preference for very strong sweet solutions, respond particularly well to naltrexone. Considerable research is being conducted to find genetic markers for better response to naltrexone, but no solid conclusions can yet be made.

Dosage

The standard dose of naltrexone has been 50 mg daily, usually starting at 25 mg for the first day or two. Naltrexone treatment can start as soon as the liver function test results are known. Patients should not be sent for detoxification and/or alcohol-free detention.

Naltrexone should be taken only on days when alcohol drinking occurs or at least is expected to occur. The naltrexone pill should be taken approximately an hour before the first drink of the day. It can be taken in the morning (there still will be a blockade of opioid receptors that evening) but at that time patients may not have an accurate perception of whether they are likely to be drinking that day or not. It is, therefore, generally recommended to postpone taking naltrexone until an hour before the first expected drink.

Although there are advantages to skipping naltrexone on days when drinking does not occur, it does not matter if patients occasionally take naltrexone without drinking. In contrast, it is very important that patients never drink without taking naltrexone. Patients should be told that the Golden Rule in treatment is **Never Drink Alcohol Without Taking Naltrexone First**. This is especially important during the first week after a break in long-term naltrexone administration because of pharmacologically enhanced reinforcement and learning at this time (as discussed below). The naltrexone treatment continues indefinitely, but the frequency of taking naltrexone automatically decreases month after month as the number of drinking days per week decreases. Results show that after three months, naltrexone usage was down to 2.1 pills per week, and that by three years it was about 1 pill per week. Even if patients have eventually quit drinking completely, they should continue to carry a naltrexone pill with them just in case an occasion arises when they want to drink again. Such occasions are more likely on holidays and especially holidays on which drinking traditionally takes place in the culture.

Information for Patients

Patients should be instructed always to take naltrexone before drinking. They should not be instructed to abstain. Instead, patients should continue drinking in the manner and in the locations in which they are accustomed to drinking. The only limitation is that they should avoid drinking more than usual at any one time: alcohol poisoning is still a danger.

Strong instructions should be given against drinking and driving and similarly against using machinery while intoxicated. Naltrexone does not block alcohol intoxication. Instead, there are indications it may enhance certain forms of intoxication, such as impairment of peripheral vision and divided attention, that are particularly hazardous for driving.

Patients usually have been told to record their drinking and naltrexone use daily in a diary. Although this practice has been partly in order to document the effects of the treatment, it is believed (although not proven) that keeping a Drinking Diary is also useful and beneficial for the patients.

Clinical trials have now demonstrated that naltrexone is effective without intensive counseling and that the particular form of counseling that alone reduces drinking does not improve the results with naltrexone. Minimal medical supervision should be maintained. Counseling aimed at improving compliance (to always take naltrexone before drinking) is probably beneficial, as it helps at adapting to a new life in which alcohol drinking is not the primary focus. The efficacy of both forms of counseling, however, has yet to be established scientifically.

Several clinicians have felt that it was beneficial if patients understood the physiological basis for alcoholism and for the extinction produced with naltrexone. Therefore, it might be useful for the physician to examine the illustrations in Appendix B, for example, which show the learning of alcoholism and how extinction occurs. Then, if necessary, the physician can help patients understand these concepts.

Pharmacologically Enhanced Reinforcement of Healthy Alternative Behaviors

Patients should be told that, while they are on naltrexone, they should avoid behaviors other than alcohol drinking that release endorphins. Otherwise, these other behaviors can also be weakened, which would be detrimental. Instead, it would be beneficial to have the other behaviors strengthened so they can compete with alcohol drinking and help fill the void as drinking is extinguished. This is made possible by practicing these alternative behaviors during pauses in naltrexone treatment.

The body reacts to having the opioid receptors blocked by naltrexone by increasing the number of these receptors, that is, upregulation. This has now been shown in various species, including human beings. So long as the naltrexone is present, there is no effect, but for a period of several days after stopping naltrexone the patient is super-sensitive to endorphins. Behaviors that release endorphins will produce enhanced reinforcement during this period. It is very important that patients do not drink alcohol during pauses in naltrexone treatment. Instead, patients should practice healthy alternative behaviors that release endorphins during these pauses.

In practice, patients at the beginning of treatment are asked to make a list of behaviors that they find pleasant, and then avoid taking part in those that release endorphins while on naltrexone. The physician can help identify which behaviors release endorphins. Then, after a few weeks of drinking alcohol while on naltrexone, the patient is advised to have a weekend without naltrexone and without alcohol, starting on Friday evening. (If the patient then finds the craving is too strong, the pause should be postponed and naltrexone resumed immediately.) Saturday is a washout day. On Sunday afternoon, still with no alcohol and no naltrexone, the patient actively chooses to take part in one or more of the healthy alternative behaviors. Usually, patients report that doing so is extremely pleasant. On Monday, the patient can go back to naltrexone and drinking.

Subsequently, this procedure should be repeated over and over, with the number of days off of naltrexone increased progressively, and the variety of alternative healthy behaviors expanded. Eventually, the periods off of naltrexone and drinking expand to fill most or all of the week.

Naltrexone should not be administered with a specified fixed time limit. If naltrexone is provided, say, for only three months, most patients will improve for that period of time, and then afterward relearn the drinking behavior. Within a few months, they will be back to where they started. Having just a short pause in drinking may be beneficial for the liver, but otherwise has little impact on the health of the individual. Naltrexone is a lifetime commitment. The commitment consists generally, however, of just carrying the pill around all the time just in case the patient drinks.

Package Insert for Naltrexone

[NOTES in italics have been added to the insert]

Depade® (naltrexone hydrochloride tablets, USP)
(25 mg, 50 mg and 100 mg)
Rx only

DESCRIPTION

Depade® (naltrexone hydrochloride tablets, USP), an opioid antagonist, is a synthetic congener of oxymorphone with no opioid agonist properties. Naltrexone differs in structure from oxymorphone in that the methyl group on the nitrogen atom is replaced by a cyclopropylmethyl group. Naltrexone hydrochloride is also related to the potent opioid antagonist, naloxone, or n-allylno-roxymorphone.

Naltrexone hydrochloride has the chemical name of 17-(cyclopropylmethyl)-4, 5•-epoxy-3, 14-dihydroxymorphinan-6-one hydrochloride.

It has the following structural formula:

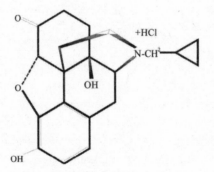

NALTREXONE HYDROCHLORIDE
$C_{20}H_{23}NO_4 \cdot HCl$ MW=377.86

Naltrexone hydrochloride is a white, crystalline compound. The hydrochloride salt is soluble in water to the extent of about 100 mg/mL. Naltrexone Hydrochloride Tablets, USP for oral administration are available as film coated tablets, containing 25 mg, 50 mg, or 100 mg of naltrexone hydrochloride.

In addition, each tablet contains the following inactive ingredients: crospovidone, hydroxypropyl methylcellulose, lactose monohydrate, magnesium stearate, microcrystalline cellulose, polyethylene glycol, polysorbate 80, silicon dioxide, titanium dioxide, yellow iron oxide and red iron oxide.

CLINICAL PHARMACOLOGY

Pharmacodynamic Actions: Naltrexone is a pure opioid antagonist. It markedly attenuates or completely blocks, reversibly, the subjective effects of intravenously administered opioids.

When co-administered with morphine, on a chronic basis, naltrexone blocks the physical dependence to morphine, heroin and other opioids. Naltrexone has few, if any, intrinsic actions besides its opioid blocking properties. However, it does produce some pupillary constriction, by an unknown mechanism.

The administration of naltrexone is not associated with the development of tolerance or dependence. In subjects physically dependent on opioids, naltrexone will precipitate withdrawal symptomatology.

Clinical studies indicate that 50 mg of naltrexone hydrochloride will block the pharmacologic effects of 25 mg of intravenously administered heroin for periods as long as 24 hours. Other data suggest that doubling the dose of naltrexone hydrochloride provides blockade for 48 hours, and tripling the dose of naltrexone hydrochloride provides blockade for about 72 hours.

Naltrexone blocks the effects of opioids by competitive binding (i.e., analogous to competitive inhibition of enzymes) at opioid receptors. This makes the blockade produced potentially surmountable, but overcoming full naltrexone blockade by administration of very high doses of opiates has resulted in excessive symptoms of histamine release in experimental subjects.

The mechanism of action of naltrexone in alcoholism is not understood; however, involvement of the endogenous opioid system is suggested by preclinical data. Naltrexone, an opioid receptor antagonist, competitively binds to such receptors and may block the effects of endogenous opioids. Opioid antagonists have been shown to reduce alcohol consumption by animals, and naltrexone has been shown to reduce alcohol consumption in clinical studies. *[NOTE: The mechanism of action for naltrexone in opiate dependence was shown to be extinction (Renault, 1980). Preclinical and clinical results support the conclusion that the primary action of naltrexone in alcoholism is also extinction of the drug-taking behaviors made while the medication blocks reinforcement (Sinclair, 2001).]*

Naltrexone is not aversive therapy and does not cause a disulfiram-like reaction either as a result of opiate use or ethanol ingestion.

Pharmacokinetics: Naltrexone is a pure opioid receptor antagonist. Although well absorbed orally, naltrexone is subject to significant first pass metabolism with oral bioavailability estimates ranging from 5% to 40%. The activity of naltrexone is believed to be due to both parent and the 6-β-naltrexol metabolite. Both parent drug and metabolites are excreted primarily by the kidney (53% to 79% of the dose), however, urinary excretion of unchanged naltrexone accounts for less than 2% of an oral dose and fecal excretion is a minor elimination pathway. The mean elimination half-life (T-1/2) values for naltrexone and 6-β-naltrexol are 4 hours and 13 hours, respectively. Naltrexone and 6-β-naltrexol are dose proportional in terms of AUC and Cmax over the range of 50 to 200 mg and do not accumulate after 100 mg daily doses.

Absorption: Following oral administration, naltrexone undergoes rapid and nearly complete absorption with approximately 96% of the dose absorbed from the gastrointestinal tract. Peak plasma levels of both naltrexone and 6-β-naltrexol occur within one hour of dosing.

Distribution: The volume of distribution for naltrexone following intravenous administration is estimated to be 1350 liters. In vitro tests with human plasma show naltrexone to be 21% bound to plasma proteins over the therapeutic dose range.

Metabolism: The systemic clearance (after intravenous administration) of naltrexone is ~3.5 L/min, which exceeds liver blood flow (~1.2 L/min). This suggests both that naltrexone is a highly extracted drug (>98% metabolized) and that extra-hepatic sites of drug metabolism exist. The major metabolite of naltrexone is 6-β-naltrexol. Two other minor metabolites are 2-hydroxy-3-methoxy-6-β-naltrexol and 2-hydroxy-3-methyl-naltrexone. Naltrexone and its metabolites are also conjugated to form additional metabolic products.

Elimination: The renal clearance for naltrexone ranges from 30 to 127 mL/min and suggests that renal elimination is primarily by glomerular filtration. In comparison, the renal clearance for 6-β-naltrexol ranges from 230 to 369 mL/min, suggesting an additional renal tubular secretory mechanism. The urinary excretion of unchanged naltrexone accounts for less than 2% of an oral dose; urinary excretion of unchanged and conjugated 6-β-naltrexol accounts for 43% of an oral dose. The pharmacokinetic profile of naltrexone suggests that naltrexone and its metabolites may undergo enterohepatic recycling.

Hepatic and Renal Impairment: Naltrexone appears to have extrahepatic sites of drug metabolism and its major metabolite undergoes active tubular secretion (see **Metabolism** above). Adequate studies of naltrexone in patients with severe hepatic or renal impairment have not been conducted (see **PRECAUTIONS: Special Risk Patients**).

Clinical Trials:
Alcoholism: The efficacy of naltrexone as an aid to the treatment of alcoholism was tested in placebo-controlled, outpatient, double blind trials. These studies used a dose of naltrexone hydrochloride 50 mg once daily for 12 weeks as an adjunct to social and psychotherapeutic methods when given under conditions that enhanced patient compliance. Patients with psychosis, dementia, and secondary psychiatric diagnoses were excluded from these studies.

In one of these studies, 104 alcohol-dependent patients were randomized to receive either naltrexone hydrochloride 50 mg once daily or placebo. In this study, naltrexone proved superior to placebo in measures of drinking including abstention rates (51% vs. 23%), number of drinking days, and relapse (31% vs. 60%). In a second study with 82 alcohol-dependent patients, the group of patients receiving naltrexone were shown to have lower relapse rates (21% vs. 41%), less alcohol craving, and fewer drinking days compared with patients who received placebo, but these results depended on the specific analysis used. *[NOTE: The insert fails to mention the most highly significant results from this clinical trial (O'Malley et al., 1992): the effect of the clinical protocol. The trial tested two protocols: COPING in which the patients generally drank while on naltrexone, and SUPPORTIVE in which patients were given strong support of abstinence while on naltrexone. The efficacy of naltrexone was strongly dependent upon the protocol. All of the significant benefits of naltrexone over placebo were in the COPING group. There were no significant benefits of naltrexone over placebo in the SUPPORTIVE group. Therefore, do not administer naltrexone along with instructions that demand complete abstinence. Instead use a protocol that allows drinking to occur while naltrexone is in the body.]*

The clinical use of naltrexone as adjunctive pharmacotherapy for the treatment of alcoholism was also evaluated in a multicenter safety study. This study of 865 individuals with alcoholism included patients with comorbid psychiatric conditions, concomitant medications, polysubstance abuse and HIV disease. Results of this study demonstrated that the side effect profile of naltrexone appears to be similar in both alcoholic and opioid dependent populations, and that serious side effects are uncommon.

In the clinical studies, treatment with naltrexone supported abstinence, prevented relapse and decreased alcohol consumption. In the uncontrolled study, the patterns of abstinence and relapse were similar to those observed in the controlled studies. Naltrexone was not uniformly helpful to all patients, and the expected effect of the drug is a modest improvement in the outcome of conventional treatment.

Treatment of Opioid Addiction:

Naltrexone has been shown to produce complete blockade of the euphoric effects of opioids in both volunteer and addict populations. When administered by means that enforce compliance, it will produce an effective opioid blockade, but has not been shown to affect the use of cocaine or other non-opioid drugs of abuse.

There are no data that demonstrate an unequivocally beneficial effect of naltrexone on rates of recidivism among detoxified, formerly opioid-dependent individuals who self-administer the drug. The failure of the drug in this setting appears to be due to poor medication compliance.

The drug is reported to be of greatest use in good prognosis opioid addicts who take the drug as part of a comprehensive occupational rehabilitative program, behavioral contract, or other compliance-enhancing protocol. Naltrexone, unlike methadone or LAAM (levo-alphaacetyl-methadol), does not reinforce medication compliance and is expected to have a therapeutic effect only when given under external conditions that support continued use of the medication.

Individualization of Dosage:
DO NOT ATTEMPT TREATMENT WITH NALTREXONE UNLESS, IN THE MEDICAL JUDGEMENT OF THE PRESCRIBING PHYSICIAN, THERE IS NO REASONABLE POSSIBILITY OF OPIOID USE WITHIN THE PAST 7 to 10 DAYS. IF THERE IS ANY QUESTION OF OCCULT OPIOID DEPENDENCE, PERFORM A NALOXONE CHALLENGE TEST.

Treatment of Alcoholism:
The placebo-controlled studies that demonstrated the efficacy of naltrexone as an adjunctive treatment of alcoholism used a dose regimen of naltrexone hydrochloride 50 mg once daily for up to 12 weeks. Other dose regimens or durations of therapy were not studied in these trials. *[NOTE: Recent clinical trials (e.g., Anton et al., 2006) have now shown that naltrexone is effective along with only minimal medical supervision and does not have to be used with within a comprehensive program of alcoholism treatment. The medication produces significant benefits without intensive counseling, and counseling did not improve the results from naltrexone. It remains to be determined whether the result is specific to the particular form of counseling used. It is possible that other forms of counseling might combine to improve the results with naltrexone.]*

Physicians are advised that 5% to 15% of patients taking naltrexone for alcoholism will complain of non-specific side effects, chiefly gastrointestinal upset. Prescribing physicians have tried using an initial 25 mg dose, splitting the daily dose, and adjusting the time of dosing with limited success. No dose or pattern of dosing has been shown to be more effective than any other in reducing these complaints for all patients. *[NOTE: The frequency of side effects is affected by the protocol. These results are found when naltrexone is first introduced to patients who are not still actively drinking. When naltrexone was given to alcohol dependent patients without prior alcohol detoxification and with a protocol that allowed continued drinking while on the medication, the frequency of reporting side effects was reduced to the same level as with placebo (Heinälä et al., 2001).]*

Treatment of Opioid Dependence:

Once the patient has been started on naltrexone hydrochloride, 50 mg once a day will produce adequate clinical blockade of the actions of parenterally administered opioids. As with many non-agonist treatments for addiction, naltrexone is of proven value only when given as part of a comprehensive plan of management that includes some measure to ensure the patient takes the medication.

A flexible approach to a dosing regimen may be employed to enhance compliance. Thus, patients may receive 50 mg of naltrexone hydrochloride every weekday with a 100 mg dose on Saturday or patients may receive 100 mg every other day, or 150 mg every third day. Several of the clinical studies reported in the literature have employed the following dosing regimen: 100 mg on Monday, 100 mg on Wednesday, and 150 mg on Friday. This dosing schedule appeared to be acceptable to many naltrexone patients successfully maintaining their opioid-free state.

Experience with the supervised administration of a number of potentially hepatotoxic agents suggests that supervised administration and single doses of naltrexone hydrochloride higher than 50 mg may have an associated increased risk of hepatocellular injury, even though three times a week dosing has been well tolerated in the addict population and in initial clinical trials in alcoholism. Clinics using this approach should balance the possible risks against the probable benefits and may wish to maintain a higher index of suspicion for drug-associated hepatitis and ensure patients are advised of the need to report non-specific abdominal complaints (see **PRECAUTIONS: Information for Patients**).

INDICATIONS AND USAGE

Naltrexone hydrochloride tablets are indicated:

In the treatment of alcohol dependence and for the blockade of the effects of exogenously administered opioids. Naltrexone hydrochloride tablets have not been shown to provide any therapeutic benefit except as part of an appropriate plan of management for the addictions.

CONTRAINDICATIONS
Naltrexone is contraindicated in:

1) Patients receiving opioid analgesics.

2) Patients currently dependent on opioids, including those currently maintained on opiate agonists [e.g., methadone or LAAM (levo-alpha-acetyl-methadol)].

3) Patients in acute opioid withdrawal (see **WARNINGS**).

4) Any individual who has failed the naloxone challenge test or who has a positive urine screen for opioids.

5) Any individual with a history of sensitivity to naltrexone or any other components of this product. It is not known if there is any cross-sensitivity with naloxone or the phenanthrene containing opioids.

6) Any individual with acute hepatitis or liver failure.

WARNINGS
Hepatotoxicity:

Naltrexone has the capacity to cause hepatocellular injury when given in excessive doses.

Naltrexone is contraindicated in acute hepatitis or liver failure, and its use in patients with active liver disease must be carefully considered in light of its hepatotoxic effects.

The margin of separation between the apparently safe dose of naltrexone and the dose causing hepatic injury appears to be only five-fold or less. Naltrexone does not appear to be a hepatotoxin at the recommended doses.

Patients should be warned of the risk of hepatic injury and advised to stop the use of naltrexone and seek medical attention if they experience symptoms of acute hepatitis.

Evidence of the hepatotoxic potential of naltrexone is derived primarily from a placebo controlled study in which naltrexonehydrochloride was administered to obese subjects at a dose approximately five-fold that recommended for the blockade of opiate receptors (300 mg per day). In that study, 5 of 26 naltrexone recipients developed elevations of serum transaminases (i.e., peak ALT values ranging from a low of 121 to a high of 532; or 3 to 19 times their baseline values) after three to eight weeks of treatment. Although the patients involved were generally clinically asymptomatic and the transaminase levels of all patients on whom follow-up was obtained returned to (or toward) baseline values in a matter of weeks, the lack of any transaminase elevations of similar magnitude in any of the 24 placebo patients in the same study is persuasive evidence that naltrexone is a direct (i.e., not idiosyncratic) hepatotoxin.

This conclusion is also supported by evidence from other placebo controlled studies in which exposure to naltrexone hydrochloride at doses above the amount recommended for the treatment of alcoholism or opiate blockade (50 mg/day) consistently produced more numerous and more significant elevations of serum transaminases than did placebo. Transaminase elevations in 3 of 9 patients with Alzheimer's Disease who received naltrexone hydrochloride (at doses up to 300 mg/day) for 5 to 8 weeks in an open clinical trial have been reported.

Although no cases of hepatic failure due to naltrexone administration have ever been reported, physicians are advised to consider this as a possible risk of treatment and to use the same care in prescribing naltrexone as they would other drugs with the potential for causing hepatic injury.

Unintended Precipitation of Abstinence:

To prevent occurrence of an acute abstinence syndrome, or exacerbation of a pre-existing subclinical abstinence syndrome, patients must be opioid-free for a minimum of 7 to 10 days before starting naltrexone. Since the absence of an opioid drug in the urine is often not sufficient proof that a patient is opioid-free, a naloxone challenge should be employed if the prescribing physician feels there is a risk of precipitating a withdrawal reaction following administration of naltrexone. The naloxone challenge test is described in the DOSAGE AND ADMINISTRATION section.

Attempt to Overcome Blockade:

While naltrexone is a potent antagonist with a prolonged pharmacologic effect (24 to 72 hours), the blockade produced by naltrexone is surmountable. This is useful in patients who may require analgesia, but poses a potential risk to individuals who attempt, on their own, to overcome the blockade by administering large amounts of exogenous opioids. Indeed, any attempt by a patient to overcome the antagonism by taking opioids is very dangerous and may lead to a fatal overdose. Injury may arise because the plasma concentration of exogenous opioids attained immediately following their acute administration may be sufficient to overcome the competitive receptor blockade. As a consequence, the patient may be in immediate danger of suffering life endangering opioid intoxication (e.g., respiratory arrest, circulatory collapse). Patients should be told of the serious consequences of trying to overcome the opiate blockade (see PRECAUTIONS, Information for Patients).

There is also the possibility that a patient who had been treated with naltrexone will respond to lower doses of opioids than previously used, particularly if taken in such a manner that high plasma concentrations remain in the body beyond the time that naltrexone exerts its therapeutic effects. This could result in potentially life-threatening opioid intoxication (respiratory compromise or arrest, circulatory collapse, etc.). Patients should be aware that they may be more sensitive to lower doses of opioids after naltrexone treatment is discontinued.

Ultra Rapid Opioid Withdrawal:
Safe use of naltrexone in rapid opiate detoxification programs has not been established (see **ADVERSE REACTIONS**).

PRECAUTIONS
General:
When Reversal of Naltrexone Blockade Is Required: In an emergency situation in patients receiving fully blocking doses of naltrexone, a suggested plan of management is regional analgesia, conscious sedation with a benzodiazepine, use of non-opioid analgesics or general anesthesia.

In a situation requiring opioid analgesia, the amount of opioid required may be greater than usual, and the resulting respiratory depression may be deeper and more prolonged.

A rapidly acting opioid analgesic which minimizes the duration of respiratory depression is preferred. The amount of analgesic administered should be titrated to the needs of the patient. Non-receptor mediated actions may occur and should be expected (e.g., facial swelling, itching, generalized erythema, or bronchoconstriction) presumably due to histamine release.

Irrespective of the drug chosen to reverse naltrexone blockade, the patient should be monitored closely by appropriately trained personnel in a setting equipped and staffed for cardiopulmonary resuscitation.

Accidentally Precipitated Withdrawal: Severe opioid withdrawal syndromes precipitated by the accidental ingestion of naltrexone have been reported in opioid-dependent individuals. Symptoms of withdrawal have usually appeared within five minutes of ingestion of naltrexone and have lasted for up to 48 hours. Mental status changes including confusion, somnolence and visual hallucinations have occurred. Significant fluid losses from vomiting and diarrhea have required intravenous fluid administration. In all cases patients were closely monitored and therapy with non-opioid medications was tailored to meet individual requirements.

Use of naltrexone does not eliminate or diminish withdrawal symptoms. If naltrexone is initiated early in the abstinence process, it will not preclude the patient's experience of the full range of signs and symptoms that would be experienced if naltrexone had not been started. Numerous adverse events are known to be associated with withdrawal.

Special Risk Patients:
Renal Impairment: Naltrexone and its primary metabolite are excreted primarily in the urine, and caution is recommended in administering the drug to patients with renal impairment.

Hepatic Impairment: Caution should be exercised when naltrexone hydrochloride is administered to patients with liver disease. An increase in naltrexone AUC of approximately 5- and 10-fold in patients with compensated and decompensated liver cirrhosis, respectively, compared with subjects with normal liver function has been reported. These data also suggest that alterations in naltrexone bioavailability are related to liver disease severity.

Suicide: The risk of suicide is known to be increased in patients with substance abuse with or without concomitant depression. This risk is not abated by treatment with naltrexone (see **ADVERSE REACTIONS**).

Information for Patients: It is recommended that the prescribing physician relate the following information to patients being treated with naltrexone:

You have been prescribed Depade® (naltrexone hydrochloride tablets, USP) as part of the comprehensive treatment for your alcoholism or drug dependence. You should carry identification to alert medical personnel to the fact that you are taking naltrexone. A naltrexone medication card may be obtained from your physician and can be used for this purpose. Carrying the identification card should help to ensure that you can obtain adequate treatment in an emergency. If you require medical treatment, be sure to tell the treating physician that you are receiving naltrexone therapy.

You should take naltrexone as directed by your physician. If you attempt to self-administer heroin or any other opiate drug, in small doses while on naltrexone, you will not perceive any effect. Most important, however, if you attempt to self-administer large doses of heroin or any other opioid (including methadone or LAAM) while on naltrexone, you may die or sustain serious injury, including coma.

[NOTE: These last two sentences, underlined in the original, are essentially the same used as instructions in the first controlled clinical trial of naltrexone for opiate dependence (Renault, 1980) in order to prevent patients from using heroin or other opiates while on naltrexone. The insert fails to mention that naltrexone produced significant benefits only in the subgroup of patients who disobeyed these instructions and self-administered opiates while on the medication.]

Naltrexone is well-tolerated in the recommended doses, but may cause liver injury when taken in excess or in people who develop liver disease from other causes. If you develop abdominal pain lasting more than a few days, white bowel movements, dark urine, or yellowing of your eyes, you should stop taking naltrexone immediately and see your doctor as soon as possible.

Laboratory Tests: A high index of suspicion for drug-related hepatic injury is critical if the occurrence of liver damage induced by naltrexone is to be detected at the earliest possible time. Evaluations, using appropriate batteries of tests to detect liver injury are recommended at a frequency appropriate to the clinical situation and the dose of naltrexone.

Naltrexone does not interfere with thin-layer, gas-liquid, and high pressure liquid chromatographic methods which may be used for the separation and detection of morphine, methadone or quinine in the urine. Naltrexone may or may not interfere with enzymatic methods for the detection of opioids depending on the specificity of the test. Please consult the test manufacturer for specific details.

Drug Interactions: Studies to evaluate possible interactions between naltrexone and drugs other than opiates have not been performed. Consequently, caution is advised if the concomitant administration of naltrexone and other drugs is required.

The safety and efficacy of concomitant use of naltrexone and disulfiram is unknown, and the concomitant use of two potentially hepatotoxic medications is not ordinarily recommended unless the probable benefits outweigh the known risks.

Lethargy and somnolence have been reported following doses of naltrexone and thioridazine.

Patients taking naltrexone may not benefit from opioid containing medicines, such as cough and cold preparations, antidiarrheal preparations, and opioid analgesics. In an emergency situation when opioid analgesia must be administered to a patient receiving naltrexone, the amount of opioid required may be greater than usual, and the resulting respiratory depression may be deeper and more prolonged (see **PRECAUTIONS**).

Carcinogenesis, Mutagenesis and Impairment of Fertility: The following statements are based on the results of experiments in mice and rats. The potential carcinogenic, mutagenic and fertility effects of the metabolite 6-β-naltrexol are unknown.

In a two-year carcinogenicity study in rats, there were small increases in the numbers of testicular mesotheliomas in males and tumors of vascular origin in males and females. The incidence of mesothelioma in males given naltrexone at a dietary dose of 100 mg/kg/day (600 mg/m²/day; 16 times the recommended therapeutic dose, based on body surface area) was 6%, compared with a maximum historical incidence of 4%. The incidence of vascular tumors in males and females given dietary doses of 100 mg/kg/day (600 mg/m^2/day) was 4%, but only the incidence in females was increased compared with a maximum historical control incidence of 2%. There was no evidence of carcinogenicity in a two-year dietary study with naltrexone in male and female mice.

There was limited evidence of a weak genotoxic effect of naltrexone in one gene mutation assay in a mammalian cell line, in the Drosophila recessive lethal assay, and in non-specific DNA repair tests with *E. coli*. However, no evidence of genotoxic potential was observed in a range of other in vitro tests, including assays for gene mutation in bacteria, yeast, or in a second mammalian cell line, a chromosomal aberration assay, and an assay for DNA damage in human cells. Naltrexone did not exhibit clastogenicity in an *in vivo* mouse micronucleus assay.

Naltrexone (100 mg/kg/day [600 mg/m^2/day] PO; 16 times the recommended therapeutic dose, based on body surface area) caused a significant increase in pseudopregnancy in the rat. A decrease in the pregnancy rate of mated female rats also occurred. There was no effect on male fertility at this dose level. The relevance of these observations to human fertility is not known.

Pregnancy: Category C. Naltrexone has been shown to increase the incidence of early fetal loss when given to rats at doses ≥30 mg/kg/day (180 mg/m^2/day; 5 times the recommended therapeutic dose, based on body surface area) and to rabbits at oral doses ≥60 mg/kg/day (720 mg/m^2/day; 18 times the recommended therapeutic dose, based on body surface area). There was no evidence of teratogenicity when naltrexone was administered orally to rats and rabbits during the period of major organogenesis at doses up to 200 mg/kg/day (32 and 65 times the recommended thereapeutic dose, respectively, based on body surface area).

Rats do not form appreciable quantities of the major human metabolite, 6-β-naltrexol; therefore, the potential reproductive toxicity of the metabolite in rats is not known.

There are no adequate and well-controlled studies in pregnant women. Naltrexone should be used during pregnancy only if the potential benefit justifies the potential risk to the fetus.

Labor And Delivery: Whether or not naltrexone affects the duration of labor and delivery is unknown.

Nursing Mothers: In animal studies, naltrexone and 6-β-naltrexol were excreted in the milk of lactating rats dosed orally with naltrexone. Whether or not naltrexone is excreted in human milk is unknown. Because many drugs are excreted in human milk, caution should be exercised when naltrexone is administered to a nursing woman.

Pediatric Use: The safe use of naltrexone in pediatric patients younger than 18 years old has not been established.

ADVERSE REACTIONS

During two randomized, double-blind placebo-controlled 12 week trials to evaluate the efficacy of naltrexone as an adjunctive treatment of alcohol dependence, most patients tolerated naltrexone well. In these studies, a total of 93 patients received naltrexone hydrochloride at a dose of 50 mg once daily. Five of these patients discontinued naltrexone because of nausea. No serious adverse events were reported during these two trials.

While extensive clinical studies evaluating the use of naltrexone in detoxified, formerly opioid-dependent individuals failed to identify any single, serious untoward risk of naltrexone use, placebo-controlled studies employing up to five-fold higher doses of naltrexone hydrochloride (up to 300 mg per day) than that recommended for use in opiate receptor blockade have shown that naltrexone causes hepatocellular injury in a substantial proportion of patients exposed at higher doses (see **WARNINGS** and **PRECAUTIONS: Laboratory Tests**).

Aside from this finding, and the risk of precipitated opioid withdrawal, available evidence does not incriminate naltrexone, used at any dose, as a cause of any other serious adverse reaction for the patient who is "opioid free." It is critical to recognize that naltrexone can precipitate or exacerbate abstinence signs and symptoms in any individual who is not completely free of exogenous opioids.

Patients with addictive disorders, especially opioid addiction, are at risk for multiple numerous adverse events and abnormal laboratory findings, including liver function abnormalities. Data from both controlled and observational studies suggest that these abnormalities, other than the dose-related hepatotoxicity described above, are not related to the use of naltrexone.

Among opioid free individuals, naltrexone administration at the recommended dose has not been associated with a predictable profile of serious adverse or untoward events. However, as mentioned above, among individuals using opioids, naltrexone may cause serious withdrawal reactions (see **CONTRAINDICATIONS, WARNINGS, DOSAGE AND ADMINISTRATION**).

Reported Adverse Events:
Naltrexone has not been shown to cause significant increases in complaints in placebo-controlled trials in patients known to be free of opioids for more than 7 to 10 days. Studies in alcoholic populations and in volunteers in clinical pharmacology studies have suggested that a small fraction of patients may experience an opioid withdrawal-like symptom complex consisting of tearfulness, mild nausea, abdominal cramps, restlessness, bone or joint pain, myalgia, and nasal symptoms. This may represent the unmasking of occult opioid use, or it may represent symptoms attributable to naltrexone. A number of alternative dosing patterns have been recommended to try to reduce the frequency of these complaints (see **Individualization of Dosage**).

Alcoholism:
In an open label safety study with approximately 570 individuals with alcoholism receiving naltrexone, the following new-onset adverse reactions occurred in 2% or more of the patients: nausea (10%), headache (7%), dizziness (4%), nervousness (4%), fatigue (4%), insomnia (3%), vomiting (3%), anxiety (2%) and somnolence (2%).

Depression, suicidal ideation, and suicidal attempts have been reported in all groups when comparing naltrexone, placebo, or controls undergoing treatment for alcoholism.

RATE RANGES OF NEW ONSET EVENTS

	Naltrexone	Placebo
Depression	0 to 15%	0 to 17%
Suicide Attempt/Ideation	0 to 1%	0 to 3%

Although no causal relationship with naltrexone is suspected, physicians should be aware that treatment with naltrexone does not reduce the risk of suicide in these patients (see **PRECAUTIONS**).

Opioid Addiction:
The following adverse reactions have been reported both at baseline and during the naltrexone clinical trials in opioid addiction at an incidence rate of more than 10%:

Difficulty sleeping, anxiety, nervousness, abdominal pain/ cramps, nausea and/or vomiting, low energy, joint and muscle pain, and headache.

The incidence was less than 10% for:

Loss of appetite, diarrhea, constipation, increased thirst, increased energy, feeling down, irritability, dizziness, skin rash, delayed ejaculation, decreased potency, and chills.

The following events occurred in less than 1% of subjects:

Respiratory: nasal congestion, itching, rhinorrhea, sneezing, sore throat, excess mucus or phlegm, sinus trouble, heavy breathing, hoarseness, cough, shortness of breath.

Cardiovascular: nose bleeds, phlebitis, edema, increased blood pressure, non-specific ECG changes, palpitations, tachycardia.

Gastrointestinal: excessive gas, hemorrhoids, diarrhea, ulcer.

Musculoskeletal: painful shoulders, legs or knees; tremors, twitching.

Genitourinary: increased frequency of, or discomfort during, urination; increased or decreased sexual interest.

Dermatologic: oily skin, pruritus, acne, athlete's foot, cold sores, alopecia.

Psychiatric: depression, paranoia, fatigue, restlessness, confusion, disorientation, hallucinations, nightmares, bad dreams.

Special senses: eyes—blurred, burning, light sensitive, swollen, aching, strained; ears—"clogged," aching, tinnitus.

General: increased appetite, weight loss, weight gain, yawning, somnolence, fever, dry mouth, head "pounding," inguinal pain, swollen glands, "side" pains, cold feet, "hot spells."

Post-marketing Experience: Data collected from post-marketing use of naltrexone show that most events usually occur early in the course of drug therapy and are transient. It is not always possible to distinguish these occurrences from those signs and symptoms that may result from a withdrawal syndrome. Events that have been reported include anorexia, asthenia, chest pain, fatigue, headache, hot flashes, malaise, changes in blood pressure, agitation, dizziness, hyperkinesia, nausea, vomiting, tremor, abdominal pain, diarrhea, elevations in liver enzymes or bilirubin, hepatic function abnormalities or hepatitis, palpitations, myalgia, anxiety, confusion, euphoria, hallucinations, insomnia, nervousness, somnolence, abnormal thinking, dyspnea, rash, increased sweating, and vision abnormalities.

Depression, suicide, attempted suicide and suicidal ideation have been reported in the post-marketing experience with naltrexone used in the treatment of opioid dependence. No causal relationship has been demonstrated. In the literature, endogenous opioids have been theorized to contribute to a variety of conditions. In some individuals the use of opioid antagonists has been associated with a change in baseline levels of some hypothalamic, pituitary, adrenal, or gonadal hormones. The clinical significance of such changes is not fully understood.

Adverse events, including withdrawal symptoms and death, have been reported with the use of naltrexone in ultra rapid opiate detoxification programs. The cause of death in these cases is not known (see **WARNINGS**).

Laboratory Tests: With the exception of liver test abnormalities (see **WARNINGS and PRECAUTIONS**), results of laboratory tests, like adverse reaction reports, have not shown consistent patterns of abnormalities that can be attributed to treatment with naltrexone.

Idiopathic thrombocytopenic purpura was reported in one patient who may have been sensitized to naltrexone in a previous course of treatment with naltrexone. The condition cleared without sequelae after discontinuation of naltrexone and corticosteroid treatment.

DRUG ABUSE AND DEPENDENCE

Naltrexone is a pure opioid antagonist. It does not lead to physical or psychological dependence. Tolerance to the opioid antagonist effect is not known to occur.

OVERDOSAGE

There is limited clinical experience with naltrexone overdosage in humans. In one study, subjects who received 800 mg daily naltrexone hydrochloride for up to one week showed no evidence of toxicity.

In the mouse, rat and guinea pig, the oral LD_{50}s were 1,100 to 1,550 mg/kg; 1,450 mg/kg; and 1,490 mg/kg; respectively. High doses of naltrexone hydrochloride (generally $\geq$1,000 mg/kg) produced salivation, depression/reduced activity, tremors, and convulsions. Mortalities in animals due to high-dose naltrexone administration usually were due to clonic-tonic convulsions and/or respiratory failure.

Treatment Of Overdosage: In view of the lack of actual experience in the treatment of naltrexone hydrochloride overdose, patients should be treated symptomatically in a closely supervised environment. Physicians should contact a poison control center for the most up-to-date information.

DOSAGE AND ADMINISTRATION

IF THERE IS ANY QUESTION OF OCCULT OPIOID DEPENDENCE, PERFORM A NALOXONE CHALLENGE TEST AND DO NOT INITIATE NALTREXONE THERAPY UNTIL THE NALOXONE CHALLENGE IS NEGATIVE.

Treatment of Alcoholism:
A dose of 50 mg once daily is recommended for most patients (see Individualization of Dosage). The placebo-controlled studies that demonstrated the efficacy of naltrexone hydrochloride as an adjunctive treatment of alcoholism used a dose regimen of naltrexone hydrochloride 50 mg once daily for up to 12 weeks. Other dose regimens or durations of therapy were not evaluated in these trials.

A patient is a candidate for treatment with naltrexone if:

- the patient is willing to take a medicine to help with alcohol dependence
- the patient is opioid free for 7 to 10 days
- the patient does not have severe or active liver or kidney problems (Typical guidelines suggest liver function tests no greater than 3 times the upper limits of normal, and bilirubin normal.)
- the patient is not allergic to naltrexone, and no other contraindications are present

Refer to **CONTRAINDICATIONS, WARNINGS, and PRECAUTIONS** Sections for additional information.

Naltrexone should be considered as only one of many factors determining the success of treatment of alcoholism. Factors associated with a good outcome in the clinical trials with naltrexone were the type, intensity, and duration of treatment; appropriate management of comorbid conditions; use of community-based support groups; and good medication compliance. To achieve the best possible treatment outcome, appropriate compliance-enhancing techniques should be implemented for all components of the treatment program, especially medication compliance.

Treatment of Opioid Dependence:
Initiate treatment with naltrexone using the following guidelines:

1. Treatment should not be attempted unless the patient has remained opioid-free for at least 7 to 10 days. Self-reporting of abstinence from opioids in opioid addicts should be verified by analysis of the patient's urine for absence of opioids. The patient should not be manifesting withdrawal signs or reporting withdrawal symptoms.

2. If there is any question of occult opioid dependence, perform a naloxone challenge test. If signs of opioid withdrawal are still observed following naloxone challenge, treatment with naltrexone should not be attempted. The naloxone challenge can be repeated in 24 hours.

3. Treatment should be initiated carefully, with an initial dose of 25 mg of naltrexone hydrochloride. If no withdrawal signs occur, the patient may be started on 50 mg a day thereafter.

Naloxone Challenge Test: The naloxone challenge test should not be performed in a patient showing clinical signs or symptoms of opioid withdrawal, or in a patient whose urine contains opioids. The naloxone challenge test may be administered by either the intravenous or subcutaneous routes.

Intravenous:
Inject 0.2 mg naloxone.
Observe for 30 seconds for signs or symptoms of withdrawal.
If no evidence of withdrawal, inject 0.6 mg of naloxone.
Observe for an additional 20 minutes.
Subcutaneous:
Administer 0.8 mg naloxone.
Observe for 20 minutes for signs or symptoms of withdrawal.
Note: Individual patients, especially those with opioid dependence, may respond to lower doses of naloxone. In some cases, 0.1 mg IV naloxone has produced a diagnostic response.

Interpretation of the Challenge: Monitor vital signs and observe the patient for signs and symptoms of opioid withdrawal. These may include but are not limited to: nausea, vomiting, dysphoria, yawning, sweating, tearing, rhinorrhea, stuffy nose, craving for opioids, poor appetite, abdominal cramps, sense of fear, skin erythema, disrupted sleep patterns, fidgeting, uneasiness, poor ability to focus, mental lapses, muscle aches or cramps, pupillary dilation, piloerection, fever, changes in blood pressure, pulse or temperature, anxiety, depression, irritability, backache, bone or joint pains, tremors, sensations of skin crawling, or fasciculations. If signs or symptoms of withdrawal appear, the test is positive and no additional naloxone should be administered.

Warning: If the test is positive, do NOT initiate naltrexone therapy. Repeat the challenge in 24 hours. If the test is negative, naltrexone therapy may be started if no other contraindications are present. If there is any doubt about the result of the test, hold naltrexone and repeat the challenge in 24 hours.

Alternative Dosing Schedules

Once the patient has been started on naltrexone hydrochloride, 50 mg every 24 hours will produce adequate clinical blockade of the actions of parenterally administered opioids (i.e., this dose will block the effects of a 25 mg intravenous heroin challenge). A flexible approach to a dosing regimen may need to be employed in cases of supervised administration. Thus, patients may receive 50 mg of naltrexone hydrochloride every weekday with a 100 mg dose on Saturday, 100 mg every other day, or 150 mg every third day. The degree of blockade produced by naltrexone may be reduced by these extended dosing intervals.

There may be a higher risk of hepatocellular injury with single doses above 50 mg, and use of higher doses and extended dosing intervals should balance the possible risks against the probable benefits (see **WARNINGS** and **Individualization of Dosage**).

Patient Compliance:

Naltrexone should be considered as only one of many factors determining the success of treatment. To achieve the best possible treatment outcome, appropriate compliance-enhancing techniques should be implemented for all components of the treatment program, including medication compliance.

HOW SUPPLIED

Depade® (naltrexone hydrochloride tablets, USP) 25 mg are available as a pink film coated capsule-shaped tablet with a convex surface, debossed with a number "25" on one side, and "DEPADE" on the other side.

Bottles of 30 . . . . .NDC 0406-0089-03

Depade® (naltrexone hydrochloride tablets, USP) 50 mg are available as a yellow film coated capsule-shaped tablet with a convex surface, debossed with a number "50" and a full bisect in between the 5 and 0 on one side and "DEPADE" on the other side.

Bottles of 30 . . . . .NDC 0406-0092-03
Bottles of 100 . . . . NDC 0406-0092-01

Depade® (naltrexone hydrochloride tablets, USP) 100 mg are available as a beige film coated capsule-shaped tablet with a convex surface, debossed with a number "100" and a partial score above and below the middle 0 on one side and "DEPADE" with a partial score on the other side.

Bottles of 30 . . . . .NDC 0406-0119-03

Bottles of 100 . . . . NDC 0406-0119-01

Storage: Store at 20°C to 25°C (68°F to 77°F) [see USP Controlled Room Temperature].

Depade® is a registered trademark of Mallinckrodt Inc.

Mallinckrodt Inc.

St. Louis, MO 63134, U.S.A.

Appendices

APPENDIX A

Results with Naltrexone and Nalmefene: Clinical Trials and Reviews

March, 2012

Notes <u>underlined</u> represent evidence that naltrexone and nalmefene are safe and produce significant benefits when extinction is possible (n=90; 66 with alcoholism). The notes are in chronological order with the most recent trials at the end of the list.

Notes in italics indicate evidence that naltrexone and nalmefene are not effective when extinction is not possible (e.g., during abstinence) (n=36; 34 with alcohol).

Notes in bold are from reviews or meta-analyses, all of which conclude naltrexone is effective (n=27).

Notes with results contrary to extinction or unclear are in the regular Arial font (n=5). (One found benefits in delaying first sampling, one with coping failed to get significant benefits, and three were unclear about the protocol.) (Long-lasting implant/injection studies are evaluated only as to whether the treatment was effective because the antagonist was always present.)

When the same trial has been published in several abstracts and articles, they are all listed under the same number, separated by the ¶ symbol.

SUMMARY: When extinction was possible, 90 out of 91 clinical trials found significant benefits from the opioid antagonist. When extinction was not possible, 36 out of 37 trials found no significant benefits from the opioid antagonist.

1. Renault, P.F. (1978). Treatment of heroin-dependent persons with antagonists: Current status. *Bulletin on Narcotics* 30: pp. 21–29. ¶ Renault, P.F. (1980). Treatment of heroin dependent persons with antagonists: Current status. In: *Naltrexone: Research Monograph* 28, Willett, R. E. and Barnett, G. (eds.). Washington, DC: National Institute of Drug Abuse, pp. 11–22. First clinical trial of naltrexone and until recently the only controlled trial for opiate addiction. Large double-blind placebo-controlled (DBPC) trial (n=197) plus 1005 open-label patients. Naltrexone was effective but only in patients who disobeyed instructions not to use opiates while on medication. *Not effective with abstinence.* It was concluded that naltrexone works by extinction. Basis for FDA acceptance of naltrexone for opiate addiction.

2. Volpicelli, J.R., O'Brien, C.P., Alterman, A.I., and Hayashida, M. (1990). Naltrexone and the treatment of alcohol dependence: Initial observations. In: *Opioids, Bulimia, and Alcohol Abuse & Alcoholism*, Reid, L.D. (ed.). New York: Springer Verlag (1990), pp. 195–214. ¶ Volpicelli, J.R., Alterman, A.I., Hayashida, M., and O'Brien, C.P. (1992). Naltrexone in the treatment of alcohol dependence. *Archives of General Psychiatry* 49: pp. 876–880. First DBPC clinical trial for alcoholism. Naltrexone was safe and effective, with the primary effects being found in patients drinking while on medication, as required by extinction. *No significant benefits before first drink on Naltrexone.*

3. O'Malley, S., Jaffe, A., Chang, G., Witte, G., Schottenfeld, R.S., and Rounsaville, B.J. (1990). Naltrexone. The treatment of alcohol dependence. In: *Opioids, Bulimia, and Alcohol Abuse & Alcoholism*, Reid, L.D. (ed.). New York: Springer Verlag; pp. 149–157. ¶ O'Malley, S.S., Jaffe, A.J., Chang, G., Schottenfeld, R.S., Meyer, R.E., and Rounsaville, B. (1992). Naltrexone and coping skills therapy for alcohol dependence. *Archives of General Psychiatry* 49: pp. 881–887. The other DBPC trial in addition to Volpicelli used for FDA approval of naltrexone for

alcoholism. Naltrexone was safe and effective in "Coping" groups inadvertently encouraged to break abstinence, *but there were no significant benefits in "Supportive" groups with instructions to abstain. No significant benefits before first drink on naltrexone. Significant interactions indicating naltrexone is better with Coping than Supportive therapy.*

4. Mason, B.J., Ritvo, E.C., Salvato, F., Zimmer, E., Goldberg, G., and Welch, B. (1993). Nalmefene modification of alcohol dependence: A pilot study. Proceedings of American Psychiatric Association Annual Meeting, San Francisco, CA, May 1993: p. 170 (abstract NR442). ¶ Mason, B.J., Ritvo, E.C., Salvato, F.R., and Goldberg, G. (1994). Preliminary dose finding for nalmefene treatment of alcoholism. *Alcoholism: Clinical and Experimental Research* 18: p. 464 (abstract 270). ¶ Mason, B.J.; Ritvo, E.C.; Morgan, R.O.; Salvato, F.R.; Goldberg, G.; Welch, B.; and Mantero Atienza, E. (1994). A double blind, placebo controlled pilot study to evaluate the efficacy and safety of oral nalmefene HCL for alcohol dependence. *Alcoholism: Clinical and Experimental Research* 18: pp. 1162–1167. Small DBPC trial showing nalmefene (similar to naltrexone) is safe and effective in treating alcoholism. *No significant benefits before first drink on nalmefene; the article says this finding confirms Sinclair's hypothesis that the medication is working through extinction.*

5. Bohn, M.J. and Kranzler, H.R. (1993). Randomized trial of safety and efficacy of 25 vs 50 mg naltrexone and brief counseling to reduce heavy drinking. Proceedings of the Research Society on Alcoholism (RSA) Meeting, Miami, FL, June 19–24, 1993. ¶ Bohn, M.J., Kranzler, H.R., Beazoglou, D., and Staehler, B.A. (1994). Naltrexone and brief counseling to reduce heavy drinking. *The American Journal on Addictions* 3: pp 91–99. Naltrexone was safe and effective in open-label study for reducing drinking and craving when used without detoxification and with instructions not to abstain but to try to cut down drinking. Protocol similar to that used by Sinclair in preclinical studies and in the Sinclair Method. "Several subjects reported subjective alterations in desire for carbohydrated-rich foodstuffs and sex."

6. Agosti, V. (1994). The efficacy of controlled trials of alcohol misuse treatments in maintaining abstinence. *International Journal of Addictions* 29: pp. 759–769. ¶ Agosti, V. (1995). The efficacy of treatment in reducing alcohol consumption: A meta-analysis. *International Journal of Addictions* 30: pp. 1067–1077. **Meta-analyses of all alcoholism treatment methods for which control data were provided. Concluded that the best method was naltrexone combined with a coping with drinking protocol.**

7. Sinclair, J.D. (1995). The story in Finland behind the new naltrexone treatment for alcoholism (and how I got the patent for it). *Life and*

Education In Finland 3/95: pp. 2–16. **Popular review concluding naltrexone is safe and effective.**

8. Agosti V. (1995). The efficacy of treatment in reducing alcohol consumption: A meta analysis. *International Journal of Addictions* **30**: pp. 1067–1077. <u>Naltrexone with coping with drinking is effective and safe.</u>

9. World Health Organization (1996). Programme on Substance Abuse, Pharmacological Treatment of substance use disorders: International issues in medications development. WHO/PSA/96.10 <u>General review concluding: "One medication, naltrexone, has been identified as a safe and effective treatment for alcohol dependence." (p. 24).</u>

10. Mason, B. (1996). Dosing issues in the pharmacotherapy of alcoholism. *Alcoholism: Clinical and Experimental Research* **20**: pp. 10A–16A. <u>Small study showing doses of 20 mg and 80 mg of nalmefene are well tolerated, concluding that 80 mg was the optimal dose 100% completing trial and 62% having a stable response (no more than 2 heavy drinking days (>4 drinks for men, >3 drinks for women).</u>

11. Monti, P.M., Rohsenow, D.J., Swift, R.M., Abrams, D.B., Colby, S.M., Mueller, T.I., Brown, R.A., and Gordon, A. (1996). Effects of naltrexone on urge to drink during alcohol cue exposure: preliminary results. *Alcoholism: Clinical and Experimental Research* **20** (supplement): p. 92A. <u>After seeing their own usual alcoholic beverage, naltrexone patients had significantly smaller urge to drink than did placebo patients.</u>

12. Anton, R.F., Romach, M.K., Kranzler, H.R., Pettinati, H., O'Malley, S., and Mann, K. (1996). Pharmacotherapy of alcoholism—10 years of progress. *Alcoholism: Clinical and Experimental Research* **20**: pp. 172A–175A. **Review concluding naltrexone is safe and effective especially in alcoholics with a family history of alcoholism.**

13. O'Malley, S. S., Jaffe, A. J., Chang, G., Rode, S., Schottenfeld, R. S., Meyer, R. E., and Rounsaville, B. (1996). Six-month follow-up of naltrexone and psychotherapy for alcohol dependence. *Archives of General Psychiatry* **53**: pp. 217–224. <u>Significant benefits from naltrexone continue for months after the end of treatment in Coping with Drinking group,</u> *but no significant benefits with abstinence.*

14. Litten, R.Z., Croop, R. S., Chick, J., McCaul, M.E., Mason, B., and Sass, H. (1996). International update: New findings on promising medications. *Alcoholism: Clinical and Experimental Research* **20**: pp. 216A–218A. <u>Preliminary reports from the British naltrexone trial, the Baltimore naltrexone trial, and the Miami nalmefene trial, all with significant benefits, as well as the large-scale DuPont open label study showing safety for naltrexone.</u>

15. O'Malley, S.S., Jaffe, A.J., Rode, S., and Rounsaville, B.J. (1996). Experience of a "slip" among alcoholics treated with naltrexone or placebo. *American Journal of Psychiatry*, 153: pp. 281–283. *Naltrexone patients drink the same as placebo patients on first day of a slip (before extinction),* but the naltrexone patients subsequently are less likely to relapse into heavy drinking and have lower craving.

16. Croop, R.S., Faukner, E.B., Labriola, D.F., and the Naltrexone Usage Study Group (1997). The safety profile of naltrexone in the treatment of alcoholism: Results from a multicenter usage study. *Archives of General Psychiatry* 54: pp. 1130–1135. The large DuPont safety study showing naltrexone was safe and effective.

17. Maxwell, S. and Shinderman, M.S. (1997). Naltrexone in the treatment of dually-diagnosed patients. *Journal of Addictive Diseases* 16: A27, p. 125. ¶ Maxwell, S. and Shinderman M.S. (2000). Use of naltrexone in the treatment of alcohol use disorders in patients with concomitant severe mental illness. *Journal of Addictive Diseases* 19: pp. 61–69. Naltrexone was safe and effective in dual diagnosis alcoholics who were allowed to drink while on medication *but it was not effective in regular alcoholics who were told to abstain while on medication.* Discussion concludes the results support Sinclair's hypothesis that naltrexone works by extinction.

18. Volpicelli, J.R., Rhines, K.C., Rhines, J.S., Volpicelli, L.A., Alterman, A.I., and O'Brien, C.P. (1997). Naltrexone and alcohol dependence: Role of subject compliance. *Archives of General Psychiatry* 54: pp. 737–742. Naltrexone was safe and effective, but poor compliance limited results. *No significant benefits before first drink in total population, but when only compliant patients examined,* there was a significant benefit before the reported first drink.

19. Oslin, D., Liberto, J., O'Brien, C.P., Krois, S., and Norbeck J. (1997). Naltrexone as an adjunct treatment for older patients with alcohol dependence. *American Journal of Geriatric Psychiatry* 5: pp. 324–332. Naltrexone was safe and effective in older patients who drank, *but of no benefit until the first drink on medication.*

20. Lifrak, P.D., Alterman, A.I., OBrien, C.P., and Volpicelli, J.R. (1997). Naltrexone for alcoholic adolescents. *American Journal of Psychiatry* 154: pp. 439–440. Naltrexone was safe and effective in adolescent alcoholics.

21. Kranzler, H.R., Tennen, H., Penta, C., and Bohn, M. J. (1997). Targeted naltrexone treatment of early problem drinkers. *Addictive Behaviors* 22: pp. 431–436. ¶ Kranzler, H.R., Tennen, H., Blomqvist et al. (2001). Targeted naltrexone treatment for early problem drinkers. *Alcoholism: Clinical and Experimental Research* 25 (supplement 5): p. 144A. First trial to give naltrexone only when patients were drinking,

in accord with the Sinclair Method; naltrexone was safe and produced significant benefits, *but none before first drink while on medication.*

22. O'Connor, P.G., Farren, C.K., Rounsaville, B.J., and O'Malley, S.S. (1997). A preliminary investigation of the management of alcohol dependence with naltrexone by primary care providers. *American Journal of Medicine* 103: pp. 477–482. Open label study concluding: "Naltrexone and counseling by primary care providers appeared to be both feasible and effective."

23. McCaul, M.E., Wand, G.S., Sullivan, J., Mummford, G., and Quigley, J. (1997). Beta-naltrexol level predicts alcohol relapse. *Alcoholism: Clinical and Experimental Research* 21: p. 32A. Naltrexone was safe and effective in patients with higher levels of the metabolite, beta-naltrexol and with higher dose (100 mg). Benefits no longer significant at 6 months.

24. Balldin, J., Berglund, M., Borg, S., Månsson, M., Berndtsen, P., Franck, J., Gustafsson, L., Halldin, J., Hollstedt, C., Nilsson, L-H., and Stolt, G. (1997). A randomized 6 month double-blind placebo-controlled study of naltrexone and coping skills education programme. *Alcohol and Alcoholism* 32: p. 325. ¶ Månsson, M., Balldin, J., Berglund, M., and Borg, S. (1999). Six-month follow-up of interaction effect between naltrexone and coping skills therapy in outpatient alcoholism treatment. *Alcohol and Alcoholism* 34: p. 454. ¶ Månsson, M., Balldin, J., Berglund, M., and Borg, S. (1999). Interaction effect between naltrexone and coping skills. Treatment and follow-up data. Abstract to "Evidence Based Medicine of Naltrexone in Alcoholism," satellite symposium to the 7th Congress of the European Society for Biomedical Research on Alcoholism, Barcelona, Spain, June 16–19, 1999. Swedish dual DBPC clinical trial showing naltrexone was safe and effective with "coping" instructions *but not effective with abstinence.*

25. Sinclair, D. (1997). Development in Finland of the extinction treatment for alcoholism with naltrexone. *Psychiatrica Fennica* 28: pp. 76–97. ¶ Sinclair, J.D. (1998). Pharmacological extinction of alcohol drinking with opioid antagonists. *Arqivos de Medicina* 12 (Supplement 1): pp. 95–98. ¶ Sinclair, J.D., Kymäläinen, O., Hernesniemi, M., Shinderman, M. S., and Maxwell S. (1998). Treatment of alcohol dependence with naltrexone utilizing an extinction protocol. Abstracts: 38th Annual Meeting, National Institute of Mental Health (NIMH)-sponsored New Clinical Drug Evaluation Unit (NCDEU) Program, Boca Raton, FL, June 10–13, 1998. ¶ Sinclair, J.D. (1998). New treatment options for substance abuse from a public health viewpoint. *Annals of Medicine* 30: pp. 406–411. Publication of the highly significant reductions

in craving and drinking found in the first Finnish clinics using the
Sinclair Method.

26. Rybakowski, J.K., Ziólkowski, M., and Volpicelli, J.R. (1997). A study
of lithium, carbamazepine and naltrexone in male patients with alcohol dependence—results of four months of treatment. Abstract from
the annual meeting of the European Society for Biomedical Research
on Alcoholism. *Naltrexone with support of abstinence was not effective.*

27. Sinclair, J.D., Kymäläinen, O., and Jakobson, B. (1998). Extinction of
the association between stimuli and drinking in the clinical treatment
of alcoholism with naltrexone. *Alcoholism: Clinical and Experimental
Research* 22 (supplement): p. 144A. Naltrexone treatment significantly reduced the ability of all sorts of stimuli (positive affect, negative
affect, and neutral) to trigger drinking, in accord with a prediction of
the extinction hypothesis.

28. Anton, R. (1998). Naltrexone compared to placebo when combined
with cognitive behavioral therapy in the treatment of outpatient alcoholics. Presented at the Ninth Congress of the International Society for
Biomedical Research on Alcoholism (ISBRA), Copenhagen, Denmark,
June 27–July 2, 1998. ¶ Anton, R. (1999). Neurobiologial approach
to alcoholism therapy: The role of naltrexone. Abstract to "Evidence
Based Medicine of Naltrexone in Alcoholism," satellite symposium
to the 7th Congress of the European Society for Biomedical Research
on Alcoholism, Barcelona, Spain, June 16–19, 1999. ¶ Anton, R.F.,
Moak, D.H., Waid, L.R., Latham, P.K., Malcolm, R.J., and Dias, J.K.
(1999). Naltrexone and cognitive behavioral therapy for the treatment of outpatient alcoholics: Results of a placebo-controlled trial.
American Journal of Psychiatry 156: pp. 1758–1764. DBPC trial showing naltrexone with coping to be safe and effective. *No benefit before
first drink on medication.*

29. Hersh, D., Van Kirk, J.R., and Kranzler, H.R. (1998). Naltrexone
treatment of comorbid alcohol and cocaine use disorders.
Psychopharmacology (Berlin, Germany) 139: pp. 44–52. Small study
with no significant benefits of naltrexone over placebo in patients addicted to both alcohol and cocaine.

30. Sinclair, J.D. (1998). From optimal complexity to the naltrexone
extinction of alcoholism. In: Viewing Psychology as a Whole: The
Integrative Science of William N. Dember. Hoffman, R., Sherrick, M.F.,
and Warm, J.S. (eds.), Washington, D.C.: American Psychological
Association, pp. 491–508. **Review concluding naltrexone is effective
and works by extinction.**

31. O'Malley, S. (ed.) (1998). *Naltrexone and Alcoholism Treatment.*
Rockville, MD: U.S. Department of Health and Human Services,
Public Health Service. Treatment Improvement Protocol (TIP) Series

Vol. 28. Book showing safety and efficacy of naltrexone and how it has been used. Includes "Why Isn't Naltrexone More Widely Used" on p. 75.

32. Kim, S.W. (1998). Opioid antagonists in the treatment of impulse-control disorders. *Journal of Clinical Psychiatry* 59: pp. 159–164. In three case studies, naltrexone helped decrease impulse-control disorders (case 1: pathological gambling + compulsive shopping; case 2: bulimia nervosa + compulsive shopping + cocaine & narcotic abuse; case 3: kleptomania + washing syndrome + hoarding syndrome).

33. Heinälä, P., Alho, H., Kuoppasalmi, K., Sinclair, D., Kiianmaa, K., and Lönnqvist, J. (1999). Use of naltrexone in the treatment of alcohol dependence—a double-blind placebo-controlled Finnish trial. *Alcohol and Alcoholism* 34: p. 433. ¶ Heinälä, P., Alho, H., Kuoppasalmi, K., Lönnqvist, J., Sinclair, D., and Kiianmaa, K. (1999). Naltrexone in alcoholism treatment: Patient efficacy and compliance. In: New Research. Program and Abstracts. American Psychiatric Association 1999. Annual Meeting, Washington, D.C., May 15–20, 1999. ¶ Alho, H., Heinälä, P., Kiianmaa, K., and Sinclair, J.D. (1999). Naltrexone for alcohol dependence: double-blind placebo-controlled Finnish trial. *Alcoholism: Clinical and Experimental Research* 23: p. 46A (abstract 246). ¶ Heinälä, P., Alho, H., Kuoppasalmi, K., Lönnqvist, J., Kiianmaa, K., and Sinclair, J.D. (2000). Targeted naltrexone with coping therapy for controlled drinking, without prior detoxification, is effective and particularly well tolerated: An 8-month controlled trial. Abstract to 10th Congress of the International Society for Biomedical Research on Alcoholism (ISBRA 2000), Yokohama, Japan, July 2–8, 2000. ¶ Heinälä, P., Alho, H., Kiianmaa, K., Lönnqvist, J., Kuoppasalmi, K., and Sinclair, J.D. (2001). Targeted use of naltrexone without prior detoxification in the treatment of alcohol dependence: A factorial double-blind placebo-controlled trial. *Journal of Clinical Psychopharmacology* 21: pp. 287–292. Finnish dual DBPC clinical trial. The Sinclair Method was tested (with no prior detoxification, instructions aimed at controlled drinking, naltrexone given only when drinking, and naltrexone continued for 8 months) and shown to be particularly safe and to produce significant benefits over placebo. *Naltrexone was also tested with abstinence and found to be slightly worse than placebo and to produce significantly more side effects than when used with controlled drinking.*

34. Garbutt, J.C., West, S.L., Carey, T.S, Lohr, K.N., and Crews, F.T. Agency for Health Care Policy and Research, AHCPR (1999). Evidence Report/Technology Assessment: Number 3: Pharmacotherapy for Alcohol Dependence. Pharmacological Treatment of Alcohol Dependence: A Review of the Evidence. *JAMA* 281: pp. 1318–1325. **Review of all**

pharmaceutical treatments for alcoholics, concluding that naltrexone is safe and effective, and with better evidence than any other medication.

35. Mason, B.J., Salvato, F.R., Williams, L.D., Ritvo, E.C., and Cutler, R.B. (1999). A double-blind, placebo-controlled study of oral nalmefene for alcohol dependence. *Archives of General Psychiatry* 56: pp. 719–725. Second nalmefene study, DBPC trial showing it to be safe and effective, *but not beneficial until first drink on medication.*

36. Rubio, G. (1999). How to use naltrexone in different alcoholic patient groups. Abstract to "Evidence Based Medicine of Naltrexone in Alcoholism," satellite symposium to the 7th Congress of the European Society for Biomedical Research on Alcoholism, Barcelona, Spain, June 16–19, 1999. Open-label but placebo-controlled study showing naltrexone was safe and effective. *No benefit until first drink on medication.*

37. Swift, R.M. (1999). Drug therapy for alcohol dependence. *New England Journal of Medicine* 340: pp. 1482–1490. **Review concluding, "Of all drugs studied for the treatment of alcohol dependence, the evidence of efficacy is strongest for naltrexone and acamprosate."**

38. Batel, P., Lancrenon, S., and Baconnet, B. (1999). Compliance, tolerance and outcome of 3 months naltrexone treatment among 215 alcohol dependents. *Alcohol and Alcoholism* 34: p. 452 (abstract 125). Open label showing good compliance in 76% of patients and relapse to heavy drinking most likely in poor compliers.

39. Knox, P.C., and Donovan, D.M. (1999). Using naltrexone in inpatient alcoholism treatment. *Journal of Psychoactive Drugs* 31(4): pp. 373–388. *DBPC study of 63 alcoholics showing naltrexone with abstinence (in an inpatient program) was of no benefit.*

40. Oslin, D.W., Pettinati, H.M., Volpicelli, J.R., Wolf, A.L., Kampman, K.M., and O'Brien, C.P. (1999). The effects of naltrexone on alcohol and cocaine use in dually addicted patients. *Journal of Substance Abuse and Treatment* 16: pp. 163–167. Naltrexone produced significant decreases in alcohol and cocaine use.

41. Morris, P. (1999). A controlled trial of naltrexone for alcohol dependence: An Australian perspective. Presented at the 1999 Scientific Meeting of the Research Society on Alcoholism, Santa Barbara, CA, June 26–July 1, 1999. ¶ Morris, P.L.P., Hopwood, M., Whelan, G., Gardiner, J., and Drummond, E. (2001). Naltrexone for alcohol dependence: A randomised controlled trial. *Addiction* 96: pp. 1565–1573. Naltrexone was safe and effective with coping with drinking protocol. *No benefit until first drink on medication.*

42. Dannon, P.N., Iancu, I., and Grunhaus, L. (1999). Naltrexone treatment in kleptomanic patients. *Human Psychopharmacology* 14: pp.

583–585. Case study reporting two kleptomanic patients successfully treated with naltrexone.

43. Sinclair, J.D., Sinclair, K., and Alho, H. (2000). Long-term follow up of continued naltrexone treatment. *Alcoholism: Clinical and Experimental Research* 24 (supplement): p. 182A. (S16:4) Significant benefits of naltrexone are still present three years after start of treatment in patients always taking medication before drinking, on craving, drinking levels, and liver damage markers.

44. World Health Organization (2000). Management of substance dependence. Review Series. A systematic review of opioid antagonists for alcohol dependence, 4. WHO/MSD/MSB 00.4. Naltrexone is effective in treating alcoholism.

45. Chick, J., Anton, R., Checinski, K., Croop, R., Drummond, D.C., Farmer, R., Labriola, D., Marshall, J., Moncrieff, J., Morgan, M.Y., Peters, T., and Ritson, B. (2000). A multicenter, randomized, double-blind, placebo-controlled trial of naltrexone in the treatment of alcohol dependence or abuse. *Alcohol and Alcoholism* 35: pp. 587–593. DBPC trial showing naltrexone was safe and effective in complying patients. *No benefit until after first drink on medication.*

46. Kranzler, H., Modesto-Lowe, V., and VanKirk, J. (2000). Naltrexone vs. nefazadone for treatment of alcohol dependence. *Neuropsychopharmacology* 22: pp. 493–503. DBPC trial failed to find significant benefit from naltrexone with Cognitive Behavioral Therapy, but same subjects contributed to significant naltrexone effect in Oslin et al., 2003.

47. Auriacombe, M., Robinson, M., Grabot, D., and Tignol, J. (2000). Naltrexone is ineffective to prevent relapse to alcohol in a realistic outpatient setting. A double blind one-year controlled study. Abstract to the 62nd Meeting of the College on Problems of Drug Dependence, Bal Harbour, FL, June 17–22, 2000. *Naltrexone with support of abstinence therapy was ineffective.*

48. Pettinati, H.M., Volpicelli, J.R., Pierce, J.D., Jr., and O'Brien, C.P. (2000). Improving naltrexone response: An intervention for medical practitioners to enhance medication compliance in alcohol dependent patients. *Journal of Addictive Diseases* 19: pp. 71–83. DBPC 12 trial with naltrexone plus BRENDA or Cognitive Behavioral Therapy. Naltrexone significantly better than placebo: lack of relapse to heavy drinking = 90% in naltrexone group vs 61.4% (or 11.4% reported online) with placebo, p<0.001. BRENDA produced significantly better compliance and staying in treatment but BRENDA plus naltrexone not yet analyzed.

49. O'Malley, S.S. (2001). Getting beyond the research clinic studies: comments on Morris et al. (2001). *Addiction* 96: pp. 1859–1860. Author

points out that the main effect was in patients who sample alcohol while on medication.

50. Ceccanti, M., Nocente, R., Calducci, G., Deiana,L., Attilia, M.L., Sasso, G.F., Sebastiani, G., Ulanio, F., and Goriale, G. (2001). Naltrexone ed alcol: Esperienze cliniche in Italia. *Medicina delle Tossicodipendenze– Italian Journal of the Addictions* 30: pp. 47–50. Single-blind, randomized trial on over 60 outpatients, showed that naltrexone was not more effective than placebo in treating alcoholics. This probably was done with instructions to abstain, but the article does not say what instructions were given, so this is classified as unclear.

51. Kranzler, H.R., and Van Kirk, J. (2001). Efficacy of naltrexone and acamprosate for alcoholism treatment: A meta-analysis. *Alcoholism: Clinical and Experimental Research* 25: pp. 1335–1341. **Review concluding naltrexone is safe and generally effective.**

52. Anton, R.F., Moak, D.H., Latham, P.K., Waid, L.R., Malcolm, R.J., Dias, J.K., and Roberts, J.S. (2001). Post-treatment results of combining naltrexone with cognitive-behavior therapy for the treatment of alcoholism. *Journal of Clinical Psychopharmacology* 21: pp. 72–77. Naltrexone was safe and effective. Benefits continue after termination of medication but eventually disappear, in accord with extinction.

53. Monti, P.M., Rohsenow, D.J., Swift, R. M., Gulliver, S.B., Colby, S.M., Mueller, T.I., Brown, R.A., Gordon, A., Abrams, D.B., Niaura, R.S., and Asher, M.K. (2001). Naltrexone and cue exposure with coping and communication skills training for alcoholics: Treatment process and 1-year outcomes. *Alcoholism: Clinical and Experimental Research* 25: pp. 1634–1647. Naltrexone plus Coping therapy was safe and effective. *No benefit until first drink on medication.*

54. Rubio, G., Jiménez-Arriero, A., Ponce, G., and Palomo, T. (2001). Naltrexone versus acamprosate: one year follow-up of alcohol dependence treatment. *Alcohol and Alcoholism* 36: pp. 419–425. Naltrexone was safe and effective with Coping with Drinking protocol. *No benefit until first drink on medication.*

55. Monterosso, J.R., Flannery, B.A., Pettinati, H.M., Oslin, D.W., Rukstalis. M., O'Brien, C.P., and Volpicelli, J.R. (2001). Predicting treatment response to naltrexone: the influence of craving and family history. *American Journal of Addiction* 10: pp. 258–268. Naltrexone was safe and effective, especially with a high craving and a family history of alcoholism.

56. Sinclair, J.D. (2001). Evidence about the use of naltrexone and for different ways of using it in the treatment of alcoholism. *Alcohol and Alcoholism* 36: pp. 2–10. **Review concluding that naltrexone is safe and effective but only when paired with drinking; data presented of the extinction of craving from naltrexone treatment in Finland.**

57. Krystal, J.H., Cramer, J.A., Krol, W.F., Kirk, G.F., and Rosenheck, R.A. (2001). Naltrexone in the treatment of alcohol dependence. *New England Journal of Medicine* 345: pp. 1734–1739. DBPC trial of naltrexone with abstinence on 627 veterans found no significant benefits over placebo. ¶ Sinclair, J.D., Alho, H., and Shinderman, M. (2002). Treatment of alcoholism: Efficacious use of naltrexone. *New England Journal of Medicine* 17: p.1330. **Explanation for why naltrexone with abstinence was not effective.**

58. Streeton, C., and Whelan, G. (2001). Naltrexone, a relapse prevention maintenance treatment of alcohol dependence: A meta-analysis of randomized controlled trials. *Alcohol and Alcoholism* 36: pp. 544–552. Meta-analysis of all published and unpublished trials concluded naltrexone was safe and effective in alcoholism treatment.

59. Gual, S.A. (2001). Evolucion clinica del alcoholismo tratado con naltrexona. Efectividad y seguridad en una muestra de 198 pacientes. *Medicina clinica* (Barcelona, Spain) 16: pp. 526–532. Open-label study showing safety of naltrexone.

60. Schmitz, J.M., Stotts, A.L., Rhoades, H.M., and Grabowski, J. (2001). Naltrexone and relapse prevention treatment for cocaine-dependent patients. *Addictive Behavior* 26: pp. 167–180. Dual DBPC at University of Texas showed naltrexone was safe and effective in treating cocaine addiction when used with a Coping protocol, *but naltrexone tended to be worse than placebo when used with abstinence.*

61. Kim, S.W. and Grant, J.E. (2001). An open naltrexone treatment study in pathological gambling disorder. *International Clinical Psychopharmacology* 16: pp. 285–289. Open label, showing naltrexone was safe and effective in treating gambling.

62. Kim, S.W., Grant, J.E., Adson, D.E., and Shin, Y.C. (2001). Double-blind naltrexone and placebo comparison study in the treatment of pathological gambling. *Biological Psychiatry* 49: pp. 914–921. DBPC trial showing naltrexone was safe and effective in treating gambling.

63. Mäkelä, R., Kallio, A., and Karhuvaara, S. (2001). Nalmefene in the treatment of heavy drinking. Programme & Abstracts of the 2001 ISAM Meeting, September 12–14, Trieste, Italy. ¶ Mäkelä, R. (2002). Multisite study of nalmefene for the treatment of heavy alcohol drinkers with impaired control. Presented at the 25th Annual Scientific Meeting of the Research Society on Alcoholism, San Francisco, CA, June 28–July 3, 2002. Nalmefene was safe and effective, especially in family history positive alcoholics, without extensive counseling.

64. Anton, R. (2002). Multisite study of nalmefene combined with modified motivational enhancement therapy in the treatment of outpatient alcoholics. Presented at the 25th Annual Scientific Meeting of the Research Society on Alcoholism, June 28–July 3, 2002, San Francisco,

CA. <u>Nalmefene was safe,</u> *but with "Motivational Enhancement Therapy (MET)" it was not significantly effective, probably because this therapy is generally enhancement of motivation for abstinence (see reference 78, below).*

65. Guardia, J. (2002). A double-blind placebo-controlled study of naltrexone in the treatment of alcohol-dependence. Results from a multicenter clinical trial. Proceedings of the 25th Annual Scientific Meeting of the Research Society on Alcoholism, San Francisco, CA, June 28–July 3, 2002. ¶ Guardia J., Caso, C., Arias, F., Gual., A., Sanahuja, J., Ramirez, M., Mengual, I., Gonzalvo, B., Segura, L., Trujols, J., and Casas, M. (2002). A double-blind, placebo-controlled study of naltrexone in the treatment of alcohol-dependence disorder: results from a multicenter clinical trial. *Alcoholism: Clinical and Experimental Research* 26: pp. 1381–1387. <u>Naltrexone was safe and effective in 202 patients reducing relapses to heavy drinking.</u> *No benefit until first drink while on medication.*

66. Kiefer, F. (2002). Randomized controlled trial of naltrexone, acamprosate, and the combination in the treatment of alcoholism. Proceedings of the 25th Annual Scientific Meeting of the Research Society on Alcoholism, San Francisco, CA, June 28–July 3, 2002. ¶ Kiefer, F., Jahn, H., Tarnaske, T., Helwig, H., Briken, P., Holzbach, R., Kampf, P., Stracke, R., Baehr, M., Naber, D., and Wiedemann, K. (2003). Comparing and combining naltrexone and acamprosate in relapse prevention of alcoholism: A double-blind, placebo-controlled study. *Archives of General Psychiatry* 60: pp. 92–99. ¶ Lesch, O.M. Diagnostic categories. European College of Neuropsychopharmacology Consensus Meeting, Nice, France, March 12–14, 2003. <u>DBPC study showing naltrexone was safe and effective alone and in combination with acamprosate, with naltrexone alone, or in combination with acamprosate better than acamprosate alone. An analysis of the results by Lesch showed that naltrexone benefited those who drank while on the medication</u> *but not those getting it with abstinence; acamprosate produced benefits with abstinence.*

67. Rukstalis, M. (2002). Comparing responses to alcohol, naltrexone in males and females. Proceedings of the 25th Annual Scientific Meeting of the Research Society on Alcoholism, San Francisco, CA, June 28–July 3, 2002. <u>Naltrexone was equally effective in men and women.</u>

68. Berglund, M. (2002). Medications for alcohol dependence. Treatment of Alcohol Abuse: An Evidence-based Review, from The Swedish Council on Technology in Health Care (SBU) Proceedings of the 25th Annual Scientific Meeting of the Research Society on Alcoholism, San Francisco, CA, June 28–July 3, 2002, p. 43. Berglund, M., Thelander, S., Salaspuro, M., Franck, J., Andréasson, S., and Öjehagen, A. (2003).

Treatment of alcohol abuse: An evidence-based review. *Alcoholism: Clinical and Experimental Research* 27: pp. 1645–1656. A search of all published and unpublished evidence showed naltrexone and acamprosate are the only medications for alcoholism with well-documented benefits. Naltrexone has been effective except when used with support of abstinence. In the 2003 report, a statistical analysis showed significantly better results with Coping/Cognitive Behavioral Therapy (CBT) than with Supportive therapy (p<0.05), and the meta-analysis showed a significant benefit over placebo with CBT.

69. Alkermes, Inc., press release. (2002). Alkermes reports positive results of phase II clinical trial of Vivitrex® for alcohol dependency at annual meeting of the American College of Neuropsychopharmacology. Jan. 3, 2002. <u>The company's sustained-release naltrexone was found to be safe and effective in treating alcoholism</u>.

70. Gastpar, M., Bonnet, U., Böning, J., Mann, K., Schmidt, L.G., Soyka, M., Wetterlingm,T., Kielstein, V., Labriola, D., and Croop. R. (2002). Lack of efficacy of naltrexone in the prevention of alcohol relapse, results from a German multicenter study. *Journal of Clinical Psychopharmacology* 22: pp. 592–598. *DBPC trial with strict abstinence, finding no benefit of naltrexone over placebo.*

71. Latt, N.C., Jurd, S., Houseman, J., and Wutzke, S.E. (2002). Naltrexone in alcohol dependence: a randomised controlled trial of effectiveness in a standard clinical setting. *The Medical Journal of Australia* 176: pp. 530–534. <u>DBPC trial without counseling found naltrexone to be safe and effective</u>.

72. Leavitt, S.B. (2002). Evidence for the efficacy of naltrexone in the treatment of alcohol dependence (alcoholism). Addiction Treatment Forum (March), Special Report. Available on the Internet at http://www.atforum.com/SiteRoot/pages/addiction_resources/naltrexoneWhitePaper.pdf **Review concluding naltrexone is safe and effective, except in combination with support of abstinence.**

73. Grant, J.E. and Kim, S.W. (2002). Effectiveness of pharmacotherapy for pathological gambling: A chart review. *Annals of Clinical Psychiatry* 14: pp. 155–161. <u>Open label naltrexone very effective against pathological gambling: 90.9 % success rate, vs. 45.5% for SSRI</u>.

74. Sinclair, J.D. and Salimov, R.M. (2002). New effective method of treatment of addiction to alcohol: extinction with the help of opiate receptor antagonists (in Russian). *Narcologia* 5: pp. 37–40. **Review concluding naltrexone is safe, effective, and works with extinction.**

75. Raymond, N.C,. Grant, J.E., and Coleman, R. (2002). Treatment of compulsive sexual behaviour with naltrexone and serotonin reuptake

inhibitors: two case studies. *International Clinical Psychopharmacology* 17: pp. 201–205. <u>Two case studies: naltrexone suppressed compulsive sexual behavior and urges in both the man and the woman, plus cocaine use in the woman.</u>

76. BioTie Therapies Corp., press release, April 24 (2003). Phase III clinical studies in alcoholism and alcohol abuse. http://www.biotie. com/en/research/dependence-disorders/nalmefene.html. <u>Large DBPC clinical trial found nalmefene without psychosocial therapy reduced heavy drinking days by half, highly significant difference from placebo. 570 patients in Finland and UK. Highly significantly greater reduction in heavy drinking days than with placebo. Also significantly more nalmefene than placebo patients rated much improved or very much improved in both Finland and UK separately and together.</u>

77. BioTie Therapies Corp, press release, May 30 (2003). ¶ Grant, J.E., Potenza, M.N., Hollander, E., Cunningham-Williams, R., Nurminen, T., Smits, G., and Kallio, A. (2006). Multicenter investigation of the opioid antagonist nalmefene in the treatment of pathological gambling. *American Journal of Psychiatry* 163: pp. 303–312. <u>Phase II DBPC trial with 207 subjects found 20 mg nalmefene tolerated well and effective in improving patient condition, in reducing compulsive feelings about gambling and thoughts about gambling; the level with nalmefene was about half that in the placebo group; 50 and 100 mg caused too many side effects.</u>

78. Anton, R.F., Moak, D.M., Latham, P.K., Myrick, D.L., and Waid, L.R. (2003). A double blind comparison of naltrexone combined with CBT or MET in the treatment of alcohol dependence. 26th Annual Scientific Meeting of the Research Society on Alcoholism, June 21–25, 2003, Fort Lauderdale, FL. *Alcoholism: Clinical and Experimental Research* 27 (supplement): p. 191A (abstract S170). <u>Dual DBPC trial showed naltrexone was effective with coping with drinking</u> *but not with Motivation Enhancement Therapy (MET). Anton in 2002 (reference 64) had gotten similar negative results with MET and nalmefene, confirming that MET is like Support of Abstinence and not a suitable protocol for opioid antagonists.*

79. O'Malley, S.S. (2003). Can alternative behavioral strategies and settings enhance the outcome of naltrexone and for whom? 26th Annual Scientific Meeting of the Research Society on Alcoholism, Fort Lauderdale, FL, June 21–25, 2003. *Alcoholism: Clinical and Experimental Research* 27 (supplement): p. 191A (abstract S172). <u>In one experiment, drinking alcohol while on naltrexone suppressed selection of further alcoholic beverages especially when the second presentation</u> *was not immediate* <u>but several hours later, showing that</u> *the effect was not from rational thinking after experiencing a lack of euphoria*

but rather caused by a slow mechanism (extinction or similar to extinction) started by the lack of reinforcement. In addition, naltrexone was effective in blocking heavy drinking in smokers taking the medicine for smoking and not intending nor instructed to reduce drinking. Author's conclusion: naltrexone should be used initially without abstinence to reduce drinking and only after that should abstinence become the goal.

80. Killeen T., Brady, K., Faldowski, R., Gold, P., Simpson, K. (2003). The effectiveness of naltrexone in a community treatment program. Abstracts of the 65th Annual Scientific Meeting, College on Problems of Drug Dependence, Bal Harbour, FL, June 14–19, 2003. ¶ Killeen, T., Brady, K., Faldowski, R., Gold, P., Simpson. K., and Anton, R. (2003). The efficacy of naltrexone in a community treatment program. *Alcoholism: Clinical and Experimental Research* 27 (supplement), p. 146a (abstract 846). DBPC trial found naltrexone significantly improved drinking-related outcomes in patients drinking during the two weeks before treatment began *but not in patients abstinent at that time of treatment onset.* Authors conclude "naltrexone may be more effective for patients who fail to abstain upon entry into treatment for alcohol abuse." Naltrexone is best for "those that are actively drinking at the time of initiation of treatment."

81. Krupitsky, E., Zvartau, E., Masalov, D., Tsoi, M., Burakov, A., Egorova, V., Didenko, T. , Romanova, T., Ivanova, E., Bespalov, A., Verbitskaya, E., Neznanov, N., Grinenko, A., and Woody, G. (2003). A double-blind, placebo controlled trial of naltrexone for heroin addiction treatment in St. Petersburg, Russia. Proceeding of NIDA-Pavlov Workshop "Pharmacotherapies for Addiction: Basic and Clinical Science," St. Petersburg, Russia, Sept. 28–Oct. 1., 2003. ¶ Krupitsky, E.M., Zvartau, E.E., Masalov, D.V., Tsoi. M.V., Burakov, A.M., Egorova, V.Y., Didenko, T.Y., Romanova, T.N., Ivanova, E.B., Bespalov, A.Y., Verbitskaya, E.V., Neznanov, N.G., Grinenko, A.Y., O'Brien, C.P., and Woody, G.E. (2004). Naltrexone for heroin dependence treatment in St. Petersburg, Russia. *Journal of Substance Abuse Treatment* 26: pp. 285–94. ¶ Krupitsky, E., Zvartau, E., Masalov, D., Tsoy, M., Burakov, A., Egorova, V., Didenko, T., Romanova, T., Ivanova, E., Bespalov, A., Verbitskaya, E.V., Neznanov, N.G., Grinenko, A.Y., O'Brien, C.P., and Woody, G.E. (2006). Naltrexone with or without fluoxetine for preventing relapse to heroin addiction in St. Petersburg, Russia. *Journal of Substance Abuse Treatment* 31: pp. 319–328. DBPC trial found *addicts sampled opiates while on naltrexone* but a significantly lower percentage than among placebo patients relapsed to full-scale drug addiction. Krupitsky agrees that results support extinction.

82. Oslin, D.W., Berrettini, W., Kranzler, H.R., Pettinati, H., Gelernter, J., Volpicelli, J.R., O'Brien, C.P. (2003). A functional polymorphism of the μ-opioid response in alcohol-dependent patients. *Neuropsychopharmacology* **28**: pp. 1546–1552. <u>Combination of three previous trials, one published positive results (Monterosso et al., 2001), one published negative results (Kranzler et al., 2000) and one unpublished. Together they showed significant benefits from naltrexone on relapse rate and time to first relapse, with significantly better results in patients with the A/G or G/G allele than the A/A allele at the gene for mu receptors, but no medication by genotype interaction.</u> *No significant effect of naltrexone on abstinence.*

83. Alkermes, Inc., press release (December 8, 2003). Alkermes Announces Statistically Significant Reduction in Heavy Drinking in Alcohol Dependent Patients in Phase III Clinical Trial of Vivitrex®. ¶ Garbutt, J.C., Kranzler, H.R., O'Malley, S.S., Gastfriend, D.R., Pettinati, H.M., Silverman, B.L., Loewy, L.W., and Ehrich, E.W. for the Vivitrex® Study Group (2005). Efficacy and tolerability of long-acting injectable naltrexone for alcohol dependence: A randomized controlled trial. *JAMA* **293**: pp. 1617–1625. <u>DBPC study of 624 alcoholics. Significant 48% reduction in drinking in slow release naltrexone-treated males, but not significant in females. Compared with placebo, 380 mg of long-acting naltrexone resulted in a 25% decrease in the event rate of heavy drinking days (P = .03)(n=205). Lower dose (190 mg) just failed to reach significance.</u> Better results with pretreatment abstinence.

84. Laaksonen E. (2004). Comparing disulfiram, acamprosate, and naltrexone treatment of alcoholism. International Society on Addictive Medicine (ISAM) meeting, Helsinki, Finland, June 2–5, 2004. <u>Naltrexone was safe and more effective than acamprosate.</u>

85. Bouza, C., Magro, A., Muñoz, A., and Amate, J.M. (2004). Efficacy and safety of naltrexone and acamprosate in the treatment of alcohol dependence: a systematic review. *Addiction* **99**: pp. 811–828. **Review concluding that "both acamprosate and naltrexone are effective as adjuvant therapies for alcohol dependence in adults. Acamprosate appears to be especially useful in a therapeutic approach targeted at achieving abstinence, whereas naltrexone seems more indicated in programmes geared to controlled consumption."**

86. Deas, D., May, K., Randall, C., Johnson, N., and Anton, R. (2005). Naltrexone treatment of adolescent alcoholics: An open-label pilot study. *Journal of Child and Adolescent Psychopharmacology* **15**: pp. 723–728. <u>Small open-label study of outpatient 13- to 17-year-old adolescent alcoholics without detox found naltrexone is safe and produced a significant reduction in alcohol drinking in the 6 weeks.</u>

87. Rubio, G., Ponce, G., Rodriquez-Jiménez, R., Jiménez-Arriero, M.A., Hoenicka, J., and Palomo, T. (2005). Clinical predictors of response to naltrexone in alcoholic patients: Who benefits most from treatment with naltrexone? *Alcohol and Alcoholism* 40: pp. 227–233. Three-month open trial in 336 men, looking at results in last 28 days. "Predictors of a positive response to NTX [naltrexone] treatment were family history of alcoholism (P = 0.010), early age at onset of drinking problems (P = 0.014) and comorbid use of other drugs of abuse (P < 0.001)," generally things that correlate with poor results in treatment.

88. Sinclair, J.D. (2005). The second generation of anti-relapse drugs: Opioidergic compounds: Clinical. In: R. Spanagel and K. Mann (eds): *Drugs for Relapse Prevention of Alcoholism*, in the series *Milestones in Drug Therapy*. Basel, Switzerland; Birkhäuser, pp. 125–134. **Review concluding "Nalmefene appears to be an appropriate medicine for preventing alcohol abuse but not for maintaining abstinence."**

89. Srisurapanont, M. and Jarusuraisin, N. (2005). Naltrexone for the treatment of alcoholism: a meta-analysis of randomized controlled trials. *International Journal of Neuropsychopharmacol* 8: pp. 267–280. **Review concluding that naltrexone is effective for preventing drinking alcoholics relapsing to heavy drinking but not for stopping the first sampling in alcoholics who are abstaining.**

90. Hernandez-Avila, C.A., Song, C., Kuo, L., Tennen, H., Armeli, S., and Kranzler. H.R. (2006). Targeted versus daily naltrexone: secondary analysis of effects on average daily drinking. *Alcoholism: Clinical and Experimental Research* 30: pp. 860–865. DBPC trial, n=150, of naltrexone with Coping with Drinking found naltrexone was effective especially with targeted use. Only targeted, not daily naltrexone helped women.

91. Anton, R.F., O'Malley, S.S., Ciraulo, D.C., Cisler, R.A., Couper, D., Donovan, D.M., Gastfriend, D.R., Hosking, J.D., Johnson, B.A., LoCastro, J.S., Longabaugh, R., Mason, B.J., Mattson, M.E., Miller, W.R., Pettinati, H.M., Randall, C.L., Swift, R., Weiss, R.D., Williams, L.D., and Zweben, A.Z., for the COMBINE Study Research Group (2006). Combined pharmacotherapies and behavioral interventions for alcohol dependence: The COMBINE study: A randomized controlled trial. *JAMA* 295: pp. 2003–2017. Largest DBPC trial in addiction (n=1383 recently detoxified alcoholics) showed naltrexone with minimal medical intervention was best at increasing days of abstinence and reducing heavy drinking days. *Intensive (20 hours) therapy without medication helped increase abstinence but did not reduce heavy drinking and did not make naltrexone better (the partially abstinence-oriented therapy actually tended to reduce the benefit). Acamprosate had*

no significant benefits and taken at the same time as naltrexone did not help naltrexone.

92. O'Neil, G., Parsons, Z., O'Neil, P., Xu, J.X., and Hulse, G. (2006). Naltrexone implants for amphetamine dependence. 3rd Stapleford International Addiction Conference on: Latest developments in effective medical treatments for addiction, Berlin, Germany, March 18–19, 2006. <u>Small open-label trial found naltrexone safe and effective in 73% of amphetamine addicts, reducing their injection days from 58.6 in the 3 months before to 17.1 in the 3 months on naltrexone (p<0.0004).</u>

93. Grüsser, S.M., Ziegler, S., Thalemann, C., and Partecke, L. (2006). Naltrexone as anticraving treatment: A psychophysiological evaluation. 3rd Stapleford International Addiction Conference on: Latest developments in effective medical treatments for addiction, Berlin, Germany, March 18–19, 2006. <u>Naltrexone implants in detoxified opiate addicts produced significantly fewer relapses than levomethadone implants, better psychological results, and subsequently less emotional-motivational involvement when seeing stimuli related to opiate use.</u>

94. Singh, J. (2006). Naltrexone implants—an Indian experience. 3rd Stapleford International Addiction Conference on: Latest developments in effective medical treatments for addiction, Berlin, Germany, March 18–19, 2006. <u>Naltrexone implants worked well in patients who had been abusing opiates or partial opiate agonists (pentazocine, buprenorphine).</u>

95. Kunøe, N., Lobmaier, P., and Waal, H. (2006). A matched case-control study of naltrexone implants for relapse prevention in detoxified opioid addicts. 3rd Stapleford International Addiction Conference on: Latest developments in effective medical treatments for addiction, Berlin, Germany, March 18–19, 2006. <u>Controlled pilot study suggesting "that naltrexone implants are an effective aid in preventing opioid relapse after completion of inpatient treatment."</u>

96. Revill, J. (2006). An audited 24 month comparison of the George O'Neill 3-vial naltrexone implant with supervised methadone, in a general practice population. 3rd Stapleford International Addiction Conference on: Latest developments in effective medical treatments for addiction, Berlin, Germany, March 18–19, 2006. <u>100% of 25 naltrexone patients but only 26% of 25 adequate-dose methadone patients had urines clear of illicit opiates at the end of 2 years.</u>

97. Grant, J.E., Potenza, M.N., Hollander, E., Cunningham-Williams, R., Nurminen, T., Smits, G., and Kallio, A. (2006). Multicenter investigation of the opioid antagonist nalmefene in the treatment of pathological gambling. *American Journal of Psychiatry* 163: pp. 303–312.

¶ Grant, J.E., Odlaug, B.L., Potenza, M.N., Hollander, E., and Kim, S.W. (2010). Nalmefene in the treatment of pathological gambling: A multi-centre, double-blind, placebo-controlled study. *The British Journal of Psychiatry* 197: pp. 330–331. DBPC showing nalmefene produced significant reduction in severity of pathological gambling: success rate ("much improved") =59.2% with nalmefene; 34% with placebo. The low dose (25 mg) was efficacious and well tolerated; higher doses produced intolerable side effects. 66% dropout rate (reported in study 17).

98. Somaxon (press release). Somaxon Pharmaceuticals Reports Positive Results From a Pilot Phase 2 Study of Oral Nalmefene in Smoking Cessation, San Diego, CA, July 26, 2006. DBPC study of 76 smokers; first report found no significant benefits from nalmefene but notes that one of the two nalmefene groups (40 mg) was numerically superior to placebo group (80 mg was not). Second report of the same DBPC trial reanalyzed, showing patients actually taking 40 mg nalmefene for a week did significantly better than placebo.

99. Morley, K.C., Teesson, M., Reid, S.C., Sannibale, C., Thomson, C., Phung, N., Weltman, M., Bell, J.R., Richardson, K., and Haber, P.S. (2006). Naltrexone versus acamprosate in the treatment of alcohol dependence: A multi-centre, randomized, double-blind, placebo-controlled trial. *Addiction* 10: pp. 1451–1462. DBPC on 169 Australian alcoholics finds naltrexone significantly delays relapse to heavy drinking *but not time to first drink.* "The results of this study support the efficacy of naltrexone in the relapse prevention of alcoholism amongst those with low levels of clinical depression and alcohol dependence severity. No effect of acamprosate was found in our sample."

100. Comer, S.D., Sullivan, M.A., Yu, E., Rothenberg, J.L., Kleber, H.D., Kampman, K., Dachis, C., and O'Brian, C.P. (2006). Injectable, sustained-release naltrexone for the treatment of opioid dependence: A randomized, placebo-controlled trial. *Archives of General Psychiatry* 63: pp. 210–218. DBPC with 2 doses of sustained-release naltrexone in 60 patients for 8 weeks. In a dose-dependent manner, naltrexone significantly improved retention in the study, and, when missing urine samples were considered positive, was safe and effective in reducing use of opioids, methadone, cocaine, benzodiazepines, and amphetamine.

101. O'Malley, S.S., Sinha, R., Grilo, C.M., Capone, C., Farren, C.K., McKee, S.A., Rounsaville, B.J., and Wu, R. (2007). Naltrexone and cognitive behavioural coping skills therapy for the treatment of alcohol drinking and eating disorders features in alcohol-dependent women: A randomized controlled trial. *Alcoholism, Clinical and Experimental Research* 31: pp. 625–634. DBPC on 103 women

alcoholics, 29 comorbid with eating disorders. "Naltrexone may be of benefit to women who are unable to maintain total abstinence from alcohol." Among those drinking, naltrexone significantly delayed the time to the second relapse and the time to the third relapse *but had no effect on the abstinence rate.* There was a tendency (p=0.06) for more loss of weight (body mass index) with naltrexone than with placebo. Both groups had improvement in eating disorders, but there were no significant differences between groups.

102. Baros, A.M., Lathan, P.K., Moak, D.H., Voronin, K., and Anton, R.F. (2007). What role does measuring medication compliance play in evaluating the efficacy of naltrexone? *Alcoholism, Clinical and Experimental Research* 31: pp. 596–603. DBPC on 160 patients with coping. Naltrexone significantly better than placebo in the most compliant patients, with about twice as much treatment effect than in the less compliant patients.

103. Gelernter, J., Gueorguieva, R., Kranzler, H.R., Zhan, H., Cramer, J., Rosenheck, R., and Krystal, J.H. (2007). Opioid receptor gene (OPRM1, OPRK1, and OPRD1) variants and response to naltrexone treatment for alcohol dependence: Results from the VA Cooperative Study. *Alcoholism, Clinical and Experimental Research* 31: 555–563. DBPC study of 215 subjects who gave DNA samples from the previously reported trial (#54). "Although NTX [naltrexone] had no significant effect on relapse to heavy drinking in the overall sample in CSP 425 [#54], it significantly reduced relapse in the subgroup that provided DNA for analysis." There were no published interactions with receptor type but a significant effect with the OPRD1 T921, helping the GG and AG genotypes but not with the AA homozygotic genotype.

104. Karhuvaara, S., Simojoki, K., Antti, V., Rosberg, M., Löyttyniemi, E., Nurminen, T., Kallio, A., and Rauno, R. (2007). Targeted nalmefene with simple medical management in the treatment of heavy drinkers: A randomized double-blind placebo-controlled multicenter study. *Alcoholism: Clinical and Experimental Research* 31: pp. 1–9. DBPC trial on 403 subjects for 7 months without intensive counseling, nalmefene decreased drinking more than placebo (p=0.0065), reduced the risk of heavy drinking 32.4% (95% CI: 14.2–46.8%; p=0.003) more than placebo, and progressively reduced markers that increased in placebo group (GGT p=0.009 and ALT p=0.002).

105. Toneatto, T., Brands, B., Selby, P., and Sinclair, D. (2007). A randomized, double-blind, placebo-controlled trial of naltrexone in the treatment of concurrent alcohol dependence and pathological gambling. Preliminary report at http://clinicaltrials.gov/ct/show/NCT0032680 7;jsessionid=5057BD239D3C012928C684806432A673?order=20.

Naltrexone failed to provide significant benefits in patients with both alcoholism and pathological gambling.

106. Jayaram-Lindström, N., Wennberg, P., Hurd, Y.L., and Franck, J. (2004). Effects of naltrexone on the subjective response to amphetamine in healthy volunteers. *Journal of Clinical Psychopharmacology* 24: pp. 665–669. ¶ Jayaram-Lindström, N., Konstenius, M., Eksborg, S., Beck, O., Hammarberg, A., and Franck, J. (2008). Naltrexone attenuates the subjective effects of amphetamine in patients with amphetamine dependence. *Neuropsychopharmacology* 33: pp. 1856–1863 (advance online publication 24 October 2007; doi: 10.1038/sj.npp.1301572.) DBPC on 20 subjects. "Pretreatment with naltrexone also significantly blocked the craving for dexamphetamine (p<0.001). . . .The potential of naltrexone as an adjunct pharmaceutical for amphetamine dependence is promising."

107. Jayaram-Lindström, N, Wennberg, P., Hurd, Y.L., and Franck J. (2005). An open clinical trial of naltrexone for amphetamine dependence: compliance and tolerability. *Nordic Journal of Psychiatry* 59: pp. 167–171. ¶ Jayaram-Lindström, N., Hammarberg, A., Beck, O., and Franck, J. (2008). Naltrexone for the treatment of amphetamine dependence: A randomized placebo-controlled trial. *American Journal of Psychiatry* 165: pp. 1442–1448 (doi:10.1176/appi.ajp.2008.08020304) ¶ Jayaram-Lindström, N. (2007). Evaluation of naltrexone as a treatment for amphetamine dependence. Dissertation from Karolinska University Hospital, presented Dec. 18, 2007. ¶ Jayaram-Lindström, N., Hammarberg, A., Beck, O., and Franck, J. (2008). Naltrexone for the treatment of amphetamine dependence: A randomized, placebo-controlled trial. *American Journal of Psychiatry* 165: pp. 1442–1448. After tests with volunteers and a compliance test with amphetamine addicts, a 12 week randomized DBPC clinical trial on addicts eventually reduced craving and produced fewer urine positives for amphetamines. Swedish medical council gave this work the award for the best clinical study in 2007.

108. Pallesen, S., Molde, H., Arnestad, H.M., Laberg, J.C., Skutle, A., Iversen, E., Støylen, I.J., Kvale, G., and Holsten, F. (2007). Outcome of pharmacological treatments of pathological gambling: A review and meta-analysis. *Journal of Clinical Psychopharmacology* 27: pp. 357–364. **Pharmacological intervention (including studies with opiate antagonists, antidepressants, and mood stabilizers) produced a significant effect size (0.78; 95% confidence interval 0.62–0.92) relative to no treatment/placebo. "Pharmacological intervention may be an adequate treatment alternative in pathological gambling."**

109. Laaksonen, E., Koski-Jännes, A., Salaspuro, M., Ahtinen, H., and Alho H. (2007). A randomized, multicenter, open-label, comparative

trial of disulfiram, naltrexone and acamprosate in the treatment of alcohol dependence. *Alcohol and Alcoholism* 43: pp. 53–61. Open-label comparison of disulfiram, naltrexone, and acamprosate in treating alcoholics, with no controls. All three medications produced significant reductions in drinking and improved quality of life. Naltrexone patients were instructed to drink normally but take naltrexone before drinking; disulfiram patients were instructed to abstain and warned of severe reactions if they did drink: naturally, the disulfiram patients remained abstinent longer and, especially in the earlier part of the study, drank less.

110. Pallesen, S., Molde, H., Arnestad, H.M., Laberg, J.C., Skutle, A., Iversen, E., Støylen, I.J., Kvale, G., and Holsten, F. (2007). Outcome of pharmacological treatments of pathological gambling: A review and meta-analysis. *Journal of Clinical Psychopharmacology* 27: pp. 357–364. **Meta-analysis of studies with opiate antagonists, antidepressants, and mood stabilizers showed pharmacotherapy produced a significant effect size (0.78; 95% confidence interval 0.62–0.92) relative to no treatment/placebo. "Pharmacological intervention may be an adequate treatment alternative in pathological gambling."**

111. Tidey, J.W., Monti, P.M., Rohsenow, D.J., Gwaltney, C.J., Miranda, R. Jr., McGeary. J.E., MacKillop, J., Swift, R.M., Abrams, D.B., Shiffman, S., and Paty, J.A. (2008). Moderators of naltrexone's effects on drinking, urge, and alcohol effects in non-treatment-seeking heavy drinkers in the natural environment. *Alcoholism: Clinical and Experimental Research* 32: pp. 58–66. (doi:10.1111/j.1530-0277.2007.00545.x). DBPC on 180 heavy drinkers (63% alcohol dependent) for 3 weeks found naltrexone reduced drinking days and heavy drinking days, plus craving in early onset drinkers and time between drinks in patients with more alcoholic relatives.

112. Grant, J.E., Kim, S.W., and Hartman, B.K. (2008). A double-blind, placebo-controlled study of the opiate antagonist naltrexone in the treatment of pathological gambling urges. *Journal of Clinical Psychiatry* 69: pp. 783–789. An 18 week DBPC with 3 doses of naltrexone (50, 100 and 150 mg/day) on 77 pathological gamblers. Results from the different doses did not differ but naltrexone produced significantly lower PG-YBOCS than 19 placebo patients (p=0.0097), urges to gamble (0.0057) and gambling behavior (0.0134), plus better Clinical Global–Improvement scale values (CGI-I, p=0.0080). Among 49 completers, naltrexone did better than placebo on all measures. Supports extinction, in contrast to authors' earlier studies when failure to see benefits in first week or two was blamed on the dose being too low.

113. O'Malley, S.S., Robin, R.W., Levenson, A.L., GreyWolf, I., Chance. L.E., Hodgkinson, C.A., Romano, D., Robinson, J., Meandzija, B.,

Stillner, V., Wu, R., and Goldman, D. (2008). Naltrexone alone and with sertraline for the treatment of alcohol dependence in Alaska natives and non-natives residing in rural settings: A randomized controlled trial. *Alcoholism: Clinical Experimental Research* 32: 1271 (do i:10.1111/j.1530-0277.2008.00682). DBPC trial on 101 Alaskans including 68 natives showed naltrexone produced significant benefits over placebo including total abstinence, but sertraline plus naltrexone was no better than just naltrexone.

114. Anton, R.F. (2008). Naltrexone for the management of alcohol dependence. *New England Journal of Medicine* 359:   pp. 715–721. **Review supporting use of naltrexone in light of results from Project Combine.**

115. Anton, R.F., Oroszi, G., O'Malley, S.S., Couper, D., Swift, R., Pettinati, H., and Goldman, D. (2008). An evaluation of mu-opioid receptor (OPRM1) as a predictor of naltrexone response in the treatment of alcohol dependence: results from the Combined Pharmacotherapies and Behavioral Interventions for Alcohol Dependence (COMBINE) study. *Archives of General Psychiatry* 65: pp. 135–144. The Asp40 allele is a selective marker for naltrexone efficacy, improving the success rate of naltrexone without intensive counseling to 87.1%. Naltrexone was not effective in people with the Asn40/Asn40 genotype. The Asp40 allele did not make a difference in subjects treated with naltrexone plus intensive counseling, perhaps explaining why some other trials that included counseling did not find markers.

116. Petrovic, P., Pleger, B., Seymour, B., Kloppel, S., De Martino, B., Critchley, H., Dolan, R.J. (2008). Blocking central opiate function modulates hedonic impact and anterior cingulate response to rewards and losses. *Journal of Neuroscience* 28: pp. 10509–10516 (doi:10.1523/JNEUROSCI.2807-08.2008). Naloxone blocked reward from gambling.

117. Pettinati, H.M., Kampman, K.M., Lynch, K.G., Suh, J.J., Dachis, C.A., Oslin, D.W., and O'Brien, C.P. (2008). Gender differences with high-dose naltrexone in patients with co-occurring cocaine and alcohol dependence. *Journal of Substance Abuse Treatment* 34: pp. 378–390. DBPC trial of 12 weeks with 116 men and 48 women with co-occurring cocaine and alcohol dependence of 150 mg/day naltrexone plus BRENDA. Significant Gender x Medication effect for cocaine treatment, with naltrexone helping men with alcohol and cocaine but making women worse.

118. O'Brien, C. (2008). Prospects for a genomic approach to the treatment of alcoholism: *Archives of General Psychiatry* 65: pp. 132–133. **Review covering the OPRM1 marker for naltrexone efficacy.**

119. Eskapa, R. (2008). *The Cure for Alcoholism*. Dallas: BenBella Books, 320 pages. **Book telling about the effective use of naltrexone and nalmefene for extinguishing the underlying cause for craving alcohol and for being unable to control drinking.**

120. Mann, K., Kiefer, F., Lemenager, T., and Vollstädt-Klein, S. (2009). Searching for the acamprosate and naltrexone responder: results from the Predict Study 12th Congress of ESBRA, Helsinki, Finland, June 7–10, 2009. Abstracts. p. 38 (119). <u>DBPC study with medical maintenance only finds naltrexone significantly delays the first episode of heavy drinking, especially in alcoholics showing high reactions on an fMRI test to alcohol-related cues (as predicted by extinction theory).</u> *Naltrexone did not delay the time to taking the first drink.*

121. Kim, S.G.,, Kim, C.M., Choi, S.W., Jae, Y.M., Lee, H.G., Son, B.Ki., Kim, J.G., Choi, Y.S., Kim, H.O., Kim, S.Y., Oslin, D. (2009). A mu opioid receptor gene polymorphism (A118G) and naltrexone treatment response in adherent Korean alcohol-dependent patients. *Psychopharmacology* **201**: pp. 611–618. <u>Open-label study showing a higher therapeutic effect of naltrexone in Korean alcoholics with the Asp40 variant of the A118G polymorphism, consistent with results in individuals of European descent,</u> *but no differences in abstinence rates.*

122. Grant J., Kim, S., and Odlaug, B. (2009). A double-blind, placebo-controlled study of the opiate antagonist, naltrexone, in the treatment of kleptomania. *Biological Psychiatry* **65**: pp. 600–606 (DOI: 10.1016/j.biopsych.2008.11.022). <u>DBPC showing positive results from treating kleptomania with naltrexone.</u>

123. Sinclair, D. (2009). Selecting patients and replacing detoxification: How opioid antagonists work in treatment. Proceedings of the Annual Meeting of the International Society on Addiction Medicine (ISAM), Calgary, Alberta, Canada, Sept. 23–29, 2009. **Review showing that opioid antagonists have had no significant effect before the first alcohol is drunk while on the medication, in agreement with extinction theory but contrary to common practice by many clinicians.**

124. Eskapa, R. (2009). Introducing naltrexone in developing countries and among endogenous people. Proceedings of the Annual Meeting of the International Society on Addiction Medicine (ISAM), Calgary, Alberta, Canada, Sept. 23–29, 2009. <u>Naltrexone has been safe and effective, with a 75% success rate, when introduced in northern India with an extinction protocol including no prior detox and instruction to take naltrexone always before drinking but only when drinking is expected.</u>

125. Alho, H., Lahti, T., Sinclair, D., and Halme, J. (2010). Treatment of gambling dependence with naltrexone pharmacotherapy and brief intervention: preliminary results. Proceedings of the International

Gambling Conference meeting, Oakland, New Zealand, Feb. 23–26, 2010. ¶ Lahti, T., Halme, J. Pankakoski, M., Sinclair D., and Alho, H. (2010). Treatment of pathological gambling with naltrexone pharmacotherapy and brief intervention: A pilot study. *Psychopharmacology Bulletin* 43: pp. 35–44. Open-label trial of naltrexone with an extinction protocol (taken only when gambling) plus pharmacologically enhanced reinforcement of healthy alternative behaviors found highly significant decrease in reported gambling problems and reported BDI depression ratings.

Information for Prescribing Naltrexone

Dear Doctor:

The patient carrying this letter to you would like your support in a highly effective treatment for alcoholism: it is called TSM and has a 78% cure rate. It requires a prescription for naltrexone.

The FDA approved naltrexone in 1995 for use in the treatment of alcohol dependence. Important new evidence has been obtained since then about how to use naltrexone much more effectively.

First, a dual double-blind clinical trial[1] showed that the usual protocol of having patients take naltrexone while abstinent is not effective. To be effective, naltrexone and alcohol must be in the system concurrently. Therefore, naltrexone must always be taken one hour before consuming alcohol. The resulting mechanism of extinction then gradually reduces craving and drinking over several months, and produces a natural detoxification—thus avoiding the distress and complications of rapid withdrawal. The result has been replicated and is consistent with findings from nearly all of the 82 clinical trials conducted to date.[2]

Second, it is now clear that naltrexone can be prescribed by doctors without an accompanying program of intensive counseling. Naltrexone was originally approved by the FDA as an adjunct within comprehensive programs of alcoholism treatment. The results of **Project Combine (*JAMA.* 2006),** the largest clinical trial in the alcohol field, showed, however, that naltrexone was effective without the need for intensive counseling where patients are treated in general medical settings.[3]

The bottom line is that TSM has proven to be far more successful than any other treatment for alcoholism on the market to date, and your patient is keen to try this method.

Detailed information can be found in Dr. Roy Eskapa's book *The Cure for Alcoholism*; instructions to physicians can be downloaded on the internet at: www.cthreefoundation.org. Additional documentation may be requested by emailing: royeskapa@yahoo.com.

David Sinclair, Ph.D.
National Institute for Health
and Welfare (THL)
Helsinki, Finland

Stephen Cox, MD
Head of the National Anxiety Association
University of Kentucky, Lexington, KY

1 Heinälä, P., Alho, H., Kiianmaa, K., Lönnqvist, J., Kuoppasalmi, K., and Sinclair, J.D. (2001). Targeted use of Naltrexone without prior detoxification in the treatment of alcohol dependence: A factorial double-blind placebo-controlled trial. *Journal of Clinical Psychopharmacology* 21(3): 287-292.

2 Sinclair, J. D. (2001). Evidence about the use of Naltrexone and for different ways of using it in the treatment of alcoholism. *Alcohol and Alcoholism* 36: 2-10; Sinclair, D. and F.Fantozzi (2004). Relapse prevention with extinction. In: Relapse prevention in the treatment of alcohol dependence. *Personalit Dipendenze* 10 (fasc.II): 219-243.

3 Anton RF, O'Malley, SS Ciraulo DC, Cisler RA. Couper.

How Addiction to Alcohol Is Learned

(All biological images courtesy of Dr. David Sinclair)

Understanding how the Sinclair Method works is easy
once you understand how an addiction develops in the first place.

THE ILLUSTRATIONS in this appendix show the rewiring of the nervous system that causes drinking to go from a weak behavior occurring only occasionally to being such a powerful response that it is almost automatic, easily stimulated, and nearly impossible to interrupt or control. They show the development of an addiction.

Understanding Addiction and the Sinclair Method

Comprehending the process by which addiction to alcohol develops was the key for discovering the Sinclair Method. Readers using the Method should also understand the process. The Method and the mechanism of addiction are difficult to explain verbally,

but many people find them rather easy to understand from illustrations, so it is important to show them rather than just describe them.

It is hard to explain them in words because language itself imposes upon us a particular theory of what causes behavior. From ancient times people have imagined that there was a little homunculus in the head who actually saw the world and rationally decided what one

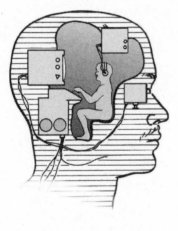

should do on the basis of expected pleasure and pain. Our language still reflects this rational-choice theory of behavior.

Once alcohol drinking has developed into alcoholism, it no longer is under rational control. Mistakenly treating alcoholism as rational behavior has probably resulted in more harm to alcoholics than any other single factor. If a homunculus rationally decides whether or not to drink on the basis of maximizing pleasure and minimizing pain, there is a simple cure for alcoholism: punish drinking; increase the pain produced by drinking. We have treated alcoholism with punishment for thousands of years. It has not worked yet. Nevertheless, we continue because it is so...rational.

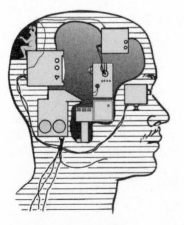

In 1981 Sinclair wrote a book with the view shown here of the homunculus, now somewhat crowded.* By then the mechanics of the visual system were understood to be something like color television, the auditory system like a stereo, and output something like a computer. Most people still tended to imagine decisions being made rationally by a homunculus. The book showed, however, that behavior could be explained as only the

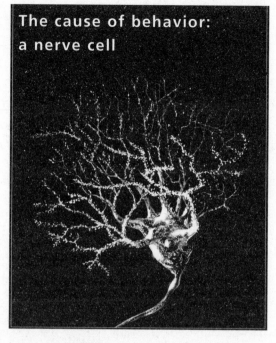

The cause of behavior: a nerve cell

output of nerve cells, without any homunculus even making the decisions and with pleasure not as a goal but an aftereffect of some behaviors.

Francis Crick (co-discoverer of the structure of DNA) called this idea the "Astonishing Hypothesis." Crick admitted, "I myself find it difficult at times to avoid the idea of a homunculus. One slips into it so easily.... People often prefer to believe that there is a disembodied soul that, in some utterly mysterious way, does the actual seeing.... Our Astonishing Hypothesis says... it's all done by nerve cells."[†]

All behavior is caused by the firing of nerve cells. This is the starting point for an understanding of addiction.

When the doctor taps your knee and your foot rises, the behavior is caused by the firing of nerve cells. That is the way you are wired.

---

* Sinclair, J. D. (1981) *The Rest Principle: A Neurophysiological Theory of Behavior*, Hillsdale, N.J.: Lawrence Erlbaum Associates.

[†] Crick, F. (1994) *The Astonishing Hypothesis*, London: Simon & Schuster, p. 258 and p. 33.

When you raise a wine glass to your lips and drink, the behavior is caused by the firing of nerve cells.

Pictures help liberate our thinking. Language alone leads us back to a rational homunculus, but the behavior of the alcoholic is not rational. Pictures free us from these restrictions, making it possible for us to understand how alcohol drinking can come to dominate our behavior.

The Scene of the Action

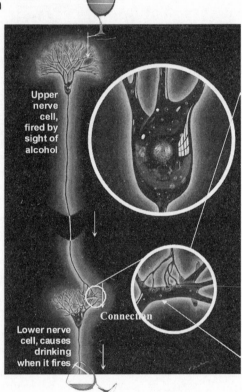

The rewiring that produces addiction occurs at the connection where one nerve cell makes another one fire.

The connection shown in the lower circle here, between a nerve cell fired by the sight of alcohol and one that triggers drinking when it fires, is initially weak. *The upper nerve cell may have to fire one hundred times to make the lower one fire and thus start drinking.* Before addiction develops, just seeing alcohol seldom results in drinking.

The addiction develops because the connection becomes more effective, until *the upper nerve cell only has to fire once to make the lower cell fire.*

In order to see the changes in the connection, we have to go closer. Imagine that you are standing on the lower nerve cell and looking off into the distance . . .

Here is what you see.

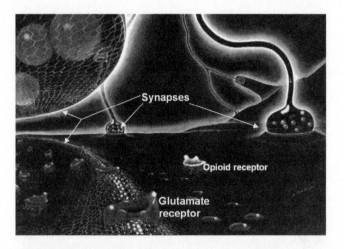

You are standing on the lower nerve cell, looking out at synapses from the upper cell. On the left, one synapse is so close that you can look inside it.

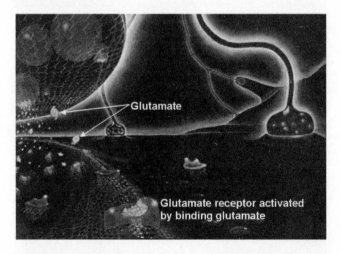

Here, the upper nerve cell has fired, releasing molecules of glutamate from the spheres where they are stored. The glutamate diffuses across the space inside of the synapse. If glutamate touches and binds to a glutamate receptor on the surface of the lower nerve cell, then the receptor is activated. *If enough receptors are activated*

(by the upper nerve cell firing one hundred times), the lower cell itself fires, and its firing causes alcohol drinking.

The alcohol is absorbed and then diffuses around the brain...

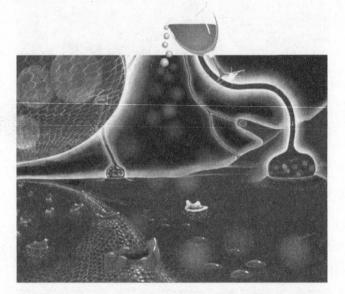

...where it causes some nerve cells (not shown) to release endorphin.

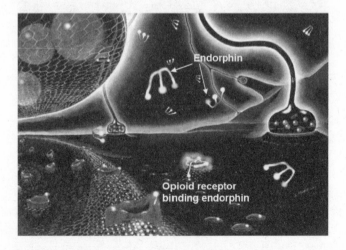

Endorphin binding to an opioid receptor triggers the mechanism called reinforcement...

Reinforcement

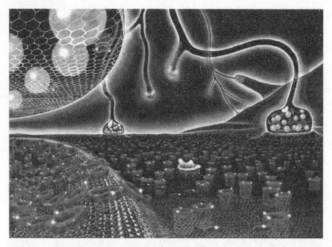

Reinforcement produces new glutamate receptors on the lower nerve cell and changes the upper one so it releases more glutamate when it fires. *Now the upper cell only has to fire ten times (not one hundred) to make the lower one fire.*

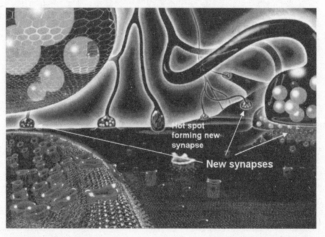

Reinforcement also produces new synapses that help the strengthened existing synapses to make the lower nerve cell fire. Repeated reinforcement causes the connection to become strong enough that the upper nerve cell *only has to fire once* to make the lower nerve cell fire and thus to start drinking. *The nervous system has become rewired so the person is now an alcoholic.*

The connection shown here—between seeing alcohol and starting to drink—is only one of many connections contributing to the development of alcoholism. For example, endorphin also reinforces the connections onto nerve cells that cause the acquisition of alcohol, and thus going to the pub or the liquor store becomes a way of life. Endorphin reinforces the connections firing nerve cells that cause thinking about alcohol. Consequently, thoughts about alcohol pop up continually and spontaneously, not because of any rational choice but because that is how the person has become wired.

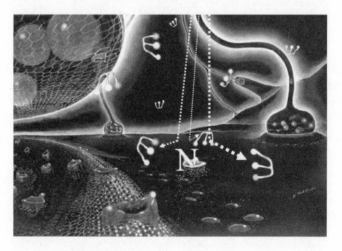

Prevention of Alcoholism

The development of alcoholism can be prevented by blocking the reinforcement from the endorphin released by alcohol.

Naltrexone or nalmefene (N), taken before drinking, blocks the opioid receptors; like putting the wrong key in a lock, it does not activate the receptor, but it blocks endorphin from binding to the receptor. The endorphin bounces off with no effect. It cannot cause reinforcement.

With the medication stopping reinforcement, the synapses from the upper nerve cell onto the lower one will not become stronger. New synapses will not form. The upper nerve cell will continue to have to fire one hundred times to make the lower one fire. Drinking remains a weak, easily controlled response. With naltrexone or nalmefene, most people can drink safely without becoming an alcoholic.

Reversal of Alcoholism

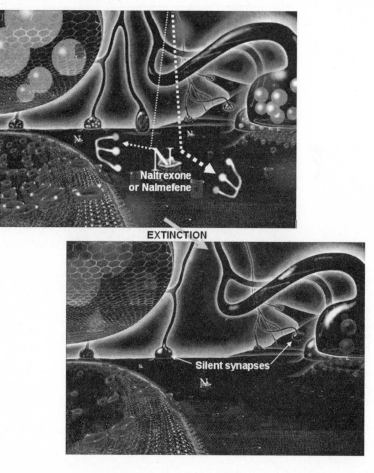

If alcoholism has already developed, taking naltrexone or nalmefene and then drinking alcohol starts a mechanism called "extinction." Extinction reverses the changes previously produced by reinforcement, thus weakening the connection between the nerve cells.

Synapses become weaker and can even be burned out completely, becoming "silent synapses." Eventually, the upper nerve cell again will have to fire one hundred or more times to make the lower nerve cell fire and produce drinking. Thus the cause of the alcoholism is removed, and controlled drinking is possible again.

APPENDIX C

Sinclair Method Awarded a U.S. Patent—Establishes the Research as the First to Suggest and Use Pharmacological Extinction for Alcoholism*

United States Patent	4,882,335
Sinclair	November 21, 1989

Method for Treating Alcohol-Drinking Response

ABSTRACT

A therapeutic method is provided for use as an adjunct in the treatment of alcoholism. The method consists of extinguishing the alcohol-drinking response of alcoholics during a relatively short period of time by having them drink alcoholic beverages repeatedly while an opiate antagonist blocks the positive reinforcement effects of ethanol in the brain.

---

* Note: Figures not included here. Download patent from: http://patft.uspto.gov/netacgi/nph-Parser?Sect1=PTO1&Sect2=HITOFF&d=PALL&p=1&u=%2Fnetahtml%2FPTO%2Fsrchnum.htm&r=1&f=G&l=50&s1=4,882,335.PN.&OS=PN/4,882,335&RS=PN/4,882,335.

Inventors:	Sinclair; John D. (Espoo, Finland)
Assignee:	Alko Limited (Helsinki, Finland)
Appl. No.:	205758
Filed:	June 13, 1988

Current U.S. Class:	514/282; 514/811
Intern'l Class:	A61k 031/44
Field of Search:	514/810,811,812,282

Other References

Chem. Abst., 106-12821P, (1987).
"Naloxone Persistently Modifies Water-Intake," *Pharmacology Biochemistry & Behaviour*, Mar. 25, 1986, vol. 29, pp. 331–334.
"Feasibility of Effective Psychopharmacological Treatments for Alcoholism," J. D. Sinclair, PhD *British Journal of Addiction*, 1987, 82, 1213–1223.

Claims

1. A method for treating alcoholism by extinguishing the alcohol-drinking response, comprising the steps of:

repeatedly administering to a subject suffering from alcoholism, an opiate antagonist selected from the group consisting of Naloxone, Naltrexone, cyclazocine, diprenorphine, etazocine, levalorphan, metazocine, nalorphine and salts thereof in a daily dosage sufficient to block the stimulatory effect of alcohol;

while the amount of antagonist in the subject's body is sufficient to block the stimulatory effect of alcohol, having the subject drink an alcoholic beverage; and

continuing the steps of administration of the opiate antagonist and drinking of an alcoholic beverage until the alcohol-drinking response is extinguished.

2. The method of claim 1 further comprising the step of punishing the patient after the alcoholic beverage is consumed, said step of punishment being selected from the group consisting of administration of electric shock, administration of emetics, and administration of an alcohol sensitizing compound.
3. The method of claim 2 wherein the alcohol sensitizing compound is disulfiram or cyanamide.
4. The method of claim 1 further comprising continuing the administration of an opiate antagonist after the alcohol-drinking response is extinguished.
5. The method in accordance with claim 1 wherein the opiate antagonist is Naloxone.
6. The method in accordance with claim 5 wherein the dose of Naloxone is from 0.2 to 30 mg daily.
7. The method in accordance with claim 1 wherein the opiate antagonist is Naltrexone.
8. The method in accordance with claim 7 wherein the dose of Naltrexone is from 20 to 300 mg daily.

Description

FIELD OF THE INVENTION
The invention is a treatment for alcohol abuse in which the alcohol-drinking response is extinguished over a limited number of sessions by being emitted while the reinforcement from alcohol is blocked with an opiate antagonist such as Naloxone or Naltrexone.

BACKGROUND OF THE INVENTION
Alcoholism is the most costly health problem in many countries. The cost, e.g., in America is estimated to be about $117,000,000,000 per year. The treatment methods currently used are not very effective. Most alcoholics drop out of treatment within a month or two. Few alcoholics, regardless of the type of treatment, are able to avoid relapses and renewed alcohol abuse.

No one is born an alcoholic. The drinking of alcohol (ethanol or ethyl alcohol) is a learned response, reinforced largely by the rewarding effects of alcohol in the central nervous system—the euphoria from lower, stimulatory doses of ethanol. An alcoholic is a person who, through an interplay of genetic and environmental factors, has had the alcohol-drinking response reinforced so often and so well that it becomes too strong for the individual to continue functioning properly in society. The strong alcohol-drinking response—i.e., the drive for alcohol—then dominates the person's behavior and life.

The current methods for treating alcoholism are not very successful probably because they do not effectively weaken the alcoholic's alcohol-drinking response. Some methods (e.g., counselling, Alcoholics Anonymous) are aimed at increasing the alcohol-ic's ability or willpower to withstand the drive for alcohol. The drive, however, is not weakened and the patient is told that he will remain an alcoholic, that is, a person with an overly strong alcohol-drinking response, for the rest of his life. These methods succeed in some alcoholics, but in most the time eventually comes when a momentary decrease in willpower causes a resumption of alcohol drinking and alcohol abuse.

Other treatments use punishment of various sorts (e.g., electric shock, disulfiram reactions, loss of a job) to try to stop alcohol drinking. Punishment is, however, a poor method for changing behaviour and has many limitations. In particular, it is ineffective when positive reinforcement is still being received for the same response that is punished. Since the treatments that punish alcohol drinking do not block the positive reinforcement of the same response coming from alcohol in the brain, they should not be expected to be very effective.

A third type of treatment has been proposed. Alcohol and opiates appear to cause positive reinforcement largely through the same neuronal system in the brain. Consequently, opiates such as morphine or methadone might be able to satisfy the drive for alcohol and thus abolish alcohol drinking. This does indeed occur in rats and other animals, and there is evidence suggesting opiates could also succeed in making alcoholics stop drinking alcohol.

The treatment probably would, however, turn alcoholics into opiate addicts, which is, of course, not a good solution.

Instead of counteracting the drive for alcohol or temporarily satisfying it, a successful treatment for alcoholics should permanently weaken the alcohol-drinking response. Fortunately, there is a well-established method for weakening a learned response: "extinction." Extinction consists of having the response emitted repeatedly in the absence of positive reinforcement.

It is relatively simple to remove external sources of positive reinforcement, such as the food a rat gets for pressing a lever or even the social reinforcement a person sometimes gets for drinking alcohol. But much of the positive reinforcement for alcohol drinking is internal, from the rewarding effects of alcohol in the brain.

The results showing that alcohol and opiates share a common mechanism of reinforcement show how the internal positive reinforcement from alcohol might be blocked. Various substances, called opiate antagonists, are able to block the receptors for opiates and thus prevent the effects of, e.g., morphine. Furthermore, there is already evidence that the two most commonly used opiate antagonists, Naloxone and Naltrexone, do block positive reinforcement from alcohol. First, they block the stimulatory effect of alcohol, which is generally thought to be related to the euphoria and positive reinforcement. (Note: Sinclair avoids the term "pleasure"—not to be confused with "positive reinforcement.") Second, it has been shown that while they are in the body they reduce voluntary alcohol drinking and intragastric self-administration of alcohol by animals.

Naloxone and Naltrexone were originally intended for use in treating overdoses of opiates (like heroin or morphine). They have since been suggested for use against a wide variety of problems including respiratory failure, anorexia nervosa, bulimia, obesity, emesis and nausea, shock, severe itching, constipation, growth of neoplasms, and sexual impotence and frigidity. There have been many studies attempting to use Naloxone to reverse alcohol intoxication and especially the coma produced by very large amounts of alcohol; although the results have been mixed and there is still controversy as to whether Naloxone can antagonize severe alcohol intoxication, it is important to note that none of these studies reported any bad effects from giving Naloxone in conjunction with alcohol. The doses of Naloxone have ranged between about 0.2 and 30 mg daily, and Naltrexone from about 20 to 300 mg daily. Other suggested uses are for the opiate antagonists in conjunction with other drugs, particularly, opiate agonists. For instance, U.S. Pat. No. 3,966,940 is for a compound containing narcotics or analgesics plus Naloxone to be given especially to narcotic addicts. In these cases the opiate or other drug is seen to be the active pharmacological agent and the opiate antagonist is included to counteract some of its effects.

Continual treatment with opiate antagonists should reduce the alcohol intake of alcoholics: so long as the antagonist is in the body, the alcoholic should have little incentive for drinking because alcohol is not rewarding. This maintenance treatment, however, has the same problem found with other long-term deterrent treatments, such as that with disulfiram: how to keep the alcoholic on the medication. Since there is still a strong drive for alcohol, the alcoholic is likely to drop out of treatment and stop taking the antagonist so that he or she can satisfy the drive by drinking again.

However, combining the well-established procedure of extinction from psychology with the pharmacological findings that opiate antagonists block reinforcement from alcohol provides a new and much more promising way of treating alcoholism. Indeed, it provides what could be called the first true cure for alcoholism. After a relatively short period of treatment during which an opiate antagonist is employed in extinction therapy, the patient is no longer an alcoholic, because the overly-strong alcohol-drinking response that made the patient be an alcoholic is extinguished. The method for using this extinction procedure is the present invention.

The idea of using extinction therapy with opiate antagonists for alcoholics has not been suggested previously. A similar idea with Naltrexone has, however, been suggested for opiate addicts (see P. F. Renault, NIDA Research Monograph No. 28, pp. 11–22, 1981), but extinction was not included in the design of the clinical tests. The patients were simply detoxified, given Naltrexone or placebo, and released. There was no program for encouraging them to take opiates while under the influence of Naltrexone, as required for extinction. Consequently, the general result was what would likely happen also with such a Naltrexone maintenance program with alcoholics: a very large percentage of the addicts dropped out, stopped taking Naltrexone, and started taking opiates again. Of the total of 1005 subjects, however, "17 of the Naltrexone and 18 of the placebo subjects actually tested the blockade by using an opiate agonist" when Naltrexone would have been active, and "in this subsample, the Naltrexone patients had significantly fewer subsequent urines positive for methadone or morphine...The pattern in the Naltrexone group was to test once or twice with heroin or methadone and then to stop. The use of these drugs in the placebo group was sporadic during the entire course of treatment... [Also, on an analog craving scale] the Naltrexone patients reported significantly less craving toward the end of their evaluation than did the placebo-treated patients."

These results suggest that Naltrexone would be much more useful against opiate addiction if the addicts were given extinction sessions in which they were encouraged to use narcotics while the positive reinforcement was blocked. Furthermore, in relation to the present invention, by showing the extinction therapy with Naltrexone does work in humans, they support the hypothesis that it would reduce alcohol abuse and the craving for alcohol in alcoholics.

The example included here shows that the extinction procedure progressively decreases and eventually almost abolishes alcohol drinking by rats and that alcohol intake remains reduced long after all Naloxone should have been removed from the body. The high predictive validity of this animal model for indicating treatments that affect human alcohol consumption is discussed in Sinclair, *British Journal of Addiction* 82, 1213–1223 (1987).

SUMMARY OF THE INVENTION
The present invention contemplates a therapeutic method, utilizing the ability of opiate antagonists to block the positive reinforcement from alcohol, to extinguish the alcohol-drinking response of

alcoholics. The extinction program consists of numerous sessions in which the alcoholic has an opiate antagonist administered and then drinks alcohol.

The extinction procedure abolishes the alcoholic's strong alcohol-drinking response. Optimally, the patient's drive for alcohol is returned to the level present before he or she ever tasted alcohol. Thus, by definition, the patient is no longer an alcoholic.

Admittedly, the patient can relearn the alcohol-drinking response and become an alcoholic again, and relearning a response that has been extinguished occurs more rapidly than the initial acquisition. But with the first-hand knowledge of the consequences of the first acquisition of alcoholism, and with even a moderate level of willpower and outside support, most alcoholics will avoid making the same mistake twice.

This extinction procedure is a useful adjunct for various other methods of treating alcoholics, including punishment of alcohol drinking, procedures to improve willpower and social rehabilitation, and maintenance procedures for preventing renewed use of alcohol. These other methods have previously been very limited because of the continuing high drive for alcohol, but they should be much more effective once the alcohol-drinking response has been extinguished.

BRIEF DESCRIPTION OF THE DRAWINGS (Drawings not reprinted here)
FIG. 1 shows the apparent extinction of alcohol drinking in Long Evans and AA rats caused by 4 daily sessions of drinking alcohol after administration of Naloxone (mean.+-.standard error).

FIG. 2 shows the apparent extinction of alcohol drinking in Wistar rats caused by 4 daily sessions when Naloxone was administered 5 minutes before the hour of drinking alcohol ("paired Naloxone" group) and the lack of effect of Naloxone injected each day 3 hours after alcohol drinking ("unpaired Naloxone" group).

FIG. 3 shows the continued reduction in alcohol drinking by the Long Evans rats that had previously undergone extinction (see FIG. 1) relative to their controls. No Naloxone was administered during this time, but the rats treated before with Naloxone drank significantly less than the controls on each of the first 7 days. They eventually returned to the control level, apparently because they were not made to abstain completely, did drink some alcohol, and thus relearned the alcohol-drinking response.

DESCRIPTION OF THE PREFERRED EMBODIMENTS

The extinction procedure can be used in all individuals classified by any of various means as alcoholics or alcohol abusers, except those in which the administration of an opiate antagonist is contraindicated and those suffering from Korsakoff's syndrome. (The extinction procedure would probably work poorly in patients with Korsakoff's syndrome.)

The patients can be interviewed to determine the alcoholic beverages they usually drink and the drinking situations in which they normally imbibe. They can then be informed that unlike most treatments, this one does not involve immediately becoming abstinent; instead, their alcohol drinking is to be slowly diminished over many days and only after that will they have to abstain. This procedure should also help to reduce the severity of withdrawal symptoms that are often produced by abrupt termination of alcohol intake.

The patient can then have an opiate antagonist administered shortly before beginning to drink an alcoholic beverage. Examples of opiate antagonists are Naloxone, Naltrexone, cyclazocine, diprenorphine, etazocine, levalorphan, metazocine, nalorphine, and their salts. The preferred opiate antagonists are Naloxone and Naltrexone, both of which have been approved for use in humans and have been shown to be free of severe side-effects. Neither is addicting or habit forming. The preferred dose range for Naloxone is 0.4 to 10 mg daily if taken by injection; the dose would have to be much larger if it were taken orally. The preferred dose range for Naltrexone is 50 to 200 mg daily. The dose administered in a specific case will depend upon the age and weight of the patient, the frequency of administration, and the route of administration, but must be sufficient to assure that the antagonist will be present in sufficient quantities in the body throughout the entire evening of alcohol drinking. The antagonist could be administered in such a way that it is continually present in the body throughout the weeks of extinction therapy. Administration in a way that allows the patient to be free of pharmacologically-active quantities of the antagonist during the following day may be preferred, since it allows the alcoholic to eat food and drink non-alcoholic beverages during the daytime without interference from the antagonist. In the latter case, the patient will be under strict orders to confine all alcohol drinking to the evening hours after the antagonist has been administered.

Examples of routes of administration for the antagonist are injection, oral consumption in any form, transdermal administration, slow-release injection, nasal administration, sublingual administration, implantable drug delivery depots, and the like. A non-obtrusive, non-painful route would be preferred.

The first extinction session (i.e., drinking after administration of the antagonist) can be conducted under close supervision in the treatment center. It is important that later extinction sessions be conducted in the same drinking situations and with the same alcoholic beverages that the patient usually has employed in the past. The stimuli from these specific beverages and situations help to elicit somewhat separate alcohol-drinking responses for the individual. For example, in a particular alcoholic, the alcohol-drinking response of having beers while watching a game on TV may be at least partly independent of his responses of imbibing cocktails at a party or drinking whiskey at a bar. Each should be extinguished in order to assure the generality of the treatment. Although the alcoholic should be encouraged to drink in the extinction sessions, there should be no social reinforcement for doing so.

The number of extinction sessions required for each patient will depend upon the severity of his or her alcoholism and the number of specific drinking situations in which the alcohol-drinking response must be extinguished. The duration of the extinction program may therefore range from about 1 to 5 weeks.

Once the alcohol-drinking response has been sufficiently weakened, the final extinction sessions could be conducted along with an element of punishment. Examples of punishment include mild electric shock when the alcohol is consumed, production of conditioned taste aversion from very large doses of alcohol with or without emetics, aversion therapy with an alcohol-sensitizing compound such as disulfiram or cyanamide, and the like.

After the final extinction session, the patient is told to abstain from all alcohol in the future. Various procedures can then be used to help ensure that the patient does in fact refrain from drinking alcohol. Such procedures include counselling, psychotherapy, family therapy, job therapy, joining Alcoholics Anonymous and the like. Efforts should also be taken to help the patient resume a normal productive life.

The patient should also be informed that although his or her alcohol-drinking response has been extinguished in the most frequently used drinking situations, it is possible that some have been missed. Consequently, if the patient anticipates or is experiencing a situation in which the response has not been extinguished, he or she should request additional extinction sessions involving this new situation. Alternatively, the patient could be kept on a maintenance program with continued administration of the opiate antagonist.

The present invention is further illustrated by the following example.

EXAMPLE
Extinction of alcohol drinking in 3 strains of rats.

Methods
The effects of drinking alcohol after being injected with Naloxone was studied in male rats of the AA strain developed for very high levels of alcohol drinking by selective breeding, in male Long Evans rats, and in male Wistar rats. In each case the animals first had several weeks of continual access to 10% (v/v) ethanol, plus food and water, during which time their alcohol drinking increased rapidly at first and eventually, after 3 to 4 weeks, approached a stable asymptotic level. They were then switched to having access to 10% alcohol for only 1 hour each day. After alcohol consumption had stabilized, the rats of each strain were divided into groups matched for alcohol consumption during the last week of 1 hour

daily access. One group in each strain was then injected with 10 mg/kg Naloxone hydrochloride 5 minutes before their hour of alcohol access for the next 4 days and a control group was injected with a similar volume of saline. There was a third group ("unpaired Naloxone") of Wistar rats that was injected with 10 mg/kg of Naloxone 3 hours after the end of their hour of alcohol access. The alcohol drinking during 1 hour on the day after the last injection was also recorded. The Long Evans rats were then switched back to continual access to alcohol and their intake measured for the next 13 days.

RESULTS

Administering Naloxone before providing access to alcohol progressively decreased alcohol drinking in all 3 strains (FIGS. 1 and 2). By the fourth day it was almost abolished in each strain, and the alcohol intake was significantly ($p<0.05$) lower than both the "pre" level (during the preceding week) and the level after the first Naloxone injection. The saline controls tended to increase their alcohol intake across days, perhaps due to the stress of injection, and drank significantly more alcohol than the rats given Naloxone before alcohol on at least the last 3 extinction days and on the "post" day, 24 hours after the last injection.

The subsequent alcohol drinking by the Long Evans rats is shown in FIG. 3. The rats subjected to extinction with Naloxone continued to drink significantly less alcohol than their saline controls on each day of the first week and then gradually returned to the control level. The latter is probably the result of relearning the alcohol-drinking response. Consistent with the common finding that a response is reacquired after extinction more rapidly than it is initially acquired, they took less than 2 weeks to reacquire the response, whereas naive Long Evans rats (i.e., ones that have never had alcohol before) require 3 to 4 weeks to reach this level of alcohol intake.

The Wistar rats given Naloxone 3 hours after alcohol drinking ("unpaired Naloxone") did not differ significantly from the controls at any time (FIG. 2); their slightly lower intake can probably be attributed to the fact that, unlike the controls, they were not stressed by injection immediately before having access to alcohol. The "unpaired Naloxone" group drank significantly more alcohol than the "paired Naloxone" group on each of the 4 extinction days. This suggests that the reduction in alcohol drinking was caused specifically by the experience acquired while Naloxone was paired with alcohol drinking.

These results are all consistent with the hypothesis that consuming alcohol while Naloxone is present causes the alcohol-drinking response to be extinguished. Water intake and body weight were not reduced and there were no indications of any effects detrimental to the health of the animals.

World Health Organization Statement on the Safety and Efficacy of Naltrexone and Open Letter from Enoch Gordis, Director, NIAAA (1995)

PROGRAMME ON SUBSTANCE ABUSE

PHARMACOLOGICAL TREATMENT OF SUBSTANCE USE DISORDERS: INTERNATIONAL ISSUES IN MEDICATIONS DEVELOPMENT

Report of a joint consultation organized by the Addiction Research Foundation, Toronto, and the WHO Programme on Substance Abuse, Geneva

Toronto, Ontario, Canada, October 1995

WORLD HEALTH ORGANIZATION

At least one medication, naltrexone, has been identified as a safe and effective treatment for alcohol dependence...The demonstration of the efficacy of naltrexone and current studies underway examining related opiate antagonists (e.g., nalmefene) might serve to encourage pharmaceutical companies that medications development in this area is possible. Disulfiram, useful for some patients, might also be effective though its efficacy has been difficult to prove in controlled trials.

DEPARTMENT OF HEALTH & HUMAN SERVICES

Public Health Service
National Institutes of Health

National Institute on Alcohol
Abuse and Alcoholism
6000 Executive Boulevard
Rockville, MD 20892-7003

FEB 6 1995

Dear Colleague:

Recently there has been a great deal of publicity in newspapers
and on television about naltrexone (REVIA™), a drug recently
approved by the Food and Drug Administration as a treatment for
alcoholism. I want to take this opportunity to share with you
information about naltrexone.

Naltrexone appears to reduce craving in many abstinent patients
and to block the reinforcing effects of alcohol in many patients
who drink. The latter effect often enables patients who drink a
small amount of alcohol to avoid full-blown relapse and lessens
the likelihood of their return to heavy drinking. However, the
mechanism of naltrexone's effect in alcoholism has not been
conclusively demonstrated.

The 3-month NIAAA-supported trials conducted at the University of
Pennsylvania and Yale University found that naltrexone cut the
rate of patient relapse by about one-half. In addition, patients
who receive naltrexone reported less alcohol craving, fewer
drinking days, and less severe alcohol-related problems than
patients treated with a placebo. Both NIAAA-supported studies
used naltrexone in combination with counseling, an important part
of the treatment regime.

The recently concluded 3-month open trials, sponsored by the
DuPont Merck Pharmaceutical Company, demonstrated that naltrexone
is safe at the prescribed dose (50 mg/day) in a large,
heterogeneous population of alcoholics in diverse treatment
modalities and settings.

NIAAA currently funds nine additional clinical trials to
determine the patient type, dose, therapy combinations, and
treatment duration with which naltrexone works best. Until
results from those studies are available, NIAAA encourages only
physicians familiar with addiction treatment to prescribe
naltrexone, only in the context of psychosocial treatments, and
only for the FDA-recommended time period. Physicians will rely
on clinical judgment to determine whether and at what point in
treatment a patient should be started on conventional treatments
or conventional treatments accompanied by naltrexone.

Approximately 1 million Americans seek alcoholism treatment each
year, many more than once. Of treated patients, approximately 50
percent relapse within the first few months of treatment. While
not a "magic bullet," naltrexone nevertheless promises to aid
many of these patients in their struggle to overcome a chronic
relapsing disease.

The addition of naltrexone to alcoholism treatment comes after
more than two decades of concerted NIAAA research on alcoholism,
alcohol abuse, and alcohol-related problems. As the Institute
celebrates its 25th anniversary this year, the technology and
knowledge acquired during the past 25 years will serve as the
basis for future advances in the prevention and treatment of
alcohol problems.

Sincerely yours,

Enoch Gordis, M.D.
Director
National Institute on
Alcohol Abuse and Alcoholism

References

Agosti, V. 1995. The efficacy of treatment in reducing alcohol consumption: A meta-analysis. *International Journal of Addictions* 30: 1067–1077.

Alcoholics Anonymous World Services, Inc., Staff. 1939. *Alcoholics Anonymous: The Story of How Many Thousands of Men and Women Have Recovered from Alcoholism.* New York: Alcoholics Anonymous World Services, Incorporated.

Alger, S. A., M. D. Schwalberg, J. M. Bigaouette, A. V. Michalek, and L. J. Howard. 1991. Effect of a tricyclic antidepressant and opiate antagonist on binge-eating behavior in normoweight bulimic and obese, binge-eating subjects. *American Journal of Clinical Nutrition* 53: 865–871.

Alho, H., P. Heinälä, K. Kiianmaa, and J. D. Sinclair. 1999. Naltrexone for alcohol dependence: Double-blind placebo-controlled Finnish trial. *Alcoholism: Clinical and Experimental Research* 23: 46A.

Altshuler, H. L., P. E. Phillips, and D. A. Feinhandler. 1980. Alteration of ethanol self-administration by Naltrexone. *Life Sciences* 26: 679–688.

Altshuler, H. L., and T. S. Shippenberg. 1982. Tetrahydroisoquinoline and opioid substrates of alcohol actions. *Progress in Clinical Biological Research* 90: 329–344.

Anton, R. 1999. Neurobiologial approach to alcoholism therapy: The role of Naltrexone. Abstract to evidence based medicine of Naltrexone in alcoholism. Satellite symposium to the 7th Congress of the European Society for Biomedical Research on Alcoholism, June 16–19, in Barcelona, Spain.

Anton, R. F., D. H. Moak, L. R. Waid, P. K. Latham, R. J. Malcolm, and J. K. Dias. 1999. Naltrexone and cognitive behavioral therapy for the treatment of outpatient alcoholics: Results of a placebo-controlled trial. *American Journal of Psychiatry* 156: 1758–1764.

Anton, R. 1998. Naltrexone compared to placebo when combined with cognitive behavioral therapy in the treatment of outpatient alcoholics. Paper presented at the 9th Congress of the International Society for Biomedical Research on Alcoholism (ISBRA), June 27–July 2, in Copenhagen, Denmark.

Anton, R. F., D. H. Moak, and P. Latham. 1995. The obsessive compulsive drinking scale: A self-rated instrument for the quantification of thoughts about alcohol and drinking behavior. *Alcoholism: Clinical and Experimental Research* 19: 92–99.

Anton, R. F. 1997. Naltrexone as adjunctive treatment to cognitive behavioral therapy for outpatient alcoholics. Paper presented at the annual meeting of the American College of Neuropsychopharmacology, December, in Waikoloa, Hawaii.

Anton, R. F. 1995. New directions in the pharmacotherapy of alcoholism. *Psychiatric Annals* 25: 353–362.

Anton, R. F., D. H. Moak, and P. K. Latham. 1996. The obsessive compulsive drinking scale: A new method of assessing outcome in alcoholism treatment studies. *Archives of General Psychiatry* 53: 225–231.

Anton, R. F., S. S. O'Malley, D. C. Ciraulo, R. A. Cisler, D. Couper, R. L. Atkinson, 1984. Endocrine and metabolic effects of opiate antagonists. *Journal of Clinical Psychiatry* 45: 20B24.

Balldin, J., M. Berglund, S. Borg, M. Månsson, P. Berndtsen, J. Franck, L. Gustafsson, J. Halldin, C. Hollstedt, L. H. Nilsson, and G. A. Stolt. 1997. A randomized 6 month double-blind placebo-controlled study of Naltrexone and coping skills education programme. *Alcohol and Alcoholism* 32: 325.

Back, R. S. 2004. Naltrexone in the Treatment of Adolescent Sexual Offenders. *Journal of Clinical Psychiatry* 65: 982–986.

Bien, T. H., W. R. Miller, and J. S. Tonigan. 1993. Brief interventions for alcohol problems: A review. *Addiction* 88: 315–335.

Bohn, M. J., D. D. Krahn, and B. A. Staehler. 1995. Development and initial validation of a measure of drinking urges in abstinent alcoholics. *Alcoholism: Clinical and Experimental Research* 19: 600–606.

Bohn, M. J., H. R. Kranzler, D. Beazoglou, and B. A. Staehler. 1994. Naltrexone and brief counseling to reduce heavy drinking: Results of a small clinical trial. *American Journal on Addictions* 3: 91–99.

Burish, T. G., S. A. Maisto, A. M. Cooper, and M. B. Sobell. 1981. Effects of voluntary short-term abstinence from alcohol on subsequent drinking patterns of college students. *Journal of Studies on Alcohol* 42: 1013–1020.

Charness, M. E. 1990. Alcohol and the brain. *Alcohol Health and Research World* 14: 85–89.

Charness, M. E., G. Hu, R. H. Edwards, and L. A. Querimit. 1993. Ethanol increases delta-opioid receptor gene expression in neuronal cell lines. *Molecular Pharmacology* 44: 1119–1127.

Charness, M. E., L. A. Querimit, and I. Diamond. 1986. Ethanol increases the expression of functional delta-opioid receptors in the neuroblastoma x glioma ng108-15 hybrid cells. *Journal of Biologic Chemistry* 261: 3164–3169.

Cloninger, C. R. 1988. Etiologic factors in substance abuse: An adoption study perspective. In *Biological vulnerability to drug abuse*, ed. R. W. Pickens and D. S. Svikis, 52–72. Rockville: National Institute on Drug Abuse.

Cloninger, C. R. 1987. Recent advances in family studies of alcoholism. *Progress in Clinical and Biological Research* 241: 47–60.

Committee on Treatment of Alcohol Problems, Institute of Medicine. 1990. *Broadening the Base of Treatment for Alcohol Problems*. Washington, DC: National Academy Press.

Cornelius, J. R., I. M. Salloum, J. G. Ehler, P. J. Jarrett, M. D. Cornelius, J. M. Perel, M. E. Thase, and A. Black. 1997. Fluoxetine in depressed alcoholics: A double-blind, placebo-controlled trial. *Archives of General Psychiatry* 54: 700–705.

Cowen, M. S., A. H. Rezvani, B. Jarrott, and A. J. Lawrence. 1999. Ethanol consumption by fawn-hooded rats following abstinence: Effect of Naltrexone and changes in mu-opioid receptor density. *Alcoholism: Clinical and Experimental Research* 23: 1008–1014.

Croop, R. S., and J. Chick. 1996. American and European clinical trials of Naltrexone. In International update: New findings on promising medications, R. Z. Litten and J. Fertig. *Alcoholism: Clinical and Experimental Research* 20: 216A–218A.

Croop, R. S., D. F. Labriola, J. M. Wroblewski, and D. W. Nibbelink. 1995. A Multicenter Safety Study of Naltrexone as Adjunctive Pharmacotherapy for Individuals with Alcoholism. Paper presented at the American Psychiatric Association's 148th annual meeting, May 20–25, in Miami, FL.

Croop, R. S., E. B. Faulkner, and D. F. Labriola. 1997. The safety profile of Naltrexone in the treatment of alcoholism: Results from a multicenter usage study. *Archives of General Psychiatry* 54: 1130–1135.

Davidson, D. and Z. Amit. 1996. Effects of Naloxone on limited-access ethanol drinking in rats. *Alcoholism: Clinical and Experimental Research* 20: 664–669.

Davidson, D., R. Swift, and E. Fitz. 1996. Naltrexone increases the latency to drink alcohol in social drinkers. *Alcoholism: Clinical and Experimental Research* 20: 732–739.

Davis, W. M., and S. G. Smith. 1974. Naloxone use to eliminate opiate-seeking behaviour: Need for extinction of conditioned reinforcement. *Biological Psychiatry* 9: 181–189.

De Waele, J. P., D. N. Papachristou, and C. Gianoulakis. 1992. The alcohol-preferring C57-L/6 mice present an enhanced sensitivity of the hypothalmic b-endorphin system to ethanol than the alcohol-avoiding DBA/2 mice. *Journal of Pharmacology and Experimental Therapeutics* 261: 788–794.

De Witte, P. 1984. Naloxone reduces alcohol intake in a free-choice procedure even when both drinking bottles contain saccharin sodium or quinine substances. *Neuropsychobiology* 12: 73–77.

Di Chiara, G. 1997. Alcohol and dopamine. *Alcohol Health and Research World* 21: 108–114.

Dickson, S. D., and C. L. Cunningham. 1996. The role of mu- and kappa-opioid receptors in ethanol-induced conditioned place preference. *Alcoholism: Clinical and Experimental Research* 20: 59A.

Donovan, D. M., D. R. Gastfriend, J. D. Hosking, B. A. Johnson, J. S. LoCastro, R. Longabaugh, B. J. Mason, M. E. Mattson, W. R. Miller, H. M. Pettinati, C. L. Randall, R. Swift, R. D. Weiss, L. D. Williams, and A. Z. Zweben. 2006. Combined pharmacotherapies and behavioral interventions for alcohol dependence: The COMBINE study: A randomized controlled trial. *Journal of the American Medical Association* 295: 2003–2017.

Doty, P., and H. de Wit. 1995. Effects of Naltrexone pretreatment on the subjective and performance effects of ethanol in social drinkers. *Behavioral Pharmacology* 6: 386–394.

Doyle, R. 1996. Deaths caused by alcohol. *Scientific American* 275: 30–31.

Elder, R. L., M. Letterman, N. E. Badia-Elder, and S. W. Kiefer. 1996. Naltrexone failed to produce conditioned taste aversion to alcohol. *Alcoholism: Clinical and Experimental Research* 20: 91A.

Farren, C. K., and S. O'Malley. 1997. Sequential use of Naltrexone in the treatment of relapsing alcoholism. *The American Journal of Psychiatry* 154: 714.

Froehlich, J. C. 1995. Genetic factors in alcohol self-administration. *Journal of Clinical Psychiatry* 56: 15–23.

Froehlich, J. C. 1997. Opioid peptides. *Alcohol Health and Research World* 21: 132–136.

Froehlich, J. C. 1996. The neurobiology of ethanol-opioid interactions in ethanol reinforcement. *Alcoholism: Clinical and Experimental Research* 20: 181A–186A.

Garbutt, J. C., S. L. West, T. S. Carey, K. N. Lohr, F. T. Crews. (1999) Evidence report/technology assessment: Number 3: Pharmacotherapy for alcohol dependence. Pharmacological treatment of alcohol dependence: A review of the evidence. *Journal of the American Medical Association* 281: 1318–1325.

Gianoulakis, C., and P. Angelogianni. 1989. Characterization of beta-endorphin peptides in the spinal cord of the rat. *Peptides* 10: 1049–1054.

Gianoulakis, C., and A. Barcomb. 1987. Effect of acute ethanol in vivo and in vitro on the beta-endorphin system in the rat. *Life Sciences* 40: 19–28.

Gianoulakis, C., B. Krishnan, and J. Thavundayil. 1996. Enhanced sensitivity of pituitary beta-endorphin to ethanol in subjects at high risk of alcoholism. *Archives of General Psychiatry* 53: 250–257.

Ginsburg, H. M. 1984. Naltrexone: Its clinical utility. In *National Institute on Drug Abuse Treatment Research Report*, 84–1358. Washington, DC: U.S. Government Printing Office.

Gladwell, Malcolm. 2005. *Blink: The Power of Thinking Without Thinking.* London: Penguin Books.

Golubchikov, V., and B. J. Rounsaville. 1996. Predictors of Naltrexone-induced nausea in alcohol-dependent subjects. *Alcoholism: Clinical and Experimental Research* 20: 91A.

Gonzales, R. A., and J. N. Jaworski.1997. Alcohol and glutamate. *Alcohol Health and Research World* 21: 120–127.

Gonzalez, J. P., and R. N. Brogden. 1988. Naltrexone. A review of its pharmacodynamic and pharmacokinetic properties and therapeutic efficacy in the management of opioid dependence. *Drugs* 35: 192–213.

Goodwin, D. W., F. Schulsinger, L. Hermansen, S. B. Guze, and G. Winokur. 1973. Alcohol problems in adoptees raised apart from alcoholic biological parents. *Archives of General Psychiatry* 28: 238–243.

Grant, B. F. 1992. DSM-III-R and proposed DSM-IV alcohol abuse and dependence, United States, 1988: A nosological comparison. *Alcoholism: Clinical and Experimental Research* 16: 1068–1077.

Gritz, E. R., S. M. Shiffman, M. E. Jarvik, J. Schlesinger, and V. C. Charuvastra. 1976. Naltrexone: Physiological and psychological effects of single doses. *Clinical Pharmacology and Therapeutics* 19: 773–776.

Heather, Nick, and Ian Robertson. 1985. *Problem Drinking: The New Approach.* Harmondsworth, England: Penguin Books.

Heinälä, P., H. Alho, K. Kuoppasalmi, J. Lönnqvist, K. Kiianmaa, and J. D. Sinclair. 2000. Targeted Naltrexone with coping therapy for controlled drinking, without prior detoxification, is effective and particularly well tolerated: An 8-month controlled trial. Abstract to 10th Congress of the

International Society for Biomedical Research on Alcoholism, July 2–July 8, Yokohama, Japan.

Heinälä, P., H. Alho, K. Kuoppasalmi, D. Sinclair, K. Kiianmaa, and J. Lönnqvist. 1999. Use of Naltrexone in the treatment of alcohol dependence—A double-blind placebo-controlled Finnish trial. *Alcohol and Alcoholism* 34: 433.

Heyser, C. J., A. J. Roberts, G. Schulteis, and G. F. Koob. 1999. Central administration of an opiate antagonist decreases oral ethanol self-administration in rats. *Alcoholism: Clinical and Experimental Research* 23: 1468–1476.

Higgins, R. L., and M. J. McCartney. 1980. Reactive effects of denying social drinkers the freedom to drink alcoholic beverages. *Journal of Studies on Alcohol* 41: 1224–1228.

Hill, K. G., and S. W. Kiefer. 1997. Naltrexone treatment increases the aversiveness of alcohol for outbred rats. *Alcoholism: Clinical and Experimental Research* 21: 637–641.

Hiller-Sturmhöfel, S. 1995. Signal transmission among nerve cells. *Alcohol Health and Research World* 19: 128.

Ho, A. K., and R. C. Chen. 1976. Interactions of narcotics, narcotic antagonists, and ethanol during acute, chronic, and withdrawal states. *Annals of the New York Academy of Sciences* 281: 297–310.

Hölter, S. M., and R. Spanagel. 1999. Effects of opiate antagonist treatment on the alcohol deprivation effect in long-term ethanol-experienced rats. *Psychopharmacology* 145: 360–369.

Horgan, C., K. C. Skwara, and L. Andersen. 1993. *Substance abuse: The nation's number one health problem: Key indicators for policy*, Jane J. Stein. Princeton: The Robert Wood Johnson Foundation.

Hyytiä, P., and J. D. Sinclair. 1993. Responding for oral ethanol after Naloxone treatment by alcohol-preferring AA rats. *Alcoholism: Clinical and Experimental Research* 17: 631–636.

Hyytiä, P. 1993. Involvement of mu-opioid receptors in alcohol drinking by alcohol-preferring AA rats. *Pharmacology, Biochemistry, and Behavior* 45: 697–702.

Hyytiä, P., K. Ingman, S. L. Soini, J. T. Laitinen, and E. R. Korpi. 1999. Effects of continuous opioid receptor blockade on alcohol intake and up-regulation of opioid receptor subtype signaling in a genetic model of high alcohol drinking. *Naunyn-Schmiedeberg's Archives of Pharmacology* 360: 391–401.

Jääskeläinen, I. P., J. Hirvonen, T. Kujala, K. Alho, C. J. Eriksson, A. Lehtokoski, E. Pekkonen, J. D. Sinclair, H. Yabe, R. Näätänen, and P. Sillanaukee. 1998. Effects of Naltrexone and ethanol on auditory event-related brain potentials. *Alcohol* 15: 105–111.

Jaffe, A. J., B. Rounsaville, G. Chang, R. S. Schottenfeld, R. E. Meyer, and

S. S. O'Malley. 1996. Naltrexone, relapse prevention, and supportive therapy with alcoholics: An analysis of patient treatment matching. *Journal of Consulting and Clinical Psychology* 64: 1044–1053.

Jaffe, J. H. 1967. Cyclazocine in the treatment of narcotic addiction. *Current Psychiatric Therapies* 7: 147–156.

Jenab, S., and C. E. Inturrisi. 1994. Ethanol and Naloxone differentially upregulate delta opioid receptor gene expression in neuroblastoma hybrid (NG108-15) cells. *Molecular Brain Research* 27: 95–102.

Judson, B. A., T. M. Carney, and A. Goldstein. 1981. Naltrexone treatment of heroin addiction: Efficacy and safety in a double-blind dosage comparison. *Drug and Alcohol Dependence* 7: 325–346.

Julius, D., and P. Renault, ed. 1976. Narcotic antagonists: Naltrexone progress report. In *National Institute on Drug Abuse Research Monograph Series*, 76–387. Rockville: National Institute on Drug Abuse.

June, H. L., S. R. McCane, R. W. Zink, P. S. Portoghese, T. -K. Li, and J. C. Froehlich. 1999. The delta 2-opioid receptor antagonist Naltriben reduces motivated responding for ethanol. *Psychopharmacology* 147: 81–89.

Keith, L. D., J. C. Crabbe, L. M. Robertson, and J. W. Kendall. 1986. Ethanol-stimulated endorphin and corticotrophin secretion in vitro. *Brain Research* 367: 222–229.

Kiianmaa, K., P. L. Hoffman, and B. Tabakoff. 1983. Antagonism of the behavioral effects of ethanol by Naltrexone in BALB/C, C57BL/6, and DBA/2 mice. *Psychopharmacology* 79: 291–294.

Kiianmaa, K., P. Hyytiä, and D. Sinclair. 1998. Dopamine and alcohol reinforcement in alcohol-preferring AA rats. *Alcoholism: Clinical and Experimental Research* 22: 155A.

King, A. C., J. R. Volpicelli, A. Frazer, and C. P. O'Brien. 1997. Effect of Naltrexone on subjective alcohol response in subjects at high and low risk for future alcohol dependence. *Psychopharmacology* 129: 15–22.

Kishline, Audrey. 1994. *Moderate drinking: The new option for problem drinkers*. Tucson: Sharp Press.

Koob, George F., and Michel Le Moal. 1997. Drug abuse: Hedonic homeostatic dysregulation. *Science* 278: 52–58.

Koob, G. F., S. Rassnick, S. Heinrichs, and F. Weiss. 1994. Alcohol: The reward system and dependence. In *Toward a molecular basis of alcohol use and abuse*, ed. B. Jansson, H. Jörnvall, U. Rydberg, L. Terenius, and B. L. Vallee, 103–114. Boston: Birkhauser-Verlag.

Kornet, M., C. Goosen, and J. M. Van Ree. 1991. Effect of Naltrexone on alcohol consumption during chronic alcohol drinking and after a period of imposed abstinence in free-choice drinking rhesus monkeys. *Psychopharmacology* 104: 367–376.

Kranzler, H. R., and R. E. Meyer. 1989. An open trial of buspirone in alcoholics. *Journal of Clinical Psychopharmacology* 9: 379–380.

Kranzler, H. R., H. Tennen, C. Penta, and M. J. Bohn. 1997. Targeted Naltrexone treatment of early problem drinkers. *Addictive Behaviors* 22: 431–436.

Kranzler, H. R., J. A. Burleson, P. Korner, F. K. Del Boca, M. J. Bohn, J. Brown, and N. Liebowitz. 1995. Placebo-controlled trial of fluoxetine as an adjunct to relapse prevention in alcoholics. *American Journal of Psychiatry* 152: 391–397.

Krishnan-Sarin, S., P. S. Portoghese, T. -K. Li, and J. C. Froehlich. 1995. The delta 2-opioid receptor antagonist Naltriben selectively attenuates alcohol intake in rats bred for alcohol preference. *Pharmacology Biochemistry and Behavior* 52: 153–159.

Krystal, J. H., J. A. Cramer, W. F. Krol, G. F. Kirk, and R. A. Rosenheck. 2001. Naltrexone in the treatment of alcohol dependence. *New England Journal of Medicine* 345: 1734–1739.

Kuhar, M. J. Basic neurobiological research: 1989–1991. Report to Congress from the Secretary, Department of Health and Human Services, National Institute on Drug Abuse, Rockville, MD.

Lazarus, Arnold A. 1981. *The practice of multimodal therapy: Systematic, comprehensive, and effective psychotherapy.* New York: McGraw Hill.

Le, A. D., and E. M. Sellers. 1994. Interaction between opiate and 5-HT3 receptor antagonists in the regulation of alcohol intake. *Alcohol and Alcoholism* 29: 545–549.

Leeson, Nick. 1997. *Rogue trader: How I brought down Barings Bank and shook the financial world.* London: Time Warner Paperbacks.

LeMarquand, D., R. O. Pihl, and S. Benkelfat. 1994. Serotonin and alcohol intake, abuse, and dependence: Clinical evidence. *Biological Psychiatry* 36: 326–337.

Leshner, A. I. 1997. Addiction is a brain disease, and it matters. *Science* 278: 45–47.

Li, X. W., T. -K. Li, and J. C. Froehlich. 1996. Alcohol alters preproenkephalin mRNA content in the shell and the core of the nucleus accumbens. *Alcoholism: Clinical and Experimental Research* 20: 53A.

Litten, R. Z., R. S. Croop, J. Chick, M. E. McCaul, B. Mason, and H. Sass. 1996. International update: New findings on promising medications. *Alcoholism: Clinical and Experimental Research* 20: 216A–218A.

Litten, R. Z., J. Allen, and J. Fertig. 1996. Pharmacotherapies for alcohol problems: A review of research with focus on developments since 1991. *Alcoholism: Clinical and Experimental Research* 20: 859–876.

Little, H. J. 1991. Mechanisms that may underlie the behavioral effects of ethanol. *Progress in Neurobiology* 36: 171–194.

Liu, X., A. R. Caggiula, S. K. Yee, H. Nobuta, A. F. Sved, R. N. Pechnick, and R. E. Poland. 2007. Mecamylamine Attenuates

Cue-Induced Reinstatement of Nicotine-Seeking Behavior in Rats. *Neuropsychopharmacology* 32: 710–718.

Lømo, T. 1978. Are there silent synapses? *Trends in Biological Sciences* 3: N9–N12.

Lozano Polo, J. L., Mora Gutiérrez, V. Martínez Pérez, J. Santamaría Gutiérrez, J. Vada Sánchez, and J. A. Vallejo Correas. 1997. [Effect of methadone or Naltrexone on the course of transaminases in parenteral drug users with hepatitis c virus infection.] *Revista Clinica Española* 197: 479–483.

Malec, T. S., E. A. Malec, and M. Doniger. 1996. Efficacy of buspirone in alcohol dependence: A review. *Alcoholism: Clinical and Experimental Research* 20: 853–858.

Månsson, M., J. Balldin, M. Berglund, and S. Borg. 1999. Interaction effect between Naltrexone and coping skills. Treatment and follow-up data. Abstract to evidence based medicine of Naltrexone in alcoholism. Satellite symposium to the 7th Congress of the European Society for Biomedical Research on Alcoholism, June 16–19, in Barcelona, Spain.

Månsson, M., J. Balldin, M. Berglund, and S. Borg. 1999. Six-month followup of interaction effect between Naltrexone and coping skills therapy in outpatient alcoholism treatment. *Alcohol and Alcoholism* 34: 454.

Marck, M. C., G. U. Liepa, S. J. Kalia, and M. C. Daoud. 1997. Investigating Differences in Hospitalized Patients Detoxified with Lorazepam vs. Phenobarbital Relative to Length of Stay, Average Total Cost, and Use of Restraints. *Journal of Addictive Diseases* 16: A23.

Marfaing-Jallat, P., D. Miceli, and J. Le Magnen. 1983. Decrease in ethanol consumption by Naloxone in naive and dependent rats. *Pharmacology Biochemistry and Behavior* 18: 537–539.

Mascott, Cynthia. HelpHorizons.com. Alcoholism and its treatment. http://www.helphorizons.com/library/search_details.htm?id=61.

Mason, B. J., F. R. Salvato, L. D. Williams, E. C. Ritvo, and R. B. Cutler. 1999. A double-blind, placebo-controlled study of oral Nalmefene for alcohol dependence. *Archives of General Psychiatry* 56: 719–724.

Mason, B. J., J. H. Kocsis, E. C. Ritvo, and R. B. Cutler. 1996. A double-blind, placebo-controlled trial of desipramine for primary alcohol dependence stratified on the presence or absence of major depression. *Journal of the American Medical Association* 275: 761–767.

Mason, B. J., E. C. Ritvo, R. O. Morgan, F. R. Salvato, G. Goldberg, B. Welch, and F. Mantero-Atienza. 1994. A double-blind, placebo-controlled pilot study to evaluate the efficacy and safety of oral Nalmefene HCL for alcohol dependence. *Alcohol: Clinical and Experimental Research* 18: 1162–1167.

Maxwell, S., and M. S. Shinderman. 1997. Naltrexone in the treatment of dually-diagnosed patients. *Journal of Addictive Diseases* 16: A27, 125.

Maxwell, S., and M. Shinderman. 1997. Naltrexone in the treatment of alcohol- dependent, mentally ill patients: A retrospective analysis of 83 cases. Paper presented at the annual meeting of the American Society of Addiction Medicine, April, in San Diego, CA.

Maxwell, S., and M. S. Shinderman. 2000. Use of Naltrexone in the treatment of alcohol use disorders in patients with concomitant severe mental illness. *Journal of Addictive Diseases* 19: 61–69.

McBride, W. J., J. M. Murphy, K. Yoshimoto, L. Lumeng, and T. -K. Li. 1993. Serotonin Mechanisms in Alcohol Drinking Behavior. *Drug Development Research* 30: 170–177.

McCaul, M. E. 1996. Efficacy of Naltrexone for alcoholics with and without comorbid opiate or cocaine dependence. In International Update: New Findings on Promising Medications, Litten, R. Z. and J. Fertig, *Alcoholism: Clinical and Experimental Research* 20: 216A–218A.

McCaul, M. E., G. S. Wand, J. Sullivan, G. Mumford, and J. and Quigley. 1997. Beta-naltrexol level predicts alcohol relapse. *Alcoholism: Clinical and Experimental Research* 21: 32A.

McGrath, P. J., E. V. Nunes, J. W. Stewart, D. Goldman, V. Agosti, K. Ocepek-Welikson, and F. M. Quitkin. 1996. Imipramine treatment of alcoholics with primary depression: A placebo-controlled clinical trial. *Archives of General Psychiatry* 53: 232–240.

Mello, N. K., J. H. Mendelson, J. C. Kuehnle, and M. S. Sellers. 1981. Operant analysis of human heroin self-administration and the effects of Naltrexone. *Journal of Pharmacology and Experimental Therapeutics* 216: 45–54.

Miller, Norman S., and Steven S. Kipnis. 1995. *Detoxification from alcohol and other drugs: A treatment improvement protocol*. Washington, DC: U.S. Government Printing Office.

Miller, William R., and Reid K. Hester. 1986. Inpatient alcoholism treatment: Who benefits? *American Psychologist* 41: 794–805.

Mitnick, Kevin D., and William L. Simon. 2002. *The Art of Deception: Controlling the human element of security*. Indianapolis: Wiley.

Morris, Philip. 1999. A controlled trial of Naltrexone for alcohol dependence: An Australian perspective. Paper presented at the 1999 Scientific Meeting of the Research Society on Alcoholism, June 26–July 1, Santa Barbara, CA.

Myers, R. D., and E. C. Critcher. 1982. Naloxone alters alcohol drinking induced in the rat by tetrahydropapaveroline (THP) infused ICV. *Pharmacology Biochemistry and Behavior* 16: 827–836.

Myers, R. D., and M. F. Lankford. 1996. Suppression of alcohol preference in high alcohol drinking rats: Efficacy of amperozide versus Naltrexone. *Neuropsychopharmacology* 14: 139–149.

Myers, R. D., S. Borg, and R. Mossberg. 1986. Antagonism by Naltrexone of voluntary alcohol selection in the chronically drinking macaque monkey. *Alcohol* 3: 383–388.

Naranjo, C. A., K. E. Kadlec, P. Sanhueza, D. Woodley-Remus, and E. M. Sellers. 1990. Fluoxetine differentially alters alcohol intake and other consummatory behaviours in problem drinkers. *Clinical Pharmacology and Therapeutics* 47: 490–498.

Naranjo, C. A., E. M. Sellers, C. A. Roach, D. V. Woodley, M. Sanchez-Craig, and K. Sykora. 1984. Zimelidine-induced variations in alcohol intake in nondepressed heavy drinkers. *Clinical Pharmacology and Therapeutics* 35: 374–381.

Naranjo, C. A., E. M. Sellers, J. T. Sullivan, D. V. Woodley, K. Kadlec, and K. Sykora. 1987. The serotonin uptake inhibitor citalopram attenuates ethanol intake. *Clinical Pharmacology and Therapeutics* 41: 266–274.

Naranjo, C. A., J. T. Sullivan, K. E. Kadlec, Woodley-Remus, D. V., G. Kennedy, and E. M. Sellers. 1989. Differential effects of viqualine on alcohol intake and other consummatory behaviors. *Clinical Pharmacology and Therapeutics* 46: 301–309.

Nash, J. Madeleine. 1997. Addicted. *Time* 149: 69–76.

National Institute on Alcohol Abuse and Alcoholism (NIAAA). 1996. Neuroscience research and medications development. *Alcohol Alert* 33.

O'Brien, C. P., L. A. Volpicelli, and J. R. Volpicelli. 1996. Naltrexone in the treatment of alcoholism: A clinical review. *Alcohol* 13: 35–39.

O'Connor, P. G., and T. R. Kosten. 1998. Rapid and ultrarapid opioid detoxification techniques. *Journal of the American Medical Association* 279: 229B–234.

O'Connor, P. G., C. K. Farren, B. J. Rounsaville, and S. S. O'Malley. 1997. A preliminary investigation of the management of alcohol dependence with Naltrexone by primary care providers. *The American Journal of Medicine* 103: 477B482.

O'Malley, S. S., A. J. Jaffe, G. Chang, R. S. Schottenfeld, R. E. Meyer, and B. Rounsaville. 1992. Naltrexone and coping skills therapy for alcohol dependence. A controlled study. *Archives of General Psychiatry* 49: 881–887.

O'Malley, S. S., A. J. Jaffe, G. Chang, S. Rode, R. S. Schottenfeld, R. E. Meyer, and B. Rounsaville. 1996. Six-month follow-up of Naltrexone and psychotherapy for alcohol dependence. *Archives of General Psychiatry* 53: 217–224.

O'Malley, S. S., R. S. Croop, J. M. Wroblewski, D. F. Labriola, and J. R. Volpicelli. 1995. Naltrexone in the treatment of alcohol dependence: A combined analysis of two trials. *Psychiatric Annals* 25: 681–688.

O'Malley, S. S., A. J. Jaffe, G. Chang, R. S. Schottenfeld, R. E. Meyer, and B. Rounsaville. 1992. Naltrexone and coping skills therapy for alcohol dependence: A controlled study. *Archives of General Psychiatry* 49: 881–887.

O'Malley, S. S., A. J. Jaffe, S. Rode, and B. J. Rounsaville. 1996. Experience of a 'slip' among alcoholics treated with Naltrexone or placebo. *American Journal of Psychiatry* 153: 281–283.

Oslin, D., J. G. Liberto, J. O'Brien, S. Krois, J. Norbeck. 1997. Naltrexone as an adjunctive treatment for older patients with alcohol dependence. *American Journal of Geriatric Psychiatry* 5: 324–332.

Overstreet, D. H., A. B. Kampov-Polevoy, A. H. Rezvani, C. Braun, R. T. Bartus, and F. T. Crews. 1999. Suppression of alcohol intake by chronic Naloxone treatment in P rats: Tolerance development and elevation of opiate receptor binding. *Alcoholism: Clinical and Experimental Research* 23: 1761–1771.

Overstreet, D. H., R. A. McArthur, J. D. Sinclair, Y. W. Lee, A. Rezvani, R. Schreiber, D. Tomkins, and W. Zieglgansberger. 1996. Alternatives to Naltrexone in animal models. *Alcoholism: Clinical and Experimental Research* 20: 231A–235A.

Parkes, H., and J. D. Sinclair. Reduction of alcohol drinking and upregulation of opioid receptors by oral naltrexone in AA rats. *Alcohol* 3: 215–21.

PDR. 1997. *Physicians' Desk Reference*. Montvale: Medical Economics Company.

Pert, C. B., G. Pasternak, and S. H. Snyder. 1973. Opiate agonists and antagonists discriminated by receptor binding in brain. *Science* 182: 1359–1361.

Pert, Candace. 1999. *Molecules of Emotion: The Science Behind Mind-Body Medicine*. New York: Touchstone.

Pettinati, H. M. 1996. Use of serotonin selective pharmacotherapy in the treatment of alcohol dependence. *Alcoholism: Clinical and Experimental Research* 20: 23A–29A.

Pickens, R. W., D. S. Svikis, M. McGue, D. T. Lykken, L. L. Heston, and P. J. Clayton. 1991. Heterogeneity in the inheritance of alcoholism. A study of male and female twins. *Archives of General Psychiatry* 48: 19–28.

Pluymen, B. 2000. *The Thinking Person's Guide to Sobriety*. New York: St Martin's Griffin.

Pomerleau, C. S., O. F. Pomerleau, and M. J. Majchrzak. 1987. Mecamylamine Pretreatment Increases Subsequent Nicotine Self-Administration as Indicated by Changes in Plasma Nicotine Level." *Psychopharmacology Berlin*. 91: 391–393.

Ramsey, N. F., M. A. Gerrits, and J. M. Van Ree. 2005. Naltrexone Affects Cocaine Self-Administration in Naïve Rats Through the Ventral Tegmental Area Rather Than Dopaminergic Target Regions. *European Neuropsychopharmacology*, 15: 297–303.

Rankin, H., R. Hodgson, and T. Stockwell. 1979. The concept of craving and its measurement. *Behaviour Research and Therapy* 17: 389–396.

Reid, L. D., L. R. Gardell, S. Chattopadhyay, and C. L. Hubbell. 1996. Periodic Naltrexone and propensity to take alcoholic beverage. *Alcoholism: Clinical and Experimental Research* 20: 1329–1334.

Reid, L. D., ed. 1990. *Opioids, Bulimia, and Alcohol Abuse and Alcoholism*, 229–246. New York: Springer.

Renault, P. F. 1980. Treatment of Heroin-Dependent Persons with Antagonists: Current Status. In *Naltrexone: Research Monograph 28*, ed. R. E. Willett and G. Barnett, 11–22. Washington, DC: U.S. Government Printing Office.

Researcher: Naltrexone Minus Drinking Equals Failure. *Alcoholism and Drug Abuse Weekly* 9: 1, 6. 1997.

Restak, Richard. 1988. *The Mind.* New York: Bantam Books.

Rice, D. P., S. Kelma, L. S. Miller, and S. Dunmeyer. 1990. *The Economic Costs to Society of Alcohol and Drug Abuse and Mental Illness: 1985.* DHHS Publication No. (ADM) 90-1694. Rockville: U.S. Department of Health and Human Services, Public Health Service, Alcohol, Drug Abuse, and Mental Health Administration.

Rounsaville, B. 1993. Pharmacologic interventions for alcohol- and cocaine-abusing individuals: A controlled study of Disulfiram vs. Naltrexone. *American Journal on Addictions* 2: 77–79.

Salloum, I. M., J. R. Cornelius, M. E. Thase, D. C. Daley, L. Kirisci, and C. Spotts. 1998. Naltrexone utility in depressed alcoholics. *Psychopharmacology Bulletin* 34: 111–115.

Sandi, C., J. Borrell, and C. Guaza. 1988. Naloxone decreases ethanol consumption within a free choice paradigm in rats. *Pharmacology Biochemistry and Behavior* 29: 39–43.

Sax, D. S., C. Kornetsky, and A. Kim. 1994. Lack of hepatotoxicity with Naltrexone treatment. *Journal of Clinical Pharmacology* 34: 898–901.

Schaler, Jeffrey. 2000. *Addiction Is a Choice.* Chicago: Open Court Publishing.

Schurman, R. A., P. D. Kramer, and J. B. Mitchell. 1985. The hidden mental health network: Treatment of mental illness by nonpsychiatric physicians. *Archives of General Psychiatry* 42: 89–94.

Senter, R. J., F. W. Smith, and S. Lewin. 1967. Ethanol ingestion as an operant response. *Psychonomic Science* 8: 291–292.

Siegel, S. 1981. Alcohol and Opiate Dependence: Revaluation of the Victorian Perspective. In vol. 9 of *Research Advances in Alcohol and Drug Problems*, ed. H. D. Cappell, F. B. Glaser, and Y. Israel et al. New York: Plenum Press.

Sillanaukee, P., K. Kiianmaa, R. Roine, and K. Seppä. 1992. Criteria of heavy drinking. [In Finnish.] *Suomen Lääkärilehti* 47: 2919–2921.

Sinclair J. D., A. Kampov-Polevoy, R. Stewart, and T. -K. Li. 1992. Taste Preferences in Rat Lines Selected for Low and High Alcohol Consumption. *Alcohol* 9: 155–160.

Sinclair, D. 1997. Development in Finland of the extinction treatment for alcoholism with Naltrexone. *Psychiatrica Fennica* 28: 76–97.

Sinclair, J. D., J. Han, and H. Alho. 1998. Oral acamprosate: Effects on voluntary alcohol drinking in rats. *Alcoholism: Clinical and Experimental Research* 22: 177A.

Sinclair, J. D., O. Kymäläinen, and B. Jakobson. 1998. Extinction of the association between stimuli and drinking in the clinical treatment of alcoholism with Naltrexone. *Alcoholism: Clinical and Experimental Research* 22: 144A.

Sinclair, J. D, K. Sinclair, and H. Alho. 2000. Continued Naltrexone: Long-term clinical follow up. Abstract to 10th Congress of the International Society for Biomedical Research on Alcoholism, July 2–8, Yokohama, Japan.

Sinclair, J. D. 1998. Pharmacological extinction of alcohol drinking with opioid antagonists. *Arqivos de medicina*. 12: 95–98.

Sinclair, J. D. 1999. New concepts for Naltrexone use. Abstract to 38th ICAA International Congress on Alcohol, Drugs and other Dependencies, August 16–20, Vienna, Austria.

Sinclair, J. D. 1978. A theory of behavior, based on rest principle control of the strength of neural connections. *Neuroscience and Biobehavioral Reviews* 2: 357–366.

Sinclair, J. D. 1996. Alcoholism: pharmacological extinction and the P-word [in Finnish]. *Työterveyslääkari* 2: 170–173.

Sinclair, J. D. 1983. "The Psychology of Alcohol" [in Finnish]. In *Alkoholi ja yhteiskunta*, ed. T. Peltoniemi and M. Voipio, 43–49. Helsinki: Otava.

Sinclair, J. D., and I. P. Jääskeläinen. 1995. Continued efficacy after Naloxone-induced suppression of alcohol drinking: Dependence upon relative timing. *Alcoholism: Clinical and Experimental Research*: 19: 13A.

Sinclair, J. D., and D. O. Bender. 1978. Compensatory behaviors: Suggestion for a common basis from deficits in hamsters. *Life Sciences* 22: 1407–1412.

Sinclair, J. D., and R. J. Senter. 1968. Development of an alcohol-deprivation effect in rats. *Quarterly Journal of Studies on Alcohol* 29: 863–867.

Sinclair, J. D., and R. J. Senter. 1967. Increased preference for ethanol in rats following alcohol deprivation. *Psychonomic Science* 8: 11–12.

Sinclair, J. D., and T. -K. Li. 1989. Long and short alcohol deprivation: Effects on AA and P alcohol-preferring rats. *Alcohol* 6: 505–509.

Sinclair, J. D. 1982. Compensatory behaviors and the rest principle. *The Behavioral and Brain Sciences* 3: 466.

Sinclair, J. D. 1990. Drugs to decrease alcohol drinking. *Annals of Medicine* 22: 357–362.

Sinclair, J. D. 1979. Ethanol intake and lithium in rats. In *Alcoholism and affective disorders: Clinical, genetic, and biochemical studies with emphasis on alcohol-lithium interaction*, ed. Donald W. Goodwin and Carlton K. Erickson, 261–283. Jamaica: Spectrum.

Sinclair, J. D. 1982. How the mind recharges batteries. *Psychology Today* 16: 96.

Sinclair, J. D. 1996. Laboratory animal research in the discovery and development of the new alcoholism treatment using opioid antagonists. In Frontiers in laboratory animal science, ed. T. Nevalainen, J. Hau and M. Sarviharju. *Scandinavian Journal of Laboratory Animal Science* 23: 379–390.

Sinclair, J. D. 1992. Method and means for treating alcoholism by extinguishing the alcohol-drinking response using a transdermally administered opiate antagonist. U.S. patent 5,096,715, filed November 20, 1989, and issued March 17, 1992.

Sinclair, J. D. 1989. Method for treating alcohol-drinking response. U.S. patent 4,882,335, filed June 13, 1988, and issued November 21, 1989.

Sinclair, J. D. 1974. Morphine suppresses alcohol drinking regardless of prior alcohol access duration. *Pharmacology, Biochemistry and Behavior* 2: 409–412.

Sinclair, J. D. 1998. New treatment options for substance abuse from a public health viewpoint. *Annals of Medicine* 30: 406–411.

Sinclair, J. D. 1998. Pharmacological extinction of alcohol drinking with opioid antagonists. *Arqivos de Medicina* 12: 95–98.

Sinclair, J. D. 1974. Rats learning to work for alcohol. *Nature* 249: 590–592.

Sinclair, J. D. 1971. The alcohol-deprivation effect in monkeys. *Psychonomic Science* 25: 21–22.

Sinclair, J. D. 1972. The alcohol-deprivation effect: Influence of various factors. *Quarterly Journal of Studies on Alcohol* 33: 769–782.

Sinclair, J. D. 1975. The effects of lithium on voluntary alcohol consumption by rats. In Vol. 24 of *The effects of centrally active drugs on voluntary alcohol consumption*, ed. J. D. Sinclair and K. Kiianmaa, 119–142. Helsinki: Finnish Foundation for Alcohol Studies.

Sinclair, J. D. 1983. The hardware of the brain. *Psychology Today* 17: 8, 11–12.

Sinclair, J. D. 1981. *The rest principle: A neurophysiological theory of behavior*. Hillsdale: Lawrence Erlbaum Associates.

Sinclair, J. D. 1986. The rest principle: An alternative rule for how the strength of neural connections is controlled. *Integrative Psychiatry* 4: 186–190.

Sinclair, J. D. 1988. The statistical model has no clothes: Multiple *t* tests are appropriate in science. *Trends in Pharmacological Sciences* 9: 12–13.

Sinclair, J. D. 1995. The story in Finland behind the new Naltrexone treatment for alcoholism (and how I got the patent for it). *Life and Education in Finland* 3: 2–16.

Sinclair, J. D., H. Scheinin, and R. Lammintausta. 1990. Method for treating alcoholism with Nalmefene. U.S. patent 5,086,058, filed June 4, 1990, and issued February 4, 1992.

Sinclair, J. D., H. Scheinin, and R. Lammintausta. 1991. Method for treating alcoholism with Nalmefene. European patent EP0531415, filed June 4, 1991, and issued December 12, 1991.

Sinclair, J. D., J. Adkins, and S. Walker. 1973. Morphine-induced suppression of alcohol drinking in rats. *Nature* 246: 425–427.

Sinclair, J. D., O. Kymäläinen, M. Hernesniemi, M. S. Shinderman, and S. Maxwell. 1998. Treatment of alcohol dependence with Naltrexone utilizing an extinction protocol. Abstracts to 38th Annual Meeting, National Institute of Mental Health (NIMH)-sponsored New Clinical Drug Evaluation Unit Program, June 10–13, Boca Raton, Florida.

Sinclair, J. D., L. Vilamo, and B. Jakobson. 1994. Selective extinction of alcohol drinking in rats with decreasing doses of opioid antagonists. *Alcoholism: Clinical and Experimental Research* 18: 489.

Sinclair, J. D., M. Rusi, M. M. Airaksinen, and H. L. Altshuler. 1982. Relating TIQ's, opiates, and ethanol. *Progress in Clinical Biological Research* 90: 365–376.

Sinclair, J. D., S. Walker, and W. Jordan. 1973. Behavioral and physiological changes associated with various durations of alcohol deprivation in rats. *Quarterly Journal of Studies on Alcohol* 34: 744–757.

Sinclair, J. D., T. -K. Li, G. L. Gessa, L. Lumeng, and D. A. Lê. 1996. High and low drinking rat lines: Contributions to current understanding and future development. *Alcoholism: Clinical and Experimental Research*, 20: 109A–112A.

Sinden, J. D., P. Marfaing-Jallat, and J. Le Magnen. 1983. The effect of Naloxone on intragastric ethanol self-administration. *Pharmacology Biochemistry and Behavior* 19: 1045–1048.

Substance Abuse and Mental Health Services Administration (SAMHSA), Office of Applied Studies, Washington, DC. 1997. *Substance Abuse Treatment and Domestic Violence: A treatment improvement protocol*. Washington, DC: U.S. Government Printing Office.

Swift, R. M., W. Whelihan, O. Kuznetsov, G. Buongiorno, and H. Hsuing. 1994. Naltrexone-induced alterations in human ethanol intoxication. *American Journal of Psychiatry* 151: 1463–1467.

Swift, R. M. 1995. Effect of Naltrexone on human alcohol consumption. *Journal of Clinical Psychiatry* 56: 24–29.

Thiagarajan, A. B., I. N. Mefford, and R. L. Eskay. 1989. Single-dose ethanol administration activates the hypothalamic-pituitary axis: Exploration of the mechanism of action. *Neuroendocrinology* 50: 427–432.

Tiihonen, J., J. Kuikka, P. Hakola, J. Paanila, J. Airaksinen, M. Eronen, and T. Hallikainen. 1994. Acute ethanol-induced changes in cerebral blood flow. *American Journal of Psychiatry* 151: 1505–1508.

Trimpey, J. 1998. Rational recovery is an effective self-help program. In *Alcohol: opposing viewpoints*, ed. S. Barbour, 135–143. San Diego: Greenhaven.

Trimpey, J. 1996. *Rational Recovery: The New Cure for Substance Addiction.* New York: Pocket.

Ulm, R. R., J. R. Volpicelli, and L. A. Volpicelli. 1995. Opiates and alcohol self-administration in animals. *Journal of Clinical Psychiatry* 56: 5–14.

Van Ree, J. M., M. A. Gerrits, and L. J. Vanderschuren. 1999. Opioids, Reward and Addiction: An Encounter of Biology, Psychology, and Medicine. *Pharmacology Reviews* 51: 341–396.

Verebey, K., J. Volavka, S. J. Mule, and R. B. Resnick. 1976. Naltrexone: Disposition, metabolism, and effects after acute and chronic dosing. *Clinical Pharmacology and Therapeutics* 20: 315–328.

Volpicelli, Joseph, and Maia Szalavitz. 2000. *Recovery options: The complete guide: How you and your loved ones can understand and treat alcohol and other drug problems.* New York: Wiley.

Volpicelli, J. R. 1995. Medical treatments for alcohol dependence. Speech delivered to Veterans' Affairs hospitals in the United States and reported by the Treatment Research Center.

Volpicelli, J. R., A. I. Alterman, M. Hayashida, and C. P. O'Brien. 1992. Naltrexone in the treatment of alcohol dependence. *Archives of General Psychiatry* 49: 876–880.

Volpicelli, J. R., and C. P. O'Brien. 1995. Introduction: Opioid involvement in alcohol dependence. *Journal of Clinical Psychiatry* 56: 3–4.

Volpicelli, J. R., K. C. Rhines, J. S. Rhines, L. A. Volpicelli, A. I. Alterman, and C. P. O'Brien. 1997. Naltrexone and alcohol dependence. Role of subject compliance. *Archives of General Psychiatry* 54: 737–742.

Volpicelli, J. R., K. L. Clay, N. T. Watson, and C. P. O'Brien. 1995. Naltrexone in the treatment of alcoholism: predicting response to Naltrexone. *Journal of Clinical Psychiatry* 56: 39–44.

Volpicelli, J. R., K. L. Clay, N. T. Watson, and L. A. Volpicelli. 1994. Naltrexone and the treatment of alcohol dependence. *Alcohol Health and Research World* 18: 272–278.

Volpicelli, J. R., K. C. Rhines, J. S. Rhines, L. A. Volpicelli, and C. P. O'Brien. 1997. Naltrexone and alcohol dependence: Role of subject compliance. *Archives of General Psychiatry* 54: 737–743.

Volpicelli, J. R., R. R. Ulm, and N. Hopson. 1991. Alcohol drinking in rats during and following morphine injections. *Alcohol* 8: 289–292.

Volpicelli, J. R., L. A. Volpicelli, and C. P. O'Brien. 1995. Medical management of alcohol dependence: Clinical use and limitations of Naltrexone treatment. *Alcohol and Alcoholism* 30: 789–798.

Wikler, W. A. 1948. Recent progress in research on the neurophysical basis of morphine addiction. *American Journal of Psychiatry* 105: 328–338.

Wikler, A., and F. T. Pescor. 1967. Classical conditioning of a morphine abstinence phenomenon, reinforcement of opioid drinking behavior and "relapse" in morphine addicted rats. *Psychopharmacologia* 10: 255–284.

Wilde, M. I., and A. J. Wagstaff. 1997. Acamprosate: A review of its pharmacology and clinical potential in the management of alcohol dependence after detoxification. *Drugs* 53: 1038–1053.

Williams, K. L., and J. H. Woods. 1999. Naltrexone reduces ethanol- and/or water-reinforced responding in rhesus monkeys: Effect depends upon ethanol concentration. *Alcoholism: Clinical and Experimental Research* 23: 1462–1467.

Yeomans, M. R., P. Wright, H. A. Macleod, and J. A. Critchley. 1990. Effects of Nalmefene on Feeding in Humans. *Psychopharmacology* 100: 426–432.

Zink, R. W., K. Rohrbach, and J. C. Froehlich. 1997. Naltrexone and Fluoxetine act synergistically to decrease alcohol intake. *Alcoholism: Clinical and Experimental Research* 21: 104A.

Endnotes

1. R. F. Anton, S. S. O'Malley, D. C. Ciraulo, R. A. Cisler, D. Couper, D. M. Donovan, D. R. Gastfriend, J. D. Hosking, B. A. Johnson, J. S. LoCastro, R. Longabaugh, B. J. Mason, M. E. Mattson, W. R. Miller, H. M. Pettinati, C. L. Randall, R. Swift, R. D. Weiss, L. D. Williams, and A. Z. Zweben, "Combined Pharmacotherapies and Behavioral Interventions for Alcohol Dependence: The COMBINE Study: A Randomized Controlled Trial," *Journal of the American Medical Association* 295 (2006): 2003–2017.
2. J. D. Sinclair, "Rats Learning to Work for Alcohol," *Nature* 249 (1974): 590–592.
3. J. D. Sinclair, J. Adkins, and S. Walker, "Morphine-Induced Suppression of Voluntary Alcohol Drinking in Rats," *Nature* 246 (1973): 425–427.
4. J. D. Sinclair, "From Optimal Complexity to the Naltrexone Extinction of Alcoholism," in *Viewing Psychology as a Whole: The Integrative Science of William N. Dember*, ed. R. Hoffman, M. F. Sherrick, and J. S. Warm (Washington, D.C.: American Psychological Association, 1998), 491–508.

   J. D. Sinclair, "Pharmacological Extinction of Alcohol Drinking with Opioid Antagonists," *Arqivos de Medicina* 12 (1998): 95–98.

   J. D. Sinclair, "New Treatment Options for Substance Abuse from a Public Health Viewpoint," *Annals of Medicine* 30 (1998): 406–411.

   J. D. Sinclair, "Evidence About the Use of Naltrexone and for

Different Ways of Using It in the Treatment of Alcoholism," *Alcohol cand Alcoholism* 36 (2001): 2–10.

5. P. Heinälä, H. Alho, K. Kiianmaa, J. Lönnqvist, K. Kuoppasalmi, and J. D. Sinclair, "Targeted Use of Naltrexone without Prior Detoxification in the Treatment of Alcohol Dependence: A Factorial Double-Blind Placebo-Controlled Trial," *Journal of Clinical Psychopharmacology* 21 (2001): 287–292.

6. Alcoholics Anonymous World Services, Inc., *The Twelve Steps and Twelve Traditions* (New York: Alcoholics Anonymous World Services, Inc., 1952).

7. J. D. Sinclair and R. J. Senter, "Development of an Alcohol-Deprivation Effect in Rats," *Quarterly Journal of Studies on Alcohol* 29 (1968): 863–867. Also see http://alcalc.oxfordjournals.org/cgi/content/full/34/4/542.

8. J. D. Sinclair, "Development in Finland of the Extinction Treatment for Alcoholism with Naltrexone," *Psychiatrica Fennica* 28 (1997): 76–97.

9. J. D. Sinclair, "The Alcohol Deprivation Effect," *Quarterly Journal of Studies on Alcohol* 33 (1972): 769–782.

10. J. D. Sinclair and R. J. Senter, "Increased preference for ethanol in rats following alcohol deprivation," *Psychonomic Science* 8 (1967): 11–12.

11. J. D. Sinclair and R. J. Senter, "Development of an Alcohol-Deprivation Effect in Rats," *Quarterly Journal of Studies on Alcohol* 29 (1968): 863–867.

12. J. D. Sinclair, "Rats Learning to Work for Alcohol," *Nature* 249 (1974): 590–592.

13. J. D. Sinclair, "A Theory of Behavior, Based on Rest Principle Control of the Strength of Neural Connections," *Neuroscience and Biobehavioral Reviews* 2 (1978): 357–366. John D. Sinclair, *The Rest Principle: A Neurophysiological Theory of Behavior* (Hillsdale: Lawrence Erlbaum Associates, 1981).

14. J. D. Sinclair et al., "Morphine-Induced Suppression of Voluntary Alcohol Drinking in Rats," *Nature* 246 (1973): 425–427. J. D. Sinclair, "Morphine Suppresses Alcohol Drinking Regardless of Prior Alcohol Access Duration." *Pharmacology, Biochemistry and Behavior* 2 (1974): 409–412.

15. J. D. Sinclair, "From Optimal Complexity to the Naltrexone Extinction of Alcoholism," in *Viewing Psychology as a Whole: The Integrative Science of William N. Dember*, ed. R. Hoffman, M. F. Sherrick, and J. S. Warm (Washington, D.C.: American Psychological Association, 1998), 491–508.

16. D. Sinclair, "Development in Finland of the Extinction Treatment for Alcoholism with Naltrexone," *Psychiatrica Fennica* 28 (1997): 76–97.

17. P. Heinälä et al., "Targeted Use of Naltrexone without Prior Detoxification in the Treatment of Alcohol Dependence: A Factorial Double-

Blind Placebo-Controlled Trial," *Journal of Clinical Psychopharmacology* 21 (2001): 287–292.

18. Ibid.

19. Ibid.

20. S. S. O'Malley, A. Jaffe, G. Chang, G. Witte, R. S. Schottenfeld, and B. J. Rounsaville, "Naltrexone in the Treatment of Alcohol Dependence," in *Opioids, Bulimia, and Alcohol Abuse and Alcoholism*, ed. L. D. Reid (New York: Springer, 1990), 149–157. S. S. O'Malley, A. J. Jaffe, G. Chang, R. S. Schottenfeld, F. E. Meyer, and B. Rounsaville, "Naltrexone and Coping Skills Therapy for Alcohol Dependence," *Archives of General Psychiatry* 49 (1992): 881– 887.

21. J. M. Schmitz, A. L. Stotts, H. M. Rhoades, and J. Grabowski, "Naltrexone and Relapse Prevention Treatment for Cocaine-Dependent Patients," *Addictive Behavior* 26 (2001): 167–180.

22. J. R. Volpicelli, A. I. Alterman, M. Hayashida, and C. P. O'Brien, "Naltrexone in the Treatment of Alcohol Dependence," *Archives of General Psychiatry* 49 (1992): 876–880.

23. S. S. O'Malley et al., "Naltrexone and Coping Skills Therapy for Alcohol Dependence," *Archives of General Psychiatry* 49 (1992): 881–887.

24. P. Heinälä, H. Alho, K. Kuoppasalmi, D. Sinclair, K. Kiianmaa, and J. Lönnqvist, "Use of Naltrexone in the Treatment of Alcohol Dependence–A Double-Blind Placebo-Controlled Finnish Trial," *Alcohol and Alcoholism* 34 (1999): 433. P. Heinälä, H. Alho, K. Kuoppasalmi, J. Lönnqvist, D. Sinclair, and K. Kiianmaa, "Naltrexone in alcoholism treatment: Patient efficacy and compliance," in *New Research. Program and Abstracts*. (American Psychiatric Association 1999 Annual Meeting, May 15–20, in Washington, DC, 1999). H. P. Alho, P. Heinälä, K. Kiianmaa, and J. D. Sinclair, "Naltrexone for Alcohol Dependence: Double-Blind Placebo-Controlled Finnish Trial," *Alcoholism: Clinical and Experimental Research* 23 (1999): 46A.

25. P. C. Knox and D. M. Donovan, "Using Naltrexone in Inpatient Alcoholism Treatment," *Journal of Psychoactive Drugs* 31 4. (1999): 373–388.

26. J. H. Krystal, J. A. Cramer, W. F. Krol, G. F. Kirk, and R. A. Rosenheck, "Naltrexone in the Treatment of Alcohol Dependence," *New England Journal of medicine* 345 (2001): 1734–1739.

27. P. F. Renault, "Treatment of Heroin-Dependent Persons with Antagonists: Current Status," in *Naltrexone: Research Monograph 28*, ed. R. E. Willett and G. Barnett (Washington, DC: U.S. Government Printing Office, 1980), 11–22.

28. J. R. Volpicelli et al., "Naltrexone in the Treatment of Alcohol Dependence," *Archives of General Psychiatry* 49 (1992): 876–880.

29. S. S. O'Malley et al., "Naltrexone and Coping Skills Therapy for Alcohol Dependence," *Archives of General Psychiatry* 49 (1992): 881–887.

30. M. J. Bohn, H. R. Kranzler, D. Beazoglou, and B. A. Staehler, "Naltrexone and Brief Counseling to Reduce Heavy Drinking," *American Journal on Addictions* 3 (1994): 91–99.

31. Balldin, J., M. Berglund, S. Borg, M. Månsson, P. Berndtsen, J. Franck, L. Gustafsson, J. Halldin, C. Hollstedt, L. H. Nilsson, and G. A. Stolt, "Randomized 6 Month Double-Blind Placebo-Controlled Study of Naltrexone and Coping Skills Education Programme," *Alcohol and Alcoholism* 32 (1997): 325.

32. S. Maxwell and M. S. Shinderman, "Naltrexone in the Treatment of Dually-Diagnosed Patients," *Journal of Addictive Diseases* 16 (1997): A27, 125.

33. H. R. Kranzler, H. Tennen, C. Penta, and M. J. Bohn, "Targeted Naltrexone Treatment of Early Problem Drinkers," *Addictive Behaviors* 22 (1997): 431–436.

34. J. Guardia, C. Caso, F. Arias, A. Gual, J. Sanahuja, M. Ramirez, I. Mengual, B. Gonzalvo, L. Segura, J. Trujols, and M. Casas, "A Double-Blind, Placebo-Controlled Study of Naltrexone in the Treatment of Alcohol-Dependence Disorder: Results from a Multicenter Clinical Trial," *Alcoholism: Clinical and Experimental Research* 26 (2002): 1381–1387.

35. P. D. Lifrak, A. I. Alterman, C. P. O'Brien, and J. R. Volpicelli, "Naltrexone for Alcoholic Adolescents," *American Journal of Psychiatry* 154 (1997): 439–440.

36. D. Oslin, J. Liberto, C. P. O'Brien, S. Krois, and J. Norbeck, "Naltrexone as an Adjunct Treatment for Older Patients with Alcohol Dependence," *American Journal of Geriatric Psychiatry* 5 (1997): 324–332.

37. M. C. Marck, G. U. Liepa, S. J. Kalia, and M. C. Daoud, "Investigating Differences in Hospitalized Patients Detoxified with Lorazepam vs. Phenobarbital Relative to Length of Stay, Average Total Cost, and Use of Restraints," *Journal of Addictive Diseases* 16 (1997): A23.

38. R. F. Anton et al., "Combined Pharmacotherapies and Behavioral Interventions for Alcohol Dependence: The COMBINE Study: A Randomized Controlled Trial," *Journal of the American Medical Association* 295 (2006): 2003–2017.

39. N. C. Latt, S. Jurd, J. Houseman, and S. E. Wutzke, "Naltrexone in Alcohol Dependence: A Randomised Controlled Trial of Effectiveness in a Standard Clinical Setting," *The Medical Journal of Australia* 176 (2002): 530–534.

40. Sakari Karhuvaara, Kaarlo Simojoki, Antti Virta, Markus Rosberg, Eliisa Löyttyniemi, Tommi Nurminen, Antero Kallio, and Rauno

Mäkelä, "Targeted Nalmefene with Simple Medical Management in the Treatment of Heavy Drinkers: A Randomized Double-Blind Placebo-Controlled Multicenter Study," *Alcoholism: Clinical and Experimental Research* 31 (No. 7) (2007): 1179–1187.

41. J. D. Sinclair, K. Sinclair, and H. Ahlo, "Long-Term Follow Up of Continued Naltrexone Treatment," *Alcoholism: Clinical and Experimental Research* 24 (2007): 182A.

42. K. C. Morely, M. Teesson, S. C. Reid, C. Sannibale, C. Thomson, N. Phung, M. Weltman, J. R. Bell, K. Richardson, and P. S. Haber, "Naltrexone Versus Acamprosate in the Treatment of Alcohol Dependence: A Multi-Centre, Randomized, Double-Blind, Placebo-Controlled Trial," *Addiction* 10 (2006): 1451–1462.

43. Janeen Interlandi, "What Addicts Need," *Newsweek*, March 3, 2008, 36–42.

44. P. F. Renault, "Treatment of heroin-dependent persons with antagonists: Current status," *Bulletin on Narcotics* 30 (1978): 21–29.

45. P. F. Renault, "Treatment of heroin-dependent persons with antagonists: Current Status," in *Naltrexone: Research Monograph 28*, ed. R. E. Willett and G. Barnett (Washington, DC: National Institute of Drug Abuse, 1980), 11–22.

46. A. Wikler, "The Theoretical Basis of Narcotic Addiction Treatment with Narcotic Antagonists," in *Narcotic Antagonists: Naltrexone Progress Report, National Institute on Drug Abuse Research Monograph Series* (Rockville, MD: National Institute on Drug Abuse, 1976), 119–122.

47. E. Krupitsky, E. Zvartau, D. Masalov, M. Tsoy, A. Burakov, V. Egorova, T. Didenko, T. Romanova, E. Ivanova, A. Bespalov, E. V. Verbitskaya, N. G. Neznanov, A.Y. Grinenko, C. P. O'Brien and G. E. Woody, "Naltrexone with or without Fluoxetine for Preventing Relapse to Heroin Addiction in St. Petersburg, Russia," *Journal of Substance Abuse Treatment* 31 (2006): 319–328.

48. Thomas Ropp, "Alternative to Alcoholism: A Little Known Drug, Naltrexone, is Hailed for its Success," *The Arizona Republic*, February 19, 1998. Can be found online at http://www.assistedrecovery. com/beta/news.htm.

49. J. D. Sinclair, "The Alcohol-Deprivation Effect in Monkeys," *Psychonomic Science* 25 (1971): 21–22.

50. http://www.vivitrol.com. Serious injection site reactions may occur with the use of injectable naltrexone www.fda.gov/medwatch

51. Cynthia Mascott, "Alcoholism and its Treatment," HelpHorizons.com, http://www.helphorizons.com/library/search_details.htm?id=61.

52. http://www.vivitrol.com. Serious injection site reactions may occur with the use of injectable naltrexone www.fda.gov/medwatch.

53. M. R. Yeomans, P. Wright, H. A. Macleod, and J. A. Critchley, "Effects

of Nalmefene on Feeding in Humans," *Psychopharmacology* 100 (1990): 426–432.

54. J. D. Sinclair, "The Psychology of Alcohol" [in Finnish], in *Alkoholi ja yhteiskunta*, ed. T. Peltoniemi and M.Voipio (Helsinki: Otava: 43–49), 1983.

55. J. Tiihonen, J. Kuikka, P. Hakola, J. Paanila, J. Airaksinen, M. Eronen, and T. Hallikainen, "Acute Ethanol-Induced Changes in Cerebral Blood Flow," *American Journal of Psychiatry* 151 (1994): 1505–1508.

56. J. D. Sinclair, "Alcoholism: Pharmacological Extinction and the P-word" [in Finnish], *Työterveyslääkäri* 2 (1996): 170–173.

57. John David Sinclair, "Second Generation Opioidergic Compounds: Clinical Data," in *Drugs for Relapse Prevention of Alcoholism*, ed. Rainer Spanagel and Karl F. Mann, in *Milestones in Drug Therapy* series, (Basal: Birkhäuser, 2005). 125–134.

58. See http://www.moderation.org/bac/bac_tables.pdf. Excerpted from *How to Control Your Drinking* by William R. Miller and Richard F. Munoz.

59. P. Sillanaukee, K. Kiianmaa, R. Roine, K. Seppä, "Criteria of heavy drinking" [in Finnish], *Suomen Lääkärilehti* 47 (1992): 2919–2921.

60. J. D. Sinclair, M. Rusi, M. M. Airaksinen, and H. L. Altshuler, "Relating TIQ's, Opiates, and Ethanol," *Progress in Clinical Biological Research* 90 (1982): 365–376.

61 I. P. Jääskeläinen, J. Hirvonen, T. Kujala, K. Alho, C. J. P. Eriksson, A. Lehtokoski, E. Pekkonen, J. D. Sinclair, H. Yabe, R. Näätänen, and P. Sillanaukee, "Effects of Naltrexone and Ethanol on Auditory Event-Related Brain Potentials," *Alcohol* 15 (1998): 105–111.

62. J. D. Sinclair, "Evidence about the Use of Naltrexone and for Different Ways of Using It in the Treatment of Alcoholism," *Alcohol and Alcoholism* 36 (2001): 2–10.

63. E. Krupitsky et al., "Naltrexone With or Without Fluoxetine for Preventing Relapse to Heroin Addiction in St. Petersburg, Russia," *Journal of Substance Abuse Treatment* 31 (2006): 319–328.

64. J. M. Schmitz et al., "Naltrexone and Relapse Prevention Treatment for Cocaine-Dependent Patients," *Addictive Behavior* 26 (2001): 167–180.

65. N. Jayaram-Lindström, P. Wennberg, Y. L. Hurd, J. Franck, "An Open Clinical Trial of Naltrexone for Amphetamine Dependence: Compliance and Tolerability," *Nordic Journal of Psychiatry* 59 (2005): 167–171. N. Jayaram-Lindström, A. Hammarberg, O. Beck, J. Franck, "Naltrexone for the Treatment of Amphetamine Dependence: A Randomized Placebo Controlled Trial" (diss., Karolinska University Hospital, 2007).

66. http://thesaurus.reference.com/browse/metamorphosis.

67. Yoshiyuki Sadamoto, *Neon Genesis Evangelion*.

68. P. F. Renault, "Treatment of Heroin-Dependent Persons with Antagonists: Current Status," in *Naltrexone: Research Monograph 28*, ed. R. E. Willett and G. Barnett (Washington, DC: U.S. Government Printing Office, 1980), 11–22.

69. E. Krupitsky et al., "Naltrexone with or without Fluoxetine for Preventing Relapse to Heroin Addiction in St. Petersburg, Russia," *Journal of Substance Abuse Treatment* 31 (2006): 319–328.

70. J. M. Van Ree, M. A. Gerrits, and L. J. Vanderschuren, "Opioids, Reward and Addiction: An Encounter of Biology, Psychology, and Medicine," *Pharmacology Reviews* 51 (1999): 341–396.

71. N. F. Ramsey, M. A. Gerrits, and J. M. Van Ree, "Naltrexone Affects Cocaine Self-Administration in Naïve Rats Through the Ventral Tegmental Area Rather Than Dopaminergic Target Regions," *European Neuropsychopharmacology*, 15 (2005): 297–303.

72. J. M. Schmitz et al., "Naltrexone and Relapse Prevention Treatment for Cocaine-Dependent Patients," *Addictive Behavior* 26 (2001): 167–180.

73. http://diss.kib.ki.se/2007/978-91-7357-449-5/thesis.pdf. See section 1.6.3, "Interaction between opioid antagonists and stimulants" in the dissertation "Evaluation of naltrexone as a treatment for amphetamine dependence."

74. http://www.vivitrol.com.

75. See the FDA site at http://www.fda.gov/cder/foi/label/2000/ 20459S2lbl.pdf and Wikipedia http://en.wikipedia.org/wiki/Revex.

76. R. S. Back, "Naltrexone in the Treatment of Adolescent Sexual Offenders," *Journal of Clinical Psychiatry* 65 (2004): 982–986.

77. R. D. Eskapa (1987) *Bizarre Sex*, London, Quatert Books.

78. http://www.suntimes.co.za/2001/10/28/news/news04.asp.

79. http://www.ncrg.org/press/jun1_01.htm, http://casinomagazine.com/ManageArticle.asp?C=280&A=1672.

80. J. E. Grant, M. N. Potenza, E. Hollander, R. Cunningham-Williams, T. Nurminen, G. Smits, and A. Kallio, "Multicenter Investigation of the Opioid Antagonist Nalmefene in the Treatment of Pathological Gambling," *American Journal of Psychiatry* 163 (2006): 303–312.

81. J. D. Sinclair, A. Kampov-Polevoy, R. Stewart, and T. -K. Li, "Taste Preferences in Rat Lines Selected for Low and High Alcohol Consumption," *Alcohol* 9 (1992): 155–160.

82. S. A. Alger, M. D. Schwalberg, J. M. Bigaouette, A. V. Michalek, and L. J. Howard, "Effect of a tricyclic antidepressant and opiate antagonist on binge-eating behavior in normoweight bulimic and obese, binge-eating subjects," *American Journal of Clinical Nutrition* 53 (1991): 865–871.

83. http://maroon.uchicago.edu/online_edition/news/2007/01/30/heroin-addiction-drug-may-help-women-stop-smoking.

84. X. Liu, A. R. Caggiula, S. K. Yee, H. Nobuta, A. F. Sved, R. N.

Pechnick, and R. E. Poland, "Mecamylamine Attenuates Cue-Induced Reinstatement of Nicotine-Seeking Behavior in Rats," *Neuropsychopharmacology* 32 (2007): 710–718.

85. C. S. Pomerleau, O. F. Pomerleau, and M. J. Majchrzak, "Mecamylamine Pretreatment Increases Subsequent Nicotine Self-Administration as Indicated by Changes in Plasma Nicotine Level," *Psychopharmacology Berl.* 91 (1987): 391–393.

86. http://www.drmirkin.com/morehealth/8432.html.

87. http://en.wikipedia.org/wiki/Internet_addiction.

88. See http://www.mitnicksecurity.com, perhaps much to US District Court Judge Mariana Pfaelzer's chagrin.

89. http://camy.org/research/status0306/status0306.pdf.

90. http://www.who.int/substance_abuse/publications/global_status_report_2004_overview.pdf.

91. http://www.niaaa.nih.gov, http://www.bma.org.uk/ap.nsf/Content/NESalcohol#OfficeofPopulationCensuses.

92. http://www.wihrd.soton.ac.uk/projx/signpost/steers/STEER_ 2001(12).pdf.

93. http://www.ias.org.uk/factsheets/health.pdf. Retrieved May 2006.

94. Ali H. Mokdad, James S. Marks, Donna F. Stroup, Julie L. Gerberding, "Actual Causes of Death in the United States, 2000," *Journal of the American Medical Association* 291 (2004) 1238–1245.

95. http://oas.samhsa.gov/nsduh/2k4nsduh/2k4Results/2k4Results. htm.

96. Full report at http://camy.org/research/status0306/status0306.pdf.

97. R. F. Anton et al., "Combined Pharmacotherapies and Behavioral Interventions for Alcohol Dependence: The COMBINE Study: A Randomized Controlled Trial," *Journal of the American Medical Association* 295 (2006): 2003–2017.

98. N. C. Latt et al., "Naltrexone in Alcohol Dependence: A Randomised Controlled Trial of Effectiveness in a Standard Clinical Setting," *The Medical Journal of Australia* 176 (11) (2002): 530–534.

99. S. Karhuvaara et al., "Targeted Nalmefene with Simple Medical Management in the Treatment of Heavy Drinkers: A Randomized Double-Blind Placebo-Controlled Multicenter Study," *Alcoholism: Clinical and Experimental Research* 31 (No. 7) (2007): 1–9.

100. D. Sinclair, F. Fantozzi, and J. Yanai, "Effective Use of Naltrexone: What Doctors and Patients Have Not Been Told" [in Italian], *Italian Journal of the Addictions* 41 (2003): 15–21.

Excerpt from
Babylon Confidential
Claudia Christian

Coming Back to Life

The Sinclair Method has successfully helped moderate alcohol drinking in Finland, where excessive alcohol use is a major national problem, as well as other countries including Israel, Russia, the Netherlands, Italy, Spain, Venezuela and Estonia. A statistical analysis of the data obtained from clinics in Finland shows highly significant reductions in alcohol drinking. The method is successful with more than 78% of alcoholics. In Florida the success rates since 2002 have been more than 85%. During the treatment program when shown on a graph a pattern emerges. It was always a classical extinction curve: drinking and craving became progressively lower with each week of treatment.

That was from a scientific article I read called "Clinical Evidence from the Sinclair Method Clinic in Sarasota, Florida." The Florida clinic was the only one in the US offering the Sinclair Method. The clinic's website said:

> Internationally hundreds of thousands of people have been helped using the Sinclair Method.
>
> More than 80% of all the clients in the program were successful in long term control of their alcohol consumption, some to acceptable levels ("Social Drinking") and others to complete abstinence. For those who desired to control their alcohol consumption, their drinking was reduced to an average of 1 drink per day. These same individuals had at one point consumed anywhere from 24 to 50 drinks or more a week. Some of the Sinclair Method's successful patients had consumed more than 200 ounces of alcohol a week prior to the program.[1]

An 80% success rate! Apart from the grim reaper, who has the only 100% guaranteed cure for addiction, I'd never heard of a treatment with such a high rate of success. What's more, the article made an astonishing claim—that the Sinclair Method was a genuine cure for alcoholism.

The word "cure" is a powerful one and can't be used lightly. The Sinclair Method makes use of a drug called naltrexone, which creates a state of pharmacological extinction in the addict's brain. It doesn't block the effect of alcohol; rather, it gradually resets the brain back to the pre-addiction condition, making it a bona fide cure.

But there was one catch: the cure only remained a cure as long as you took the pill, every time before you had a drink, for the rest of your life. Otherwise the endorphins released when drinking would not be blocked by the effect of naltrexone and would lead the brain to revert to a state of craving alcohol.

I researched naltrexone and found that it had been available and FDA-approved for the treatment of alcoholism since 1994. It was

---

[1] www.28weekrecovery.com/index_files/Page389.htm

non-addictive, and the side effects were minor and temporary—nausea, headaches, and insomnia. *Sign me up!*

The Florida clinic charged $3,800 for treatment, beyond my budget by that stage. Luckily, I found a book, *The Cure for Alcoholism* by Roy Eskapa, PhD.

The book had an introduction by David Sinclair, PhD, who developed the Sinclair Method, which described alcoholism as a learned chemical addiction of the brain. Sinclair maintains that abstinence only makes the problem worse, and I'd made the biggest mistake in the book: I'd gone stone-cold sober after every binge. The sudden deprivation of alcohol only led to stronger cravings. This not only leads to eventual relapse but also damages the brain and internal organs. What no one at rehab or detox centers ever tells you is that you can detox by gradually reducing your alcohol intake. The reason no one thinks to mention this is that most alcoholics aren't capable of doing it. But with naltrexone it's made possible by one amazing, almost unbelievable fact—that the Sinclair Method only works as a cure if the alcoholic keeps on drinking.

You take naltrexone to reduce your consumption, and at the same time it kills off your addiction. My armor was battered and hanging on by its fraying straps, but now I'd have something to fight the monster with that I'd never had before—a weapon. I'd always been on the defensive, on the back foot while the monster attacked at will. If the claims about the Sinclair Method were true, I just might be able to obliterate that bitch once and for all.

The Cure for Alcoholism contained all the information I needed to start the Sinclair Method solo. The first step was to find a doctor who would prescribe naltrexone, which costs about $30 for thirty 50 mg pills—about a dollar added to the cost of a night out. Even better, I was able to use my SAG insurance, which brought the cost down even more to $10 for thirty pills.

By taking one pill one hour before drinking I could begin the process of pharmacological extinction.

I was still not turned on by the idea of taking a pill forever, but hell, if it worked it was better than going to an AA meeting and fighting the war every fucking day for the rest of my life. And the other thing that resonated with me was the Sinclair Method's treatment of alcoholism as a disease, like diabetes or high blood pressure. It was a relief to know that someone had devised a safe, medically proven, nonaddictive way to combat it.

Following on from the use of naltrexone, the book encouraged using the beneficial effect of the drug to strengthen healthy, alternative behaviors—eating tasty meals, exercise, sports, even sex.

I went in to see my doctor, armed with a copy of *The Cure for Alcoholism*. I'd been fighting every day for the last ten years. I wanted peace, I wanted my life back, and I wasn't going to take no for an answer.

The doctor was a nice young guy who a pill-popping friend had recommended, one used to dealing with addicts. I'd seen him once before when I was suffering a combo attack of flu and alcohol withdrawal. He'd prescribed some anti-anxiety pills to deal with the monster and an antibiotic for the flu. The flu went the way of the dodo; the monster didn't bat an eyelid.

I was back and this time asking for naltrexone. I'd also printed out pages of the clinical papers I found on the Internet, and I sat with him and discussed the Sinclair Method. He looked up the drug in his pharmaceutical reference book and finally, with trepidation, he gave me the piece of paper that represented my last hope of recovery, my hopeful stay of execution.

I had to go to a compound pharmacy (one that makes special drugs to order) to fill my prescription. Within fifteen minutes I had fifteen pills. I stopped by Trader Joe's on the way home and bought a bottle of red wine and a steak. I was PMS-ing and David was out of town. It was the perfect time to schedule the first experiment.

I shook the plastic pill bottle at the traffic lights, like a witch doctor rattling bones for good luck. The wine sat next to me in the passenger seat. The way home involved driving right past the khaki-colored bus stop on Coldwater Canyon. I turned and looked at it as I drove past and was overcome with emotion. I had to pull over.

I couldn't believe that the pills could work, that I didn't need to abstain. It was too good to be true.

Nothing's for free, babe.

The very idea seemed to go against everything I'd learned at AA and in rehab and at the detox center. The monster was rattling around in my head. I was shaking, tears streaming down my face. The bus stop, the ride to rehab with Holly and my mom, the back of the rapist's van, the sight of my mom in a bloodstained shirt holding Patrick's bandana in her hand, it was all the same place— the monster's cave, its place of power—and I'd been trapped in it for so long that I didn't know if I had the courage to leave.

Claudia, honey, this is just another dead end. Everything else you've tried has failed and you know you swore never to pop pills. Throw them out the window and go home. We'll enjoy the wine together.

As soon as I got home I took the pill. It was 5:45 p.m. on February 22, 2009. I waited until 6:45 before having a glass of wine—I wanted to make sure the pill had time to work. I was nervous, but I'd gotten my courage back after the bus-stop incident. I was so hopeful!

After I drank the wine, I felt a little dizzy and found that I could only eat a little of the steak and spinach on my plate. I also felt a little stoned and not at all clear-headed.

Why are you doing this?

The monster was still posturing, but I noticed that her voice lacked power. *She* was anxious as well. I didn't dignify her with an answer, and she knew why. She knew that, more than anything, I wanted to be normal.

Soon I was struck by a revelation: *It's 7:15. I've only had one glass of red wine and don't feel like having another. By now I should be well on my way to polishing off the bottle.*

It was a week before I touched another drop—this time, three glasses of wine. I slept like crap and woke up tired and thirsty the next morning, but the monster was still silent. The binge that I was sure would overtake me like a tsunami had arrived as only a minor swell and quickly receded.

A month after that, I took my pill before having my first social drink, a glass of wine with people in my writing class. I was hyper-aware of how strange it felt to be normal. It was as if I was standing outside my body watching myself laugh and socialize. I kept waiting for the something bad to happen. Nothing did. A month earlier I'd have been on my third glass and working out how to sneak the unfinished bottle into my bag when no one was looking.

Another week passed, and I attended my first post-Sinclair dinner party with David. I found that my body was adjusting to the pill. I didn't feel so dizzy anymore.

It had been a month since I'd seen the monster in the mirror, and though she was still running around in my mind, threatening and cajoling, I could sense she was getting desperate.

Then came the real test: a trip to Napa to visit my mom and stepfather. It's feeding time in the lion enclosure and Claudia's on the menu. I took two bottles of red to last the whole trip.

And then the carnage began. My mom questioned my latest attempt to fix my life. My stepfather once again posited his carefully thought-out theory that I was injecting hard drugs. I stayed cool like Fonzie. I drank my wine, a glass a day, and returned to L.A. without going on a single binge, having tamed the lions.

It seemed that while I was on the Sinclair Method nothing could trigger me to drink. I still have cravings when I have PMS or if I have a long, difficult day, but there seems to be a disconnect between the voice of the monster and the dangerous behavior it previously triggered.

I took on another big challenge—a trip to Italy with David. Tuscany, land of the luscious red. I resigned myself to drinking only at night. No repeat of the turmoil in Tahiti. I wanted to *remember* my time in Italy.

I was still thinking like an alcoholic. I obsessively counted my supply of naltrexone, ensuring I had enough, but I was anxious without cause. I took my pill as instructed and only drank too much on one occasion—four glasses with a gorgeous meal of pasta putanesca—but even that didn't lead to a binge.

I returned from Italy triumphant, a Roman emperor having vanquished the barbarians.

By the time I'd used the Sinclair Method for six months the dizzy feeling was completely gone. I cut out drinking during the week altogether, only imbibing on weekends, and then only on a special occasions—a few glasses at a dinner party or on a getaway with

David. My desire to consume alcohol steadily declined, taking my abnormal behavior with it. I didn't feel dizzy at all or experience any side effects. My life was back to how I remembered it before the monster came along. Drinking, I could honestly take it or leave it.

But fear is the hardest of human emotions to conquer. I was still reluctant to declare total victory; I didn't want to be like George Bush and hang out the "Mission Accomplished" banner until I'd really won the war.

It wasn't that long ago that, when I wasn't thinking about what to drink or where to get it, I'd kill time calculating how many days I'd wasted recovering from binges (165) in the hope that that sheer number would deter me from wasting any more.

But my confidence slowly grew. The bottles of wine in my cabinet were only used at dinner parties. The cooking wine that I used to guzzle desperately could rest easy in my pantry beside the Marsala and Cognac—they'd only ever be used as intended, to make sauces for my recipes.

My brain was changing, and as it did I was reclaiming my life.

It took another year, watching the monster slowly wither and retreat from sight, until I made the call, the official announcement. I'd battled the monster for close to a decade, and now I'd finally won. Print the headline: "Armistice Announced—the Enemy Has Signed the Treaty—Peace at Last!"

It was the spring of 2010, I'd been on the Sinclair Method for a few months, and I was getting a manicure-pedicure at this Korean beautician's place when my phone rang. It was Adam Rifkin, my director friend from the good old days.

"Claudia, I'm working on something right now for Showtime. It's a TV version of my movie *LOOK*, do you want to be in it?"

"You've got to be kidding me!"

"It's a really funny character. Her name's Stella. I wrote her specifically for you. I'd love for you to be in it."

I was so grateful, so happy! By "funny" he meant that she was a paranoid, alcoholic cokehead and, according to the production notes, a fortysomething MILF.

"Claudia, you still there?"

I was so stunned, I'd forgotten to talk.

"I'm still here."

"It's really low budget, so there's not much money in it..."

"But I'm gonna be back on TV?"

"Yeah, you'll be on Showtime."

And there it was. My career was back. I felt the world change around me, the final piece fall into place. I knew it was real. It felt just like when I got my first role on *Dallas* all those years before. The drought had been broken.

Then another job came, voice work on a computer game, and after that another. I worked on a sci-fi short film written by an Aussie named Morgan Buchanan, who became my regular writing partner (and co-author of this book). We started writing a series of future-Rome sci-fi novels.

I had my life back. People wanted me to be in their lives. Hollywood wanted to make use of my talents. It was a rebirth in every way.

In May 2011 David and I were back in French Polynesia. Moʻorea was beautiful as I stared at its green and grey volcanic mountains from my over-the-water bungalow. I was the happiest I'd been in over a decade, an alcoholic who had found a cure.

David stood by me through the tail end of my struggle, and although he was incredibly supportive our social life had taken on a dismal atmosphere of early dinners and subdued conversation. Now we enjoyed cooking together, dinner parties, wine, and laughter. We survived the monster together and emerged from that ordeal as stronger, closer friends.

My life had come full circle. I had worked hard, taken risks, and believed in myself at the start of my career in Hollywood. I'd experienced meteoric highs and cataclysmic lows. I'd gone from a smart, attractive woman in her early thirties with a six-figure income, a mansion, and a successful career, to someone consumed by addiction, an unrecognizable creature, sneaking out, drinking spirits from a paper bag in a bus shelter. I'd gone from someone who was in love with life to a woman who was humiliated, wracked with suicidal thoughts. And now I'd been given the ultimate blessing, the ultimate miracle—a fresh start. Not the false start I used to have when I'd recover from a binge. This was real; I could feel it in my bones.

The Tahitian water is a bright, azure blue, creating an atmosphere of invigorating peace. I'm halfway through my glass of champagne. When I finish it, I'll get a massage and later go snorkeling with David in the lagoon teeming with tropical fish. I've had my pill, and the monster slumbers in the back of my brain, as if it had never been. I actually see Tahiti this time, the color, the slow pace of life, the beauty. A white seaplane flies overhead carrying passengers back to the main island of Tahiti. I'll be on that plane soon enough, heading back to star in a new film. My friends were right, this is paradise, but so is every aspect of my life now. I'm free from hell; I can finally enjoy heaven.

This was excerpted from Claudia Christian's new book, Babylon Confidential, *being released by BenBella Books in November 2012. Claudia's book shows how she successfully implemented the Sinclair Method presented in* The Cure for Alcoholism.

Index

About the Author

ROY ESKAPA, PhD, obtained a B.A. in psychology from Reed College in Portland, Oregon, and went on to complete a PhD in clinical psychology at the California School of Professional Psychology in Los Angeles (1983; licensed psychologist, New Jersey, 1988). He had a variety of postdoctoral training experiences including forensic psychology, multimodal therapy, and addiction medicine. He has published several articles and book chapters, as well as a four-hundred-page tome on forensic psychology. During the 1990s he developed a successful program for treating childhood enuresis while also working closely with Dr. David Sinclair on his research on pharmacological extinction (Sinclair Method) into the causes and solutions for alcoholism.

He is an Associate Fellow of the British Psychological Society, and is a Chartered psychologist in the UK. At present he is focused on securing greater exposure for the unequivocally cost-effective Sinclair Method in the treatment of alcoholism and other drug addictions. In addition to conducting a private one-on-one and online practice, Dr. Eskapa is available for speaking engagements and consultation to industry, government, health, and education departments, and NGOs on Sinclair's revolutionary prevention of and cure for alcoholism and other addictions.